East Asian Sexualities

East Asian Sexualities
Modernity, Gender and New Sexual Cultures

Edited by
Stevi Jackson, Liu Jieyu and Woo Juhyun

Zed Books
LONDON & NEW YORK

East Asian Sexualities: Modernity, Gender and New Sexual Cultures was first published in 2008 by Zed Books Ltd, 7 Cynthia Street, London N1 9JF, UK and Room 400, 175 Fifth Avenue, New York, NY 10010, USA

www.zedbooks.co.uk

Editorial copyright © Stevi Jackson, Liu Jieyu and Woo Juhyun 2008
Copyright in this collection © Zed Books 2008

The rights of Stevi Jackson, Liu Jieyu and Woo Juhyun to be identified as the editors of this work have been asserted by them in accordance with the Copyright, Designs and Patents Act, 1988

Designed and set in 10.5/12.5 pt Bembo by Long House, Cumbria UK
Cover designed by Andrew Corbett
Printed and bound in the UK by Biddles Ltd, King's Lynn

Distributed in the USA exclusively by Palgrave Macmillan, 175 Fifth Avenue, New York, NY 10010

A catalogue record for this book is available from the British Library
Library of Congress Cataloging in Publication Data are available

ISBN 978 1 84277 888 3 hb
ISBN 978 1 84277 889 0 pb

Contents

Note on Asian Names

With the exception of Annie Chan, Saori Kamano, Diana Khor and Stevi Jackson, all authors' names follow the East Asian convention, in which family names precede personal names. Often, when publishing in English, East Asian scholars defer to Western practice and reverse their names. In this book, in keeping with our wish to challenge Western cultural hegemony, most have retained or reverted to the Eastern practice.

Acknowledgements

We would like to thank all our friends and colleagues in the Centre for Women's Studies, University of York and the Department of East Asian Studies, University of Leeds for their encouragement and support – in particular Harriet Badger, Anne Akeroyd and Ann Kaloski-Naylor. Thanks are also due to our contributors, who have been a pleasure to work with and whose promptness in turning drafts around and responding to queries has ensured that we kept to schedule. Finally we are extremely grateful to our editor at Zed Books, Ellen McKinlay, whose enthusiasm for the project, evident from our earliest tentative discussions with her, encouraged us to pursue it. She has been immensely supportive, patient and helpful throughout the process of producing the book.

Stevi Jackson
Liu Jieyu
Woo Juhyun

Notes on Contributors

Annie Hau-nung Chan is Assistant Professor at the Department of Sociology and Social Policy, Lingnan University, Hong Kong. Her research interests include domestic work and family change, Hong Kong culture, and female sexuality. She has published articles in *Postcolonial Studies, Journal of Family and Economic Issues, International Sociology*, and *Gender, Place and Culture*. She is currently studying Hong Kong women's subjectivities and narratives as represented on the Internet.

Chen Mei-Hua holds a PhD degree in Women's Studies, University of York, UK. Her dissertation looks at the ways in which sex work locates on the intersection of gender, sexuality and class. She currently teaches courses in Feminist Theory and Gender and Work at Tunghai University, Taiwan. She has published articles on issues such as sex work and sexuality in well-known journals in Taiwan. Recently her research has concentrated on the interrelation between sex work and the gendered labour market, and on Chinese migrant sex workers in Taiwan. As a feminist activist, she also serves on the board of the Awakening Foundation, one of the most important women's organizations in Taiwan.

Cho Joo-hyun is Professor of Women's Studies and Director of the Institute for Women's Studies at Keimyung University, South Korea. She received her PhD in Sociology from the University of Illinois at Urbana-Champaign in 1988. She is the author of many books, including (with Cho Eun and Lee Jeong-ok) 근대 가족의 변모와 여성문제 [*Transformation of the Modern Family and Women's Issues*]; 여성 정체성의 정치학 [*Gender Identity Politics*]; and (with Cho Eun and Kim Eun-shil) 성해방과 성정치 [*Sexual Liberation and Sexual Politics*]. She has worked on the subjects of family violence, gender and sexuality, and the women's movement. Her current research interests are on gender and bioethics, and globalization and violence.

Ding Yu is a PhD student in the Department of Social Work at the University of Hong Kong and is researching Chinese women sex workers. She undertook her undergraduate and postgraduate education in the UK before going to Hong Kong for her PhD research. Her research interests are women's sexuality and how China's development, modernization and urbanization influence their perceptions of work and life.

Ho Sik-Ying is Associate Professor at the Department of Social Work and Social Administration, University of Hong Kong. Dr Ho is one the few recognized experts in the relatively uncharted territory of gender and sexuality studies in Hong Kong and China. Her main research and teaching interests are in the area of homosexuality, gender and sexuality issues. Besides her two theses, Dr Ho has published numerous peer-reviewed papers in journals including *Sex Roles: A Journal of Sex Research, Journal of Sex Research, Violence Against Women, Sexualities, Affilia: Journal of Women and Social Work,* and *Women's Studies International Forum.* Her important contributions to the development of a dynamic theory of gender and sexuality in the international arena are helping to problematize feminist theories and resist Western hegemonies through empirical case studies that make connections between discourses, cultural practices, political economy and social change.

Stevi Jackson is Professor of Women's Studies and Director of the Centre for Women's Studies at the University of York, UK. She works on theories of gender and sexuality and is the author of a number of books, including *Childhood and Sexuality, Heterosexuality in Question* and (with Sue Scott) *Theorizing Sexuality.* She has co-edited, with Sue Scott, *Feminism and Sexuality* and *Gender: a Sociological Reader.* She has a long-standing personal interest in East Asia, having spent formative years in Hong Kong as a teenager, and has recently developed an academic interest in the area through her research students and through contacts with East Asian feminist scholars.

Saori Kamano is a senior researcher at the National Institute of Population and Social Security Research with special interests in families, sexualities and gender. She obtained her PhD in Sociology at Stanford University in 1995 with a dissertation on 'Same-sex sexual/ intimate relationships: a cross-national analysis of the interlinkages among naming, the gender system, and gay and lesbian resistance activities'. Recently, she has been working on papers and conference presentations on such topics as 'Entering the lesbian Japan: debut stories', 'Doing couples in lesbian communities and doing lesbian couples in Japanese society', 'Housework in lesbian couples in Japan: its division, negotiation, and interpretation', and 'Lesbian couples and gay couples: how differences in social environment affect daily lives'.

Diana Khor grew up in Hong Kong, received her doctorate in Sociology at Stanford University in California, and is now a Professor at Hosei University in Tokyo, Japan. She teaches a variety of classes related to race, class and gender inequality in a cross-national and global context, and does research related to the social construction of gender, broadly conceived. She recently completed an analysis of housework division among lesbian and gay couples in Sweden (*Journal of GLBT Family Studies*), and is currently working on a project on the development of women's and gender studies in Japan. With Saori Kamano, she also co-edited a special issue of the *Journal of Lesbian Studies* in 2006, which was published simultaneously as *'Lesbians' in East Asia: Diversity, Identities, and Resistance*.

Lan Pei-Chia is Associate Professor of Sociology at National Taiwan University. She was a postdoctoral fellow at University of California, Berkeley (2000–1) and a Fulbright scholar at New York University (2006–7). Her book, *Global Cinderellas: Migrant Domestics and Newly Rich Employers in Taiwan*, won the 2007 Distinguished Book Award from the Sex and Gender Section of the American Sociological Association and the 2007 ICAS Book Prize: Best Study in Social Science from the International Convention of Asian Scholars. She has done research on gender and work in Taiwan and labour migration in Asia and is starting a new project on service work in urban China.

Lee Sung-Eun is a research fellow at the Asian Center for Women's Studies at Ewha Woman's University in South Korea and has lectured in the Department of Women's Studies at Ewha since 2003. She is a co-author of *Introducing Women's Studies in Korea* [새 여성학 강의] and also the author of 'Practical strategies against sexual harassment in Korea' (*Asian Journal of Women's Studies* 2004). Her research has focused on the conceptualization of sexual intimacy in Korean married couples and, more recently, the sexuality of the 'New Woman' in a global and historical context.

Li Yinhe was born in Beijing in 1952. She holds a PhD in Sociology from Pittsburgh University and is currently Professor in Sociology and Research Fellow of the Sociology Section, Chinese Academy of Social Sciences. Her main published books are *Reproduction and Chinese Village Culture* [生育与中国村落文化], *The Rise of Women's Power* [女性权力的崛起], *Chinese Women's Love and Sex* [中国女性的感情与性], *Homosexual Culture in China* [同性恋亚文化], *On Sex* [性的问题] and *On Gender* [性别问题].

Liu Jieyu is an Academic Fellow in the White Rose East Asia Centre, University of Leeds. She gained her Bachelor's degree from Nanjing University and her PhD from the University of York, and was a postdoctoral fellow at the University of Sussex and Lecturer in Sociology at the University of Glasgow before taking up her present post. She is the author of *Gendering Redundancy in Urban China: Women Workers of the Unlucky Generation* and of journal articles on women workers in China. She is currently researching the sexualization and aestheticization of white-collar work in China (the 'white-collar beauty' syndrome) and the aspirations of young women employed in such work.

Muta Kazue is Professor of Sociology and Gender Studies at Osaka University, Japan. Her speciality is historical sociology and gender studies. As Visiting Professor, she taught Japanese studies/gender studies courses at Columbia University in 1998 and the University of Michigan in 2004. She is the author of *Jenderkazokuwo koete* [*Gendered Family in Japan: from Past to Future*], *Jissensuru feminizumu* [*Feminist Practice*] and *Senryaku to shiteno kazoku* [*Family Politics and Women in Modern Japan*]. Her English publications includes 'The New Woman in Japan: radicalism and ambivalence toward love and sex', in Heilmann and Beetham (eds), *New Woman Hybridities: Femininity, Feminism, and International Consumer Culture, 1880–1930* and 'Images of the family in Meiji periodicals: the paradox underlying the emergence of the home', *US–Japan Women's Journal*, 7 (1994).

Shen Hsiu-hua is an Assistant Professor at the Institute of Sociology at National Tsing Hua University in Taiwan. She is a former postdoctoral fellow at the Fairbank Center for East Asian Studies at Harvard University (2003–2004) and the Asia Research Institute at the National University of Singapore (2004–2006). Her research and teaching interests include gender, migration, globalization, political sociology and qualitative research. She has published and edited works related to transnational masculinities, the international division of intimate labour, heterosexuality and migration, family–state relations, and transnational marriages. She is currently researching flexible intimacy in the global context.

Woo Juhyun completed her PhD at the University of York on narratives of sexual citizenship. She undertook her undergraduate and graduate education in the UK, but was born and raised in Korea, where she worked as a sociological researcher before returning to the UK to write her PhD. She is currently teaching sociology and women's studies at the University of York.

Introduction

Reflections on Gender, Modernity and East Asian Sexualities

STEVI JACKSON, LIU JIEYU AND WOO JUHYUN

Western feminists have been aware for several decades of the need to broaden their scholarship beyond the Euro-American axis that has defined its priorities, yet the lives of East Asian women – over a quarter of the world's women – have received little attention except from those with a specialist interest in the region. Thus, while there is now a fairly substantial body of literature on East Asian women available in the West, it has had only a marginal impact on Western women's studies and feminist theory. Most attempts to globalize feminism have been framed in terms of an opposition between First World and Third World women (Mohanty 1991) or, in more recent parlance, between North and South. While it is obviously crucial to develop feminist analyses of the widening gulf between rich and poor nations, the effect of this is to exclude East Asian women who are neither Western nor from the global South. Although East Asia is growing in global influence, it is a region about which Westerners, including feminists, know little, all too often still seeing it as mysteriously 'other'.

In putting together a collection that brings East Asian feminist scholarship to the attention of wider Western audiences, we hope to persuade them that East Asia matters and that the work of East Asian feminists should be taken seriously as part of a global feminist dialogue. Our introduction, then, is intended to provide some background information for readers unfamiliar with East Asia as well as to contextualize and draw out some of the themes discussed by individual contributors to the volume. This work, a small sample of that being produced by Chinese, Taiwanese, Japanese and Korean scholars, focuses on sexuality: a much debated and highly charged area of concern in the East as in the West. In the Western context feminists have highlighted the gendered asymmetry and inequality inherent in the social ordering of sexuality. They have, on the one hand, contested double standards of morality and sought to promote women's sexual autonomy while, on the other hand, combating sexual violence and exploitation – but with differing and often hotly disputed emphases (see Jackson and Scott 1996). While gender and sexuality are evidently interrelated, there is also considerable debate on how these terms should be defined and how their interrelationship can best be theorized (Jackson 2006a, 2006b).

Similar debates among East Asian feminists are discussed by contributors to this volume (see especially chapters 5, 6 and 7). In attempting to talk to each other across cultures, however, it should be remembered that the concepts of gender and sexuality are modern, Western constructs – and, in the case of gender, specifically Anglophone in origin. The idea of 'sexuality' as a specific, erotic, aspect of human life and being dates back only to the late nineteenth century (Heath 1982); the concept of gender, first used in the late 1960s to differentiate socio-cultural masculine and feminine identities from biological 'sex' differences (Stoller 1968), was taken up by feminists from the 1970s onwards to emphasize the social bases of the division and distinction between women and men. These terms have no pre-existing equivalents in Asian languages and do not translate easily (Lee, So-Hee 2002; Li Xiaojiang 1999); yet they have, nonetheless, been taken up and reinvented by East Asian scholars. All East Asian languages have a word for sex but the concept of sexuality, central to the project of this book, has proved particularly difficult. In Japanese and Korean, which use phonetic representation, the problem has been resolved, at least partially, by 'localizing' the English word – in Japanese it becomes *sekushuariti*.[1] In Chinese, a language based on ideographic representation of concepts (as opposed to sounds), the problem is more intractable. Here 'sexuality' has been variously translated simply as *xing* (sex), in Taiwan *xing-zhi* ('the nature of sex') or, in China, as *xing cunzai* ('the existence of sex'). None of these terms is very satisfactory. These difficulties, centring on the term 'sex' (*xing*), which means both erotic acts and male–female differences, do have a parallel in the ambiguity around 'sex' and 'sexual' in everyday English – where it can be used as a substitute for gender (the sexual division of labour) or to denote the erotic (sexual fantasies). These conflations perhaps tell us something about the social ordering of sexuality in both Eastern and Western contexts – that to be 'normally' or normatively 'sexed' (gendered) is to display appropriate masculine or feminine sexual (erotic) conduct and, in particular, to form sexual (erotic) attachments to the 'other' 'sex' (gender).

There are, then, points of both similarity and difference to be found between East Asian and Western understandings of sexuality – and similarities and differences within both regions too. The chapters in this collection speak to these varied interpretations, and thus bring East Asian perspectives to bear on issues likely to be familiar to Western readers as well as some that are less familiar. The contributors are also, in the process, addressing the gendered and sexual consequences of globalization and modernization. In so doing they collectively underline two key points: that globalization is differentially experienced in different locations and that Western modernity is not everyone's modernity.

As the contributors to this volume make clear, modernity can no longer be considered a purely Western phenomenon – East Asian nations such as Japan, South Korea and Taiwan are as modern or post-modern as the West, while China is rapidly modernizing. These nations have all modernized very quickly, however, through a 'compressed' process of socio-economic development (Chan, this volume, Chapter 10; Abelmann 2003). These transformations have had profound consequences for gender relations, in particular in the sphere of intimacy and sexuality with which we are concerned here. New sexual cultures and vocabularies have emerged; new dilemmas face women in their daily sexual lives; there are new priorities in sexual politics. We should be careful, however, not to assume that Eastern nations are simply 'catching up' with their Western counterparts, or that social trends similar to those observed in the West confirm that late modernity has the same consequences in all parts of the world. Figures on both Eastern and Western 'trends', moreover, always conceal within them considerable complexity and variability even within a single nation. While taking account of the local specificities of Asian cultures, then, we should be alert to diversity within and between Eastern nations, which also helps guard against the Western tendency to stereotype and exoticize the East.

'East' and 'West': imaginative geographies

We recognize, of course, that the binary opposition of East and West is a construction – but it is a construction with material effects. East and West are products of 'imaginative geography' (Said 1978), a geography that has arisen from the history of European colonialism and imperialism. This is reflected in conventional cartographical representations of the world, which concretize Western imaginative geography and reflect actual histories. Now, when the globe is represented flattened out, it is with the Greenwich meridian (a heritage of Britain's past maritime supremacy)[2] in the centre and the international dateline defining its edges, with the Americas positioned to the west and Asia to the east. Imaginative geography has become 'real', solidifying the relative terms East and West as absolutes.

Historically the East was subdivided, eurocentrically, into the Near, Middle and Far East. The concept of the 'Near East' has all but vanished from our contemporary vocabulary so that, aside from the distinction between Eastern and Western Europe,[3] the 'East' for most Westerners now starts in the 'Middle' East, and extends to the 'Far' East. And the East continues to trouble the West in these post-colonial times. Western powers are still trying to subdue and control the Middle East, while East Asia evokes, as perhaps it always has, more ambivalent and mixed responses. Since the last few decades of the last century this region has been challenging the West's economic supremacy. The rapid modernization of the region, which has been brought into sharper focus by China's entry on to the world economic stage, has fuelled Western interest in Asia: it cannot now be ignored or discounted. These historical developments have changed the way this particular 'East' figures in the Western imagination, but the old ideas of the East as exotically other – whether dangerously or alluringly so – persist. And the exoticized East of the Western imaginary has always been gendered and sexualized: the Japanese geisha or tragic 'Butterfly' and the coy Chinese 'lotus blossom' with her bound feet – or her evil opposite, the domineering 'dragon lady' (Lim 2005) – still figure in Western ideas of the East.[4]

The sexualized image of Asian women as docile and subservient yet skilled in erotic arts has fuelled the fantasies of many Western men, evident today in the marketing of parts of Asia for tourism in general and sex tourism in particular (O'Connell Davidson 1995), and in Western male travellers' accounts of the appeal of East Asian cities.

Westerners, however, do not hold a monopoly on imaginative geography – even if the Western version has been hegemonic. Just as the West constructs images of the East, so there are Eastern constructions of 'the West' – and these are highly contested. The paths of cultural influence between West and East have long moved in both directions (Jackson and Jaffer 2004), but they remain asymmetrical. The power and reach of Western culture industries (through film, fashion, music, women's magazines, etcetera) have given Western culture far greater penetration in the East than Eastern culture has in the other direction. This Western cultural influence can be read as a new form of imperialism or as signifying inclusion in global modernity, as a harbinger of progress or of moral contagion and corruption, as promising new freedoms or posing new risks. These competing interpretations are inflected by conceptions of modernization and Westernization, in particular whether modernization necessarily entails Westernization. How Western cultural influences are perceived, and whether they are modified, resisted or embraced, varies between and within countries, often in relation to competing ideas of national identity. And women frequently figure centrally in such national imaginaries – whether in terms of traditions to be preserved and protected, modern rights and freedoms to be promoted, or anxieties about cultural or ethnic boundaries (Lan 2008).

Alongside this, in Eastern nations, actual changes in the situation of women are occurring, and new gendered and sexual lifestyles and identities are emerging. Women are active agents in these processes, individually and collectively involved in renegotiating and reshaping their daily lives in changing conditions. In the process they are often constructing their own ideas of what it means to be modern (see, for example, Lan, this volume Chapter 1, and Ding and Ho, Chapter 6). Modernity, as Lisa Rofel points out, 'is a struggle that takes place in specific locations and a process that links together local/global configurations' (Rofel 1999: 18). Modernity, then, is not a monolithic entity – processes of modernization are complex and particular, and are enacted by both individuals and collectivities; modernity is also imagined and re-imagined from different historical and social locations. The image of modernity requires its converse – tradition or, more pejoratively, 'backwardness' – against which it is positioned. 'Tradition' is by no means fixed by the past but is constantly (re)invented from the perspective of the present to suit particular conceptions of the modern.

If modernity is locally negotiated, it follows that it might be differently gendered outside the narrow confines of the West. East Asian modernity has been built on a different history, with different cultures and traditions and also a different relationship between tradition and modernity, in part precisely because of the association between the 'Western' and the 'modern'. Aiko Tanabe and Yumiko Tokito-Tanabe (2003) argue that, while Eastern nations modernized through 'learning from and imitating the West', the maintenance of a self-identity as distinct from the West required the incorporation of tradition within modernity and vice versa. Therefore, they suggest, modern Eastern societies cannot be characterized as what Giddens (1990) terms 'post-traditional'; rather, there is a 'complex self-reflexive endeavour to position onself for *and* against "European modernity" and "indigenous tradition"' (Tanabe and Tokito-Tanabe 2003: 4, emphasis in original).

East Asia matters: some historical background

The East Asian nations with which we are concerned here have their own complex histories interwoven with each other and with differing histories of interaction with the West. The old 'Far East' long held an allure for the West as the source of exotic and desired luxuries such as silk and porcelain, but, despite their best efforts, Western nations never managed fully to colonize Asia beyond the South-East.[5] They did, however, exert a degree of dominance over China, even though only two small enclaves came directly under colonial rule: of the Portuguese in Macau and the British in Hong Kong. China, from ancient times, had widespread influence in East Asia in terms of its social and cultural values and language systems – for example through the spread of Confucianism to Korea and Japan, and the adoption of Chinese characters into written Japanese. Britain's attempts to gain access to Chinese commodities on more favourable trade terms led ultimately to China's defeat in the 1842 Opium War, after which Hong Kong was ceded to Britain (a national disgrace in Chinese eyes). By then China's influence in the region was on the wane; its Qing dynasty, seriously weakened by the beginning of the twentieth century, was finally overthrown by the nationalist revolution in 1911, ushering in a period of self-conscious modernization.

Japan, meanwhile, had long held the West at bay and during the Tokugawa period had followed a policy of isolationism. Finally, in the mid-nineteenth century, it was forced to grant trading concessions to the Western powers. During the Meiji period (1868–1912), however, Japan began modernizing and appropriating aspects of Western technology on its own terms. It renegotiated more favourable trade terms with the West and, at the beginning of the twentieth century, was becoming a colonial power in its own right. Japan annexed Taiwan (Formosa) in 1895, following war with China, and subsequently established a protectorate over Korea in 1905 before colonizing it in 1910. Japan was also challenging the West's military might, having defeated Russia in the war of 1904–5. China bore the brunt of Japan's expansionism in the 1930s: Manchuria was annexed in 1932, and open war between China and Japan erupted in 1937 – a prelude to Japan overrunning much of Asia and the Pacific during the Second World War.

Japan rose from the ashes of its eventual defeat in 1945 and the horrors of the Hiroshima and Nagasaki bombs to become a major player on the world economic stage and a peaceable democratic nation. The fortunes of its erstwhile colonies and enemies were more mixed. The nationalists in China lost the civil war with the communists after Japan's defeat and in 1949 the People's Republic of China was established. Taiwan, liberated from Japanese rule, found itself under the control of Chiang Kai-Shek's nationalist army, which retreated there after defeat by the communists and established the rival Republic of China, recognized by the United Nations until 1971 and supported by the USA until relations between the USA and the PRC were normalized in 1978. Under repressive military rule until 1987, Taiwan has since become a democracy, but remains largely unrecognized in the world as a nation in its own right. Relations between Taiwan and China have been tense throughout this period, with the latter opposing any move by the former to establish full national status – and whether it should become an independent nation remains a contested issue within Taiwan itself. Korea was partitioned following the Korean War (1950–3), with a totalitarian communist state in the north and what was effectively a military dictatorship in the South until the democratic 'revolution' of 1987. With the transition to democracy in South Korea and Taiwan, feminist campaigns had considerable impact, placing women's issues on the political agenda.

South Korea and Taiwan have now joined Japan as modern, prosperous societies (though Japan and South Korea both experienced economic crises during the 1990s). In all three countries women have made progress in education and employment, but patriarchal values and practices have by no means been eradicated and continue to mark women's lives today. In particular, as we shall see, within these East Asian capitalist democracies men's sexual 'needs' are still privileged and it remains difficult for women to attain sexual autonomy, especially if they seek to escape the institution of heterosexuality.

China's communist regime, on the other hand, initially espoused an 'official' ideology of equality between women and men, outlawing concubinage and prostitution and mobilizing women into the workforce. Yet women did not enter the labour force on equal terms with men: there remained a strict gendered division of labour in the *danwei* (work units) and women were still, in many respects (for example in the allocation of housing), considered dependants (Liu 2007). Moreover, the project of equality entailed the desexualization of women, while tight controls on personal life severely restricted sexual freedom and access to sexual knowledge. The only acceptable form of sexual activity was within monogamous marriage. Despite the rhetoric of equality women were still defined in 'scientific' terms as essentially different from and less sexual than men (Evans 1997).

China, since the 1980s, has been pursuing a policy of 'opening up' to the outside world and moving to a market economy – which has, among other things, led to the emergence of social and sexual relations across the Taiwan Strait (see Shen, Chapter 11) as well as new sexual cultures in coastal cities: for some young women, being 'sexy' and sexually more adventurous has become a badge of 'modern' status (Farrer 2002; Ding and Ho, Chapter 6, this volume). 'Opening up' has also brought with it a growing sex industry, the sexualization of women's labour (Ding and Ho, Chapter 6; Liu, Chapter 4) and a proliferation of 'sexy images' which, according to Judith Farquhar, are 'at least as important in conveying a generalized imagination of modernity and wealth as they are in stimulating erotic feeling' (2002: 216). New opportunities are available for some women, particularly the young, urban and privileged, but must be understood alongside the increasing abandonment of the old communist commitment to gender equality and a widening gulf between rich and poor.

Understanding the gendered character of everyday sexuality in East

Asia entails taking account of family structures and practices and the influence of Confucianism. Historically East Asian culture has been strongly patriarchal and patrilineal – and the latter has all the more force because families are understood not simply in terms of living relatives but as lineages, existing through time, in which living generations owe homage not only to present elders, but also to ancestors. The family, thus conceived, is also a cornerstone of Confucianism. Chinese in origin, Confucianism remains influential not only in China and Taiwan but also in Korea, and has had some influence in Japan via its historical adoption within samurai culture. The Confucian ethic privileges order and hierarchy, the needs of the collective over those of the individual, filial piety and women's obedience to men.[6] It thus leaves little scope for women's autonomy or for expressions of sexuality that are not harnessed to the needs of men and of procreation – especially the production of male children who will perpetuate the family. It has been described as 'the most patriarchal of all the major normative systems of the world' (Therborn 2004: 119).

Today Confucianism is less an explicit belief system than a set of taken-for-granted traditional assumptions about 'the way things are' (or should be). Its traces have nonetheless left their mark on East Asia. This cultural heritage has helped shape the context in which East Asian sexualities are lived and understood and in which feminists seek to advance their cause: Confucianism is thus often cited in Eastern feminist writings as a major barrier to gender equality and women's sexual autonomy. It has, however, faced challenges from modernizing projects and processes. In China Confucianism was critiqued by radical reformers from the early twentieth century onwards and came under sustained attack during the communist revolution and particularly during the Cultural Revolution. It may be argued, however, that despite this repudiation Chinese communism perpetuated some of Confucianism's key features, particularly its collectivist ethos and deference for authority – albeit the authority of the Party rather than feudal rulers. For example, the distinctive familial organization of the *danwei*, the work and residential unit fundamental to social organization in urban China prior to the 1990s, regulated women's domestic lives and their life chances. A *danwei* leader

> acted like a family elder, interfering in decisions to marry, to have a house, to have a baby and in the conduct of marital life; Confucian

familial protocols, theoretically rendered obsolete by socialism, had been redeployed in various forms in the daily practice of *danwei*'s control'. (Liu 2007: 141)

The global market economy, now dominating China as much as capitalist East Asia, might be expected to sweep aside such 'traditional' ideas, but it is unlikely to be that simple. For example, during the Party Congress of 2007, in discussing future national agendas, the state government also called for the establishment of a harmonious society, resonant with the ancient Confucian protocol. Indeed, there are signs that Confucianism itself is being rehabilitated in China.

Elsewhere, too, Confucian ethics have become embedded in the project of modernity. The corporate cultures of Japan and South Korea flourished in the 1960s and 1970s by incorporating old ideals of loyalty to the collective (the company). Only after the economic crises of the 1990s was this threatened by increasing job insecurity and competitive individualism. Individualism, which has a long history in the West, especially in Britain and the USA, is thus relatively new to Asia – gaining influence in the more thoroughly Westernized contexts of Hong Kong and Taiwan earlier than elsewhere, but even here traditional influences on familial and gender relations have not been eradicated. Moreover, as in China, 'harmony' remains a valued feature of social life, within family and workplace, and it is often incumbent on women, as subordinates, to ensure it is not disrupted (see, for example, Muta, Chapter 2; Lee, Chapter 3; and, for China, Liu, Chapter 4). Changing patterns of intimacy in East Asia, then, need to be understood in the light of the region's culture and history.

Conceptualizing intimacy and modernity: making sense of local and global change

Our premise, then, is that we inhabit *different* modernities. The theories woven around modernity in the West, which are generally presented as universal theories of the late-modern or post-modern condition, actually refer to a *particular* form of modernity, a product of local Western culture and history – and of a particular imagined tradition. They are, in short, ethnocentric. In Western academic debate the characteristics of late modernity and late capitalism, with its 'flexible' employment patterns and global flows of products, people and ideas, have been associated with 'detraditionalization' and individualization (Beck and Beck-Gernsheim 2002), a disembedding of the individual from close personal and community ties, a reflexive 'project of the self' and a 'transformation of intimacy' (Giddens 1990, 1991, 1992). There has been considerable critical engagement with these ideas on the part of Western feminists, in particular with the claims made about the impact of social change on gendered and sexual relations. While some Western feminists have taken up some of these themes, albeit critically, in arguing that we are moving towards more diverse post-modern forms of intimate relationships (Roseneil 2000; Stacey 1996), others are more cautious, suggesting that many of the claims being made do not fully capture what is happening in our intimate lives (Adkins 2002; Jamieson 1999; Smart and Shipman 2004). The scope of these debates, however, needs to be extended beyond their Western, largely Euro-American, focus.

What is of interest to feminists is the way women feature in these theoretical accounts of late modernity. Whereas the classical theorists of 'old' industrial modernity − Durkheim, Weber and Simmel − located women as outside the modernizing process, 'left behind' in their 'traditional' domestic sphere, the new generation of modernity theorists have dealt with gender rather differently. For Giddens (1991), the 'transformation of intimacy' − the shift from romantic to confluent love and the 'pure relationship' contingent on mutual satisfaction rather than lifelong commitment − is spearheaded by women, gays and lesbians forging more democratic relationships. Here women are no longer positioned outside the project of modernity but out in front. Beck and Beck-Gernsheim are in some ways closer to the old modernity theorists. In their conceptualization of individualization, detraditionalization and the 'do-it-yourself' biography, intimate relationships are changing, but with the caveat that women are not yet fully individuated. For Castells (2004), new feminist, lesbian and gay movements represent an aspect of the power of identity politics in the modern world, possibly signalling the end of patriarchalism.

There are varying degrees to which these writers have considered the world beyond the West, and varying degrees to which their claims are evidenced. Castells takes a global sweep, using examples from various regions of the world. He has also done us a service in drawing together some useful data on global trends in the process. But given that we know that 'patriarchalism' is not a monolithic entity, what does its posited end entail in different parts of the globe? Beck and Beck-Gernsheim (2002) are rooted in the West, and draw what evidence they use from there. But what does individualization mean in societies that do not share the Western individualistic heritage? What does de-traditionalization mean when the tradition in question is not a Western one?

Giddens, at the end of *The Consequences of Modernity* (1990), does briefly address the question of whether modernity is a specifically Western project. Yes, he says, in that its origins – capitalism and the nation-state – are Western; no, in the sense that globalization entails culturally diverse local adjustments; yes, in that reflexive knowledge production overrides local culture and marks a break from tradition. Thus, on balance, Giddens sees modernity as essentially Western. *The Transformation of Intimacy*, however, is entirely Western in focus and, like much of his work, has little by way of evidence to support it. What intimacy is being transformed where the tradition of romantic love, as Giddens describes it, is not part of local culture?

Some of the ideas of these theorists are being taken up by Eastern scholars to explain changes in gender relationships and family life in East Asian countries.[7] So, further questions arise: If these perspectives are problematic in Western contexts, do they have any purchase at all outside the West? What effects is modernization having on intimate gendered and sexual lives in the East, and how much do these outcomes resemble what is happening in the West? How far are changes attributable to modernization *per se* or to local conditions?

Much of the evidence for these (Western) claims about the gendered consequences of modernity comes from trends in women's labour market participation, increasing economic independence, and consequent changes in family life. Castells, for example, identifies the family as the cornerstone of patriarchalism – and the weakening of the former as presaging the demise of the latter. It is the case that certain trends observable in East Asian nations, such as women's increasing participation in the labour market, later marriage and falling fertility, are similar to those in the West, but we cannot assume that they have identical meanings or identical consequences in different regions – or even in different countries within the same region.

In capitalist East Asian nations, as in the West, the gap between men's and women's 'economic activity rates' is closing (see Castells 2004: 219–20, tables 4.13 and 4.14). It should be noted, though, that there are local variations within East Asia, just as there are in Europe. For example, fewer women are in paid work in South Korea than in neighbouring Japan (Castells 2004). There are also variations within countries, reflecting class, ethnic and rural/urban divides. Thus in China, where women have been mobilized into the labour market since the communist revolution, the modernizing project and the market economy have opened up new employment opportunities for young, educated and urban women, enabled young rural women to migrate to cities to find work, but often worsened the economic situation of older, uneducated and rural women (Liu 2007; Pun 2005; Lee 2005). In general, moreover, women still earn less than men, as they do globally.

The rise in women's employment in many parts of the world reflects a growing demand for women's labour but also, in many instances, a greater need for married women to contribute to family income as the 'flexible' global economy undermines security of employment and men's ability to earn a 'family wage' (Irwin 1999). Women are also becoming more available for employment as they spend a shorter period of their lives in child rearing. Thus changes in women's working lives interconnect with changes in domestic life.

Declining birth rates are widely agreed to be characteristic of modernity and affect East Asian countries as well as Western ones (see, for example, Cho, Chapter 7; Kamano and Khor, Chapter 8). Here too there are differences, for example, between women choosing to have only one or two children (albeit within economic and social constraints) and having that decision made for them, as in the case of China's one-child policy. Despite having fewer children and engaging in paid work, women generally retain their responsibility for domestic labour, and the ideal wife in East Asia is still expected to put husband and family first. How this domestic burden is experienced and managed, however, varies by class. Working-class women juggle the double burden of waged and domestic work, while more privileged, well-paid women reduce their domestic drudgery by buying the services of other, poorer, women in an increasingly international market (Romero 1992; Cheng 2003; Lan 2003, 2006). Wealthy women in Taiwan and Japan, for example, employ maids from the Philippines or South-East Asia (Cheng 2003; Lan 2003, 2006; see also Lan, Chapter 1, this volume). The inequality among women that this represents does nothing to undermine the inequality between women and men.

Trends in marriage and divorce are also part of the changing conditions of women's lives. More women are delaying or even eschewing marriage: falling rates of and later marriage have been recorded since the 1970s in Japan, Korea and Taiwan as well as in most Western countries, as have high rates of divorce. Again, though, there are variations between and within regions. China still has an extremely high rate of marriage, making it virtually compulsory (Liu 2004), and elsewhere in Asia marriage is still regarded as a normal and inevitable part of life. Cohabitation has become commonplace in the West (25 per cent of non-married women were cohabiting with a man in the UK in 2004), but is still less common and less socially acceptable in the East (see Kamano and Khor, Chapter 8), as is living alone. Even in the West it is only very privileged women who can maintain an independent single lifestyle at a decent standard of living – in East Asia, where most unmarried women live with their parents, living alone is an unusual choice, but is becoming more possible.

Women may, as Giddens argues, be seeking more egalitarian partnerships, but Western evidence suggests that it is the continuing lack of equality that causes much of the strain and instability in contemporary heterosexual relationships – and there are plenty of indications to suggest that this may be the case in East Asia, too. Many men, it seems, resist democratized relationships and prefer more 'traditional' heterosexual arrangements.

One strategy open to them is to turn to the global marriage market, aided by a host of international match-making organizations (Constable 2005) whereby women from poorer countries seek to improve their position by marrying men from richer nations. These men hope to 'fulfil their nostalgia for a prefeminist family romance' by marrying foreign women, in the (often false) expectation that they will be subservient (Lan 2003: 202). European and American men seek wives from Eastern Europe and Asia; men in Japan, Korea and Taiwan find brides in poorer, more 'traditional' countries in South-East Asia (Constable 2005; Suzuki 2005). There are class dimensions here – it is less privileged men, who lose out in local marriage markets, who tend to look elsewhere for wives; but more privileged men working within a transnational economy can avail themselves of the services of both a wife at home and a mistress abroad (see Shen, Chapter 11).

The idea of a 'transformation of intimacy' is closely related to the individualization thesis: the idea that increasing individuation, reflexivity and choice result in more fluid, fragile and contingent intimate relationships (Giddens 1991; Beck and Beck-Gernsheim 1995, 2002; Beck-Gernsheim 2002; Bauman 2003). The individualization thesis emphasizes a break with tradition, the erosion of normative prescription, and a disembedding of the individual from the social – all of which is seen as freeing us from social constraints. There are, however, some evident problems with this picture. First, it entails 'a rather soggy notion of "tradition"' (Pahl and Spencer 2004: 201), referring often to an unspecified past and with little foundation in historical evidence. This imaginary picture of 'traditional' European social order over-emphasizes the degree to which individuals were embedded in community and represents those communities as far more fixed and static than the accumulated historical evidence suggests (Pahl and Spencer 2004, 2006). Conversely, it downplays the continued importance of 'personal communities' of friends and kin (Pahl and Spencer 2004) and the extent to which individual conduct and the choices we make continue to be shaped by culture, social context and the immediate social milieu in which our lives are lived (Smart and Shipman 2004; Irwin 2005). Such sceptics rarely dismiss the individualization thesis altogether, but they do contest some of its claims.

Even in the West there is considerable evidence of people not only maintaining family and other personal ties but also expressing a strong sense of mutual obligation across households, while in East Asia the idea of family remains strong despite demographic trends indicative of strain within intimate relationships. Such kin ties are often an important source of social support: for example, wider kinship networks play a very important role in finding re-employment among redundant workers in the Chinese labour market (Liu 2007). With increased geographical mobility in our globalized world such ties are not only local or even national ones; kin divided by distance may retain a sense of attachment across countries and continents. Thus migrants in the UK have been found to maintain strong kin ties to their home countries (Mason 2004; Smart and Shipman 2004) and the durability of such ties has been noted in Chinese diasporic communities (Lee et al. 2002). More temporary migrants also keep up family connections: for example, a woman from the Philippines might leave children with relatives while working to support them in Saudi Arabia, Japan or Taiwan (Cheng 2003; Lan 2003).

The individualization thesis is a Western idea, formulated from within cultures with a long history of individualism (Macfarlane 1978). One aspect of this has been free choice of marriage partners and the idea that marriage should be based on love for another who complements and completes the self – though with changing conceptions of love over time (Evans 2003). It has also been associated with a long history of households based on nuclear families. Most human societies, including those of East Asia, do not share this history. The individualization thesis ignores alternative cultural traditions. As Carol Smart and Becky Shipman note, it presents a 'monochrome' picture of intimacy in the late modern world. They suggest, in the UK context, that we should not think of alternatives to Western-style intimacy as 'practices that are yet to catch up in the "individualization race"', but as 'different ways of "doing family"' (2004: 496). Similarly, we should not regard East Asian practices as simply 'lagging behind' the West, but as products of different histories and cultures.

Individualism remains problematic in East Asia. It is not universally embraced as the inalienable right of the sovereign individual, as in Western philosophy, but as something more troubling and full of contradictions. For example, in China, with the determination to develop a market economy, the state has widely promoted economic individualism, praising competition and efficiency; as a result, a self-reliant individualism is widely internalized. Yet, paradoxically, 'harmony' – requiring the individual to defer to the collective social will – remains a strong theme in official rhetoric. For women this presents both risks and opportunities. Without a fully developed social welfare system, older and less-educated women resorted to their wider family network when they were thrown out of their former jobs during the economic restructuring (Liu 2007). By contrast, the urban young women from the only-child generation enjoy unprecedented educational investment from their families, which fosters a certain self-centredness as they grow up (Tsui and Rich 2002). However, their newly gained 'individualism' is undermined by the reality of gender discrimination in China's transition to a market economy. Women, including highly educated women, are facing disadvantages in job applications. Young professional women, despite a desire for personal success and self-development, express the concern to get the best possible husband and to push him forward. These contradictory voices reflect the intermingling of past and present, of tradition and modernity, and of the tensions and frictions arising from these oppositional ideologies. Thus, the newly arising individualism among China's younger generation seems to be 'under constant negotiation with the traditional ideologies' (Liu 2007: 136).

Thus superficially similar trends in different parts of the world – later marriage, more divorce, more women working – may not have the same meaning or consequences in countries with different cultural traditions and histories. We may live in a globalized, late-modern world, but not everyone's modernity is the same (Rofel 1999) and it cannot therefore be assumed that modernization will have the same consequences for women's intimate lives world-wide. East Asian scholarship enables us to explore the extent to which universalizing claims about late-modern 'transformations of intimacy' (Giddens 1991), 'individualization' and 'de-traditionalization' (Beck and Beck-Gernsheim 2002) are specific to the West, or whether supposed global trends such as the 'end of patriarchalism' (Castells 2004) are tenable in the light of local particularities. Social change in East Asia, then, casts new light on debates about the gendered consequences of modernity and globalization, and can therefore add to the critiques of mainstream theories of modernity already developed by Western feminists.

Intimacy, sexuality and everyday life

In the West, the increasing individualization attributed to late modernity has been associated with greater sexual freedom, the breaking of the link between sex, marriage and reproduction, and the exploration of new sexual lifestyles. While some of the contributions to this volume indicate that women in East Asia are also seeking greater sexual autonomy (Lan, Chapter 1; Ding and Ho, Chapter 6; Kamano and Khor, Chapter 8) it is clear that they face considerable constraints in so doing. Other chapters draw attention to the continued strong double standards of morality (Liu, Chapter 4; Shen, Chapter 11), sexual harassment (chapters 2 and 3), and the difficulties of forging a viable feminist sexual politics (Cho, Chapter 7).

Historically, in East Asian societies, talking about sex openly was culturally taboo. Women were traditionally cast as the passive party in sexual encounters and constrained from expressing sexual desires: 'A "good woman" is per definition not a "whore" and should not take any sexual initiatives' (Micollier 2004: xvi). In the context of economic development and globalization, alternative sexual practices and sexual cultures are emerging, testing the traditional moral boundaries. However, despite economic liberalization, the scope for development of sexual discourses in East Asia is still very limited. In the Korean context Cho Joo-hyun analyses the difficulties that feminist scholars have encountered in thinking of female sexuality other than in terms of the 'pure heterosexual woman', which has inhibited the analysis of sexual diversity (see Chapter 7).

Often, until recently, it was not possible even to find a language with which to talk about sexuality in the same way as is routinely done in the West (Lee 2002). When Liu Jieyu (Chapter 4) was interviewing young women on sexual activities, in order to be culturally appropriate and 'reputable', both she and the interviewees tried hard to find words (such as 'this' or 'that') to describe what they meant without mentioning the word 'sex' explicitly. Even many of the sex workers interviewed by Chen Mei-Hua (Chapter 5) found it difficult to describe 'doing that thing'. On the other hand, women participating in research often welcome the rare opportunity to express and explore their views on sexuality, as Annie Chan found (see Chapter 10).

This cultural reticence on sexual matters does pose particular challenges to researchers attempting to explore these issues. For example, one of our contributors, Li Yinhe (Chapter 9), has undertaken pioneering work in collecting women's stories on sex and love and conducting research on homosexuality, but her work and her progressive views have proved highly controversial in China. This chapter, which she based on one of her books (Li Yinhe 1998), is rather different in style and tone from our other contributions: it is based primarily on women's stories rather than argument or analysis. While it does not conform to Western conventions of scholarship, it allows the voices of Chinese women to be heard and offers us tantalizing glimpses of the ways in which changing ideas about love and sex are impacting on their everyday lives. It is for this reason, and in recognition of the difficulty of pursuing this kind of research in China, that we have included it. In China, even more than elsewhere in East Asia, work that documents women's sexual practices is radical, new and often brave.

Even where it is hidden, however, sexuality is embedded in wider social relations and in non-sexual aspects of social life; in particular, it is enmeshed with gender relations. Feminists in the East, as in the

West, are finding themselves caught between the polarized priorities of those pursuing anti-violence and anti-exploitation agendas, on the one hand, and defenders of pleasure and diversity on the other (see Cho, Chapter 7). There is, however, as Chen Mei-Hua (Chapter 5) points out, a less explored space between these polarities where ordinary, everyday unconventional *and* conventional sexual lives go on. In order to avoid the potential traps of a polarized sexual politics it is essential to be aware of the ways in which sexual expression, whether highly normative or extravagantly transgressive, is always embedded in wider patterns of sociality. Many of the contributions in this volume tell us much about the ways in which sexual relationships and activities take place within the context of ordinary everyday lives, even where those sexualities are unconventional, as in the case of the *xiaojies* discussed by Ding and Ho (Chapter 6) or the lesbian lives described by Kamano and Khor (Chapter 8). Conversely, those seeking to live 'respectable' sexual lives can find themselves affected by less reputable arrangements, as in the case of Taiwanese 'first wives' (Chapter 11) or the Chinese 'white-collar beauties' (Liu, Chapter 4) who end up walking a fine line between respectability and disreputability.

Work, economics and sexuality

Our starting point in emphasizing the everyday dimensions of sexuality is the world of work. Yet sexuality is generally thought of as occupying a sphere of social life quite separate from that of work, something uniquely private, conventionally located in either the private domain of domesticity or the domain of leisure – particularly men's leisure. Feminists, however, have long challenged the public–private distinction on which such oppositions rest – initially in establishing women's domestic responsibilities as work, more recently (for some feminists) in reconceptualizing prostitution as work. It is now beginning to be recognized, moreover, that both paid employment and domestic work are subject to sexualization and implicated in the maintenance of normative heterosexuality.

Domestic work, as Lan Pei-Chia points out, crosses the boundaries between public and private – it takes place in the employer's private, domestic space, which becomes public work space for the employee. There she is under surveillance, and under suspicion as a potentially threatening sexualized other (see also Yeoh and Huang

1998). Migrant workers in general are often constructed as sexually predatory and promiscuous by the host community and by male members of the migrant groups, as was the case in Jacka's (2006) study of rural migrant workers in urban China. Migrant domestic workers are doubly positioned as outsiders, as alien 'others', in relation to both family and nation. Worries about the activities of female migrants lead employers to constrain the physical mobility of their employees, trying to keep them within the boundaries of the home, within the private sphere.

More generally in East Asia, work intersects with sexuality because business practice is facilitated through sexualized leisure. This creates particular problems for women white-collar workers, who are either constrained to adapt to business-related leisure in venues designed for men's sexual pleasure or miss out on networking that might be vital to the effective performance of their jobs. Just how ubiquitous this practice is in Asia is evinced by how often it is mentioned in this volume – not only in the chapter devoted to the 'office party' (Lee, Chapter 3) but also in relation to routine work (Liu, Chapter 4), sexual harassment (Chapter 2), the problems of first wives (Chapter 11), and also the work of those who provide sexual services to businessmen (chapters 5 and 6).

The link between sex work and other work is therefore particularly explicit in East Asia and raises wider questions about the sexualization of women's labour. Lee (Chapter 3) draws attention to the ways in which Korean women workers try to manage the routine sexual harassment that takes place in leisure contexts where the boundaries between 'respectable' office workers and sex workers become blurred. Similarly Liu (Chapter 4) discusses how professional women negotiated the sexualized encounters prevalent in the Chinese business culture, while trying to maintain the professional image of their white-collar occupations. As well as drawing attention to the lack of a discourse on sexuality for women, she also details the impact upon their private lives of women's involvement in these sexualized business cultures. The connection is made from the other direction by Chen Mei-Hua (Chapter 5). In explicitly addressing the services sex workers routinely provide, she demonstrates the varying professional skills this work entails and how the embodied, aestheticized and emotional labour performed by sex workers parallels other work in the service sector.

The question of whether sex work is work has been contentious within feminist movements world-wide, but the terrain of this contestation varies, influenced both by local sexual cultures and by the particularities of national regulatory regimes. Three of the chapters in this volume address the opposition between sex work as work and prostitution as sexual exploitation, demonstrating the specificities of cultural and national contexts. In the Korean case (Cho, Chapter 7), where the view that prostitution constitutes sexual exploitation has been hegemonic within the women's movement, sex workers have contested this by vociferously claiming identities as workers and drawing parallels with other forms of labour. In the case of the women working in the sex industries in the Pearl River Delta region of China (Ding and Ho, Chapter 6), however, the identity of 'sex worker' has been resisted. Where the term 'sex work' has been seen elsewhere as emphasizing the 'work' in sex work, many of these women felt it placed too much emphasis on the 'sex' at the expense of other aspects of their work – the emotional and embodied labour that Chen Mei-Hua (Chapter 5) also emphasizes. Interestingly, some defined it as not work precisely because it was not a regular, reputable job. The idea that the label 'sex worker' endows the work with dignity, so central to sex workers' movements elsewhere in Asia (and in the West) was absent from the *xiaojies'* accounts. Rather, they sought other means of establishing a positive self-identity, positioning themselves as modern and cosmopolitan. (It is possible here that an identity as 'worker' is tainted by the association with past communist glorification of the worker, which in the context of China's modernizing drive simply seems old-fashioned.)

Global flows and local change

Global late modernity is characterized by movements of people, rapid communication and flows of ideas. Some of the work contexts described above depend on migrant labour, which has become a key feature of East Asian life. The wealthy economies of Japan, South Korea and Taiwan draw in migrants from poorer South-East Asian countries such as the Philippines, Indonesia and Vietnam, while China is characterized by massive rural–urban migration, especially to coastal cities. As Lan Pei-Chia points out (Chapter 1), individual migration trajectories can be complex: a single woman in her working life may move to different countries and occupy a variety of migrant roles – as sex worker, foreign wife or domestic worker. She also highlights the complex ways in which sexuality comes into play as migrant workers traverse boundaries of nation and occupation, and between public and private space. They are also simultaneously shifting identities – for example from exoticized foreigner to global cosmopolitan. These boundary crossings entail the mobilization of complex arts of impression management as women negotiate space for themselves while maintaining relations with employers, boyfriends and girlfriends, and their families back home.

While economic motives are clearly an important driver of migration from poorer to richer regions or nations, it is clearly not economics alone that motivates women to move, but also a desire for less tangible benefits. And here modernity often figures in the imagination of the migrant – the ability to participate in a more sophisticated, cosmopolitan urban environment, including participation in more 'modern' open sexual cultures. Being away from their own homes and the surveillance of their natal families and communities can present migrant women with new opportunities for sexual experimentation and for developing a more autonomous sense of sexual subjectivity (see Lan, Chapter 1; Ding and Ho, Chapter 6).

The relation between economy and migration is also stratified. Poor women move to find work, higher pay and more exciting lives, but nonetheless generally find themselves near the bottom of the social hierarchy or precariously positioned on the ladder of upward mobility in host cities or countries. Wealthier men, on the other hand, also move for economic gain but are in a much more secure and privileged position. Here, too, there might be other attractions – in particular the well-developed sex industries offering to cater to their every desire and the freedom to pursue sexual adventures while away from their wives. The phenomenon of *bao ernai* (keeping a mistress or 'second wife') in China creates its counterpart in the 'first wife' left at home (see Shen, Chapter 11).

It is not only people who move around the region and the world, but also ideas: this is why migrants are motivated by visions of modernity and sophistication in the first place. New ideas entail new concepts – these too are sometimes borrowed from elsewhere as in the case of 'sex work' and *sekuhara* (sexual harassment). But as Muta Kazue (Chapter 2) makes clear, when concepts travel they do not remain unchanged – *sekuhara* has acquired connotations in Japan that differ from the Western meaning of 'sexual harassment' and which reflect the local conditions of its use, simultaneously de-radicalizing it and making it more deployable in the Japanese context. New terms have also been coined in East Asia, such as the ironic use of *tongzhi* (comrade) within the gay community, originally in Hong Kong, but now also in Taiwan – though lesbians use this term less often, preferring their own vocabularies (Sang 2003).

The spread of new ideas has facilitated the rise of new sexual cultures in urban centres: sometimes these borrow ideas from the West, but recast them for local use (Farrer 2002). Even in China, where the government tries to limit access to knowledge about 'decadent' sexual practices, new communications technologies as well as the demands of a market economy have begun to make it easier to evade censorship and to exchange sexual information.[8] One very significant aspect of the movement of ideas is growing evidence of a discourse of female sexual pleasure in East Asia, evident from the studies of women's sexuality in China and Hong Kong (chapters 9 and 10). Moreover, while heteronormativity is firmly entrenched in East Asia, alternative sexual cultures are emerging, most visibly in Hong Kong and Taiwan, but elsewhere too.

Feminist and sexual liberation movements strike at the heart of traditional Asian values – which is why they are often seen as unwelcome Western imports. Writing of the growth of a lesbian movement in Taiwan in the 1990s, Manuel Castells (2004) argues that this development, 'in a quasi-authoritarian political context, and amidst a deeply patriarchal culture, shows the breaking of traditional molds by global trends of identity politics' (2004: 266). But his optimism about the direction of global trends needs to be tempered. While he concedes that Asian lesbianism has been adapted to local cultural conditions, he gives insufficient attention to the ways in which both lesbian identities themselves and strategies open to lesbian activists are shaped by those local conditions. Certainly, as Castells notes, sexual liberation movements break a 'deep-seated taboo in Chinese culture' (ibid.: 268) – and in other Asian cultures. But the Asian aversion to homosexuality is not identical to homophobia in the West. Homosexuality and lesbianism are not merely objects of moral outrage – they challenge the foundations of the Asian patriarchal family. Of course they are also seen as antithetical to conservative versions of 'family values' in the West, but in East Asia, where the family as lineage is a more pressing reality, eschewing reproductive, marital relationships has more devastating consequences. To live as a gay man is to renege on the paramount filial duty of continuing the family line and ensuring parents' future status as ancestors; to live as a lesbian refuses women's part in this project, brings shame on the family, and flies in the face of all tenets of feminine virtue. Moreover, to claim a gay or lesbian identity is an assertion of individual desires over the collective, the family.

Although delayed marriage is becoming common in parts of East Asia, making single life more possible for women, to be a lesbian is still not easy. Despite Taiwan's well-developed lesbian community (at least in Taipei), lesbians can rarely be 'out' in the Western sense and often lead double lives. Even claiming public space, as in the gay pride marches held in Taiwan since 2003, may not entail public declaration of individual identity, still less being out to family and colleagues (Martin 2003; Sang 2003). Japan boasts one 'out' lesbian local politician, Kanako Otsuji, but negotiating a lesbian lifestyle remains a delicate matter where such a choice remains outside the thinkable and where living with another woman does not mean escaping pressures to marry (see Kamano and Khor, Chapter 8). In China lesbians have been subject to administrative detention and re-education as 'hooligans', and are still regarded as sick or perverted even by more liberal opinion (Evans 1997; He Xiaopei 2001). In Korea the lesbian community is almost entirely closeted, leading double lives in a very real sense. For example, having/using two names – a 'given' family name and a 'chosen' lesbian name – is common for many lesbians in South Korea (Woo 2007). Most lesbians only know each other by their 'chosen' lesbian names: they are very careful not to tell or ask each other what their 'given' (or 'real') names are. These two names reflect different sides of their lives, experienced as being mutually exclusive. She is, as her 'chosen-lesbian-fake' name, a lesbian; yet she is, as her 'given-family-real' name, to be read as being a heterosexual. If she were not, she might lose the recognition of her place in family and society – hence the campaign against outing (see Cho, Chapter 7).

Lesbians cannot count on finding sanctuary within East Asian women's movements – though some (like the Taiwanese) have been more welcoming than others. Lesbians faced opposition in the early days of Western feminism, too, but were visible participants in the movement from the beginning. In East Asia, their inclusion has been more problematic. The Korean case, documented by Cho Joo-hyun (Chapter 7) is particularly interesting since even academic feminists, influenced by Western post-modern and queer theory, have largely ignored issues confronting Korean lesbians.[9] Thus, while embracing ideas of sexual diversity and fluid sex identities, they have denied the oppression of Korean lesbians, both in spite of post-modernism (the persistence of homophobia) and because of it (the emphasis on destabilizing identity giving licence to damn Korean lesbians as insufficiently queer).

Conclusion

The ways in which Western feminist and academic ideas and concepts travel to and within East Asia should alert us to the asymmetrical flows of cultural exchange within the global order. But they also suggest that these same ideas and concepts have some purchase and explanatory power in these local contexts, and that feminists can find some common ground across our cultural differences, real and imagined, between East and West. We hope that Western readers will find much of interest here – new debates that resonate with established ones as well as new perspectives that challenge or complement Western feminist knowledge. The issues raised in this volume throw into sharp relief the interconnections between changes in the ordering of economic life and transformations of intimate life, while at the same time demonstrating that the localized, lived complexities that result cannot easily be captured through notions of a detraditionalized or post-traditional social order. They suggest that feminists in the East and West are facing some similar personal and political dilemmas posed by living in a rapidly changing global world, but that we should continue to be aware of the varying contexts in which women's lives are lived – not only between the West and the East, but within both regions.

As will be evident from the chapters in this volume, East Asian feminists are engaging with the work of their Western counterparts, and drawing on Western feminist debates in developing their own theory and politics. In so doing they are also making their work comprehensible and relevant to Western audiences. East Asian feminists have thus opened a potential dialogue with Western feminism. It is now up to Western feminists to reply.

Notes

1 Written Japanese has both an ideographic character set, adapted from Chinese, and two phonetic scripts; modern Korean has a phonetic script.

2 It is a specific history of European global exploration and adventurism that led to the definition of an arbitrary line of longitude as the 'prime meridian'; the British won the tussle with the Spanish to establish that this line ran through Greenwich rather than Cadiz.

3 The East/West distinction within Europe is defined, of course, by its own history: from the split between the eastern Orthodox and Western Roman churches, to the rise and fall of the Ottoman Empire and, more recently, to the Soviet bloc and its collapse.

4 This imagery has been slightly shifted but not displaced by the recent popularity of Chinese films, such as *Crouching Tiger, Hidden Dragon* and *House of Flying Daggers,* featuring women as heroic fighters.

5 The Dutch in Indonesia, the French in Indo-China, the Spanish in the Philippines and the British in Malaysia.

6 For example, the three obediences: of a single woman to her father, a wife to her husband, a widow to her son.

7 Key works by these scholars have been translated into Asian languages. In Korea, for example, *The Transformation of Intimacy* (Giddens 1991) was translated in 1996; *Normal Chaos of Love* (Beck and Beck-Gernsheim 1995) followed in 1999. Their central ideas and concepts – 'transformation of intimacy', 'individualization', and 'de-traditionalization' – have been utilized by many feminist scholars in analysing changed (as well as unchanged) heterosexual couple/marital relationships and family culture in Korea (Ham 2001; Lee 2006; Kim 2006).

8 For example, banned books have been circulated on the Internet – among them, Wei Hui's *Shanghai Baby.*

9 Judith Butler's *Bodies that Matter* (1993) was translated into Korean in 2003, but her *Gender Trouble* (1990) has not yet been translated. Nevertheless, Butler's conception of gender as performative was being introduced in the late 1990s; it was widely discussed and has been well received by feminists, students and academics in Korea.

References

Abelmann, Nancy (2003) *The Melodrama of Mobility: Women, Talk and Class in Contemporary South Korea.* Honolulu: University of Hawaii Press.

Adkins, Lisa (2002) *Revisions: Gender and Sexuality in Late Modernity.* Buckingham: Open University Press.

Bauman, Zygmunt (2003) *Liquid Love: on the Frailty of Human Bonds.* Cambridge: Polity.

Beck, Ulrich and Elizabeth Beck-Gernsheim (1995) *The Normal Chaos of Love,* Cambridge: Polity.

—— (2002) *Individualization*. London: Sage.

Beck-Gernsheim, Elizabeth (2002) *Reinventing the Family: In Search of New Lifestyles*. Cambridge: Polity.

Butler, Judith (1990) *Gender Trouble*. New York: Routledge.

—— (1993) *Bodies That Matter*. New York: Routledge.

Castells, Manuel (2004) *The Power of Identity*, second edition. Oxford: Blackwell.

Cheng, Shu-ju Ada (2003) 'Rethinking the globalization of domestic service: foreign domestics, state control and the politics of identity in Taiwan', *Gender and Society*, 17 (2): 166–86.

Constable, Nicole (ed.) (2005) *Cross-Border Marriages: Gender and Mobility in Transnational Asia*. Philadelphia: University of Pennsylvania Press.

Evans, Harriet (1997) *Women and Sexuality in China*. Cambridge: Polity.

Evans, Mary (2003) *Love: An Unromantic Discussion*. Cambridge: Polity.

Farquhar, Judith (2002) *Appetites: Food and Sex in Post-Socialist China*. Durham, NC: Duke University Press.

Farrer, James (2002) *Opening Up: Youth Sex Culture and Market Reform in Shanghai*. Chicago: Chicago University Press.

Giddens, Anthony (1990) *The Consequences of Modernity*. Cambridge: Polity.

—— (1991) *Modernity and Self-Identity*. Cambridge: Polity.

—— (1992) *The Transformation of Intimacy*. Cambridge: Polity.

Ham In-hui [함인희] (2001) 배우자 선택 양식의 변화: 친밀성의 혁명? ['Changes in the choices of a spouse: a revolution of intimacy?'], 족과 문화 [*Family and Culture*], 13 (2): 3–28.

He Xiaopei (2001) 'Chinese queer (*tongzhi*) women organizing in the 1990s' in Ping-Chun Hsiung, Maria Jaschok, Cecilia Milwertz and Red Chan (eds) *Chinese Women Organizing: Cadres, Feminists, Muslims, Queers*. New York: Berg, pp. 41–59.

Heath, Stephen (1982) *The Sexual Fix*. London: Macmillan.

Irwin, Sarah (1999) 'Resourcing the family: gendered claims and obligations and issues of explanation' in E. Silva and C. Smart (eds), *The New Family*. London: Sage, pp. 31–45.

—— (2005) *Reshaping Social Life*. London: Routledge.

Jacka, Tamara. (2006) *Rural Women in Urban China: Gender, Migration, and Social Change*. Armonk, NY and London: M. E. Sharpe.

Jackson, Anna and Amin Jaffer (eds) (2004) *Encounters: the Meeting of Europe and Asia 1500–1800*. London: V & A Publications.

Jackson, Stevi (2006a) 'Heterosexuality, sexuality and gender: re-thinking the intersections' in D. Richardson, J. McLaughlin and M. E. Casey (eds), *Intersections Between Feminism and Queer Theory*. Basingstoke: Palgrave, pp. 28–68.

—— (2006b) 'Gender, Sexuality and Heterosexuality: The complexity (and limits) of heteronormativity', *Feminist Theory*, 7 (1) pp. 105–21.

Jackson, Stevi and Sue Scott (1996) 'Sexual skirmishes and feminist factions: twenty-five years of debate on women and sexuality' in S. Jackson and S. Scott (eds), *Feminism and Sexuality: a Reader.* Edinburgh: Edinburgh University Press; New York: Columbia University Press, pp. 1–34.

Jamieson, Lynn (1999) 'Intimacy transformed?' *Sociology*, 33 (3): 477–94.

Kim Hye-yeong [김혜영] (2006) 한국 가족문화의 재고 – 친밀성의 부재와 허약한 가족관계 ['A revisit to Korean family culture – the lack of intimacy and poor family relationships'], 보건복지 포럼 [*Health and Welfare Policy Forum*], 115 (5): 20–34.

Lan, Pei-Chia (2003) 'Maid or madam? Filipina migrant workers and the continuity of domestic labour', *Gender and Society*, 17 (2): 187–208.

—— (2006) *Global Cinderellas*. Durham, NC: Duke University Press.

—— (2008) 'Migrant women's bodies as boundary makers: reproductive crisis and sexual control in the ethnic frontier of Taiwan', *Signs: Journal of Women in Culture and Society*, 33 (4): 833–61.

Langford, Wendy (1999) *Revolutions of the Heart*. London: Routledge.

Lee, Ching Kwan (2005) 'Livelihood struggles and market reform: (un)marking Chinese labour after state socialism'. United Nations Research Institute for Social Development Paper, available online at <http: www.unrisd.org/publications/opgp2> (accessed 2 March 2006).

Lee, Maggy, Anita Chan, Hannah Bradby and Gill Green (2002) 'Chinese migrant women and families in Britain', *Women's Studies International Forum*, 42 (1): 607–16.

Lee, So Hee (2002). 'The concept of female sexuality in Korean popular culture' in L. Kendall (ed.), *Under Construction: the Gendering of Modernity, Class and Consumption in the Republic of Korea*. Honolulu: University of Hawaii Press.

Lee Sung-eun [이성은](2006) 한국 기혼 남녀의 섹슈얼리티와 친밀성의 개념화 ['A research on sexuality and the re-construction of intimacy within married couples'], 가족과 문화 [*Family and Culture*], 18 (2): 1–36.

Li Xiaojiang (1999) 'With what discourses do we reflect on Chinese women? Thoughts on transnational feminism in China' in M. H.-H. Yang (ed.), *Spaces of Their Own: Women's Public Sphere in Transnational China*. Minneapolis, MN: University of Minnesota Press, pp. 261–77.

Li Yinhe (李银河) (1998) *Chinese Women's Viewpoints on Feelings and Sex* [*zhongguo nvxing de qinggan yu xin*, 中国女性的情感与性]. Beijing: Today's China Publishing House[今日中国出版社].

Lim, Shirley J. (2005) *A Feeling of Belonging: Asian American Women's Public Culture, 1930–1960*. New York: New York University Press.

Liu Jieyu (2004) 'Hold up the sky? Reflections on marriage in contemporary China', *Feminism and Psychology*, 14 (1): 195–202.

—— (2007) *Gender and Work in Urban China: Women Workers of the Unlucky Generation*. London: Routledge.

Macfarlane, Alan (1978) *Origins of English Individualism: Family, Property and Social Transition*. Oxford: Blackwell.

Martin, Fran (2003) *Situating Sexualities: Queer Representation in Taiwanese Fiction, Film and Public Culture*. Hong Kong: Hong Kong University Press.

Mason, Jennifer (2004) 'Managing kinship over long distances: the significance of the visit', *Social Policy and Society*, 3 (4): 421–9.

Micollier, Evelyne (2004) 'Social significance of commercial sex work: implicitly shaping a sexual culture?' in E. Micollier (ed.), *Sexual Cultures in East Asia: the Social Construction of Sexuality and Sexual Risk in a Time of AIDS*. London: RoutledgeCurzon.

Mohanty, Chandra Talpade (1991) *Third World Women and the Politics of Feminism*. Bloomington, IN: Indiana University Press.

O'Connell Davidson, Julia (1995) 'British sex tourists in Thailand' in M.Maynard and J. Purvis (eds), *(Hetero)Sexual Politics*. London: Taylor and Francis, pp. 42–64.

Pahl, Ray and Liz Spencer (2004) 'Personal communities: not simply families of "fate" or "choice"', *Current Sociology*, 52 (2): 199–221.

—— (2006) *Rethinking Friendship: Hidden Solidarities Today*. Princeton, NJ: Princeton University Press.

Pun Ngai (2005) *Made in China: Women Factory Workers in a Global Workplace*. Durham, NC: Duke University Press.

Rofel, Lisa (1999) *Other Modernities: Gendered Yearnings in China after Socialism*. Berkeley and Los Angeles, CA: University of California Press.

Romero, Mary (1992) *Maid in the USA*. New York: Routledge.

Roseneil, Sasha (2000) 'Queer frameworks and queer tendencies: towards an understanding of postmodern transformations of sexuality', *Sociological Research Online*, 5 (3) <http://www.socresonline.org.uk/5/3/roseneil.html>

Said, Edward W. (1978) *Orientalism: Western Conceptions of the Orient*. London: Routledge and Kegan Paul.

Sang, Tze-lan D. (2003) *The Emerging Lesbian: Female Same Sex Desire in Modern China*. Chicago, IL: Chicago University Press.

Smart, Carol and Beccy Shipman (2004) 'Visions in monochrome: families, marriage and the individualization thesis', *British Journal of Sociology*, 55 (4): 491–509.

Stacey, Judith (1996) *In the Name of the Family: Rethinking Family Values in the Postmodern Age*. Boston: Beacon Press.

Stoller, Robert (1968) *Sex and Gender*. New York: Science House.

Suzuki, Nobue (2005) 'Tripartite desires: Filipina–Japanese marriages and fantasies of transnational traversal' in N. Constable (ed.) *Cross-Border Marriages: Gender and Mobility in Transnational Asia*. Philadelphia: University of Pennsylvania Press, pp. 124–44.

Tanabe, Akio and Yumiko Tokita-Tanabe (2003) 'Introduction: gender and modernity in Asia and the Pacific' in Y. Hayami, A. Tanabe and T.Tokita (eds), *Gender and Modernity: Perspectives from Asia and the Pacific*. Kyoto: Kyoto University Press.

Therborn, Göran (2004) *Between Sex and Power: Family in the World, 1900–2000*. London: Routledge.

Tsui, Ming and L. Rich (2002) 'The only child and educational opportunity for girls in urban China', *Gender and Society*, 16 (1): 74–92.

Woo, Juhyun (2007) 'Sexual stories go to Westminster: narratives of sexual citizens/outsiders in Britain'. Unpublished PhD dissertation, University of York.

Yeoh, Brenda S. A. and Shirlena Huang (1998) 'Negotiating public space: strategies and styles of migrant female domestic workers in Singapore', *Urban Studies*, 35 (3): 583–602.

Part I
Sex and Work

1 Global Cinderellas: Sexuality, Power and Situational Practices across Borders

LAN PEI-CHIA

Migrant domestic workers are global Cinderellas. I use this metaphor to illuminate their experience of mobility as a paradoxical juxtaposition of emancipation and exploitation.[1] Migrant women work overseas to escape poverty and stress at home; they also embark on the journey to expand life horizons and to explore global modernity. After crossing geographical borders, they are nevertheless confined within the four walls of their employers' households and the often oppressive policy regulation of the host state. Although migrant women may improve their material lives (and those of their families at home), Cinderella's happy ending remains a fairy tale for many trapped in the diaspora.

In this chapter, I focus on two stories of migrant women, one Filipina and the other Indonesian, one divorced and the other single, to illustrate how they situate identities and negotiate sexualities in their cross-border journey. Although these women are not East Asians by origin, they emigrate to and work in East Asia. Echoing recent scholars who have criticized the territorialized social science imaginary as 'methodological nationalism' (Wimmer and Schiller 2002), I adopt a transnational framework to look at the experience of migrant women as an essential contribution to our understanding of East Asian sexualities.

These global Cinderellas do not merely leave glass slippers, awaiting the coming of a prince as their saviour. Yet neither is their story a linear transformation of embracing modernity and sexual liberation. Through the lens of sexualities, I demonstrate how migrant women in East Asia bargain with power constraints from both home and host societies and manage to improve their life chances across borders.

Negotiating sexuality transnationally

Studies of sexualities and queer theory have recently experienced a small but discernible 'transnational turn' (Povinelli and Chauncey 1999).

Scholars have paid increased attention to historical and geographical particularities of sexuality as contextualized embodiments. As Luisa Schein put it, 'sexualities are *situated*; they appear and are always lived within national, political, racial–ethnic and gender frames' (Schein 2000: 6, emphasis in original). Meanwhile, we have also witnessed the reconfiguration of local identities, desires and imaginaries in the globalized world, in which 'sexuality is negotiated, constrained, expressed and made meaningful across disparate social locations' (ibid.).

Elizabeth Povinelli and George Chauncey (1999: 446) have proposed the research agenda of 'thinking sexuality transnationally': we need to 'map the movements of people, capital, and images across national boundaries; follow the desires, aspirations, and desperations that prompted these movements, and chronicle the effects of these movements on sexual subjectivities, identification and intimate practices'. I suggest that the experiences of migrant women constitute a critical site of negotiating sexuality transnationally. They cross borders to seek financial gain as well as to explore global modernity. They return home with foreign goods, exotic experiences and reconfigured subjectivities.

Although an expanding body of literature has examined the experience of female migrant workers in Asia, their sexuality – intimate behaviours, erotic desires and sexual identities – is still under-explored terrain. Most of the existing literature looks at sexuality as a site of labour control and discipline (Constable 1997), a marker of racialized differences and ethno-national boundaries (Cheng 2006, Lan 2008), or a discursive field in which migrants negotiate moral identities between the imposed images of prostitution and sainthood (Groves and Chang 2000). Martin Manalansan (2006) has therefore sharply criticized a tendency in migration studies to relate sexuality to control and violence and fail to see migrants as active agents who possess sexual desire and erotic practice.

Mobility, either cross-border or rural-to-urban, has reconfigured the sexual subjectivities of migrant women. However, as some studies have revealed, migration is not a linear process of modernization and sexual liberation. Instead, migrant women often experience competing sets of discourses about sex, love and marriage (Ma and Cheng 2005), and they continually negotiate sexuality and identities across social settings and cultural contexts. For example, migrant workers in China not only emigrate from the countryside to cities but also traverse the conflicting moral orders of rural tradition and urban modernity (Jacka and Gaetano 2004; Pun 2005). Their liminal status allows migrant women to experience sexuality in a transient condition, such as participating in casual urban sex while still subscribing to the moral codes of traditional marriage (Ma and Cheng 2005: 311).

A few researchers have also reported a wider range of sexual practices beyond heterosexual normalcy in the journey of migrant domestic workers to Hong Kong. According to Julian McAllister Groves and Kimberly Chang (2000: 80), some married Filipinas consider lesbianism a 'safe' and 'moral' alternative to extramarital affairs with men; tomboys are desirable in the community because they are 'willing to serve' and 'protect' Filipinas. Amy Sim (2006) also discovered that single Indonesian migrant women who participate in same-sex relationships attempt to avoid the risk of pregnancy and protect the moral code at home while satisfying their needs for physical and emotional intimacy; some also view homosexuality as a 'fashionable practice' associated with Western modernity.

To examine the sexual agency of migrant women in their trans-national journey, I suggest that we look at sexualities not simply as practices situated in particular social locations and discursive contexts but also as *situational* performances in which migrant women reflexively engage themselves throughout their mobility across spatial and temporal settings. I found Erving Goffman's (1959) dramaturgical concepts 'frontstage' and 'backstage' useful in describing the situational, context-bound performances of migrant women. These 'stages' refer to the dual societies involved in their transnational lives as well as the various locales that situate their multi-layered, translocal subjectivities. Nicky Gregson and Gillian Rose (2000: 441) remind us that 'these "stages" do not preexist their performances, rather, specific performances bring these spaces into being'. The lived experiences of migrant women turn places – either private home or public space – into performative stages of identities and sexuality and sites of labour control and power struggle.

Goffman's theory has been criticized for its insufficient sensitivity to power inequality. The concept of 'power geometry' introduced by Doreen Massey (1999) sheds insight on the reality that people in distinct social locations have unequal access to and power over flows and connections facilitated by time-space compression. Professional migrants with labour market advantages can enjoy a metropolitan life on the basis of flexible citizenship (Ong 1999). Lower-end migrants, however, suffer from limited life chances circumvented by labour subordination and residency regulation in host countries. In addition, the patterns of recruitment and incorporation often differ for specific categories of women and men. Gender, in articulation with class, ethnicity, nationality, sexuality and so on, enables and constrains people's ability to move.[2] Patricia R. Pessar and Sarah J. Mahler (2003: 817), proposing the framework of 'gendered geographies of power', suggest that we study 'not only how people's social locations affect their access to resources and mobility across transnational spaces, but also their agency as initiators, refiners and transformers of these locations'. They also emphasize that 'social agency' should include *corporeal* agency such as migration as well as *cognitive* processes like imagination and mind work.

In sum, this chapter will examine the sexual agency of migrant women without losing sight of the various kinds of structural constraints they face while crossing borders and stretching life horizons. I will demonstrate how sexualities serve as a structural mechanism that contributes to the feminization of migration and a medium of power enforcing class subordination and ethnic 'otherization'. I will also explore how the social imagery of sexuality shapes the ways people think about and act toward migration and how they assert sexual agency as situational practices across social settings and geographical territories.

Female migrant workers in East Asia

The increasing prosperity of East Asia since the 1980s has stimulated substantial international migration within this region. It is estimated that the stock of temporary migrant workers in Asia, with or without legal documents, reached 6.1 million by 2000 (Battistella 2002). About one third of this migrant labour force is feminized (Yamanaka and Piper 2003). The two million women are concentrated in particular occupations, including the entertainment industry, health services, and especially domestic service. Their destinations are widely located in Hong Kong, Singapore, Taiwan, Malaysia, South Korea and Japan.

Since the early 1990s, Taiwan has become a popular destination for Asian migrant workers. The majority of migrant women are employed as domestic helpers and caretakers. In spite of stringent government controls on employer qualifications, the presence of migrant domestic workers in Taiwanese upper-class and middle-class households has rapidly expanded.[3] Of the 160,000 migrant domestic helpers and caretakers registered by the end of August 2007, nearly 60 per cent are from Indonesia, 24 per cent from Vietnam, and 16 per cent from the Philippines.[4]

This chapter is based on ethnographic research conducted in two phases. From August 1998 to July 1999 I conducted observation in a church-based non-governmental organization that provided services for migrant workers in Taipei, and interviewed 58 Filipina domestic workers. The fieldwork with Indonesian migrants was conducted from September 2002 to October 2003. I approached informants while they 'hung out' in Taipei Railway Station on Sundays and 35 in-depth interviews were conducted. I communicated with Filipinas in English and with Indonesians in Mandarin Chinese. I also took two short-term field trips in the Philippines in 1999 and 2002 and one in Indonesia in 2003.

Luisa's story

Luisa was born on the outskirts of Manila in the early 1960s. She studied in college for one year and dropped out after her father's sudden death. As the eldest of the six children in her family, she became the extension of her mother and felt compelled to support her siblings. She worked as a secretary in Manila but found the salary too meagre. She decided to apply for an entertainer's job in Japan. What appealed to her was not just the high salary but also the glamour of femininity associated with the job. 'Not everyone can go there. You need to have a pretty face, a nice body, and a beautiful smile.' She was trained to sing and dance by the recruitment agency for six months in order to receive a certificate authorized by the Philippine government. She failed the exam once and finally made it after another six months of training. She left Manila for Tokyo at the age of twenty-one.

Luisa, along with thousands of Filipinas, falls into the category of *Japayuki-san*, a term coined in Japan to describe South-East Asian women who have come to work in the 'entertainment' industry, which denotes a wide range of occupations from singing in karaoke bars, go-go dancing and hostessing, to the sale of sex services (Mackie

1998). As James A. Tyner (1996) has pointed out, the growth of 'entertainment migration' in the 1980s was related to the decline of sex tours of Japanese men to the Philippines. Campaigns against sex tourism, organized by religious and women's rights groups in both Japan and the Philippines, however, 'did not eliminate the "demand" for sexual excursions, but merely forced a shift in venue' (Tyner 1996: 84). Filipinas, whose images had been constructed as 'exotic, docile, sensual and cheerful', were imported to Japan to participate in the growing domestic sex industry.

Luisa's job was a combination of singer, dancer and hostess. After a group performance, customers made requests for particular entertainers, who were not allowed to drink liquor but only juice. The more juice a customer ordered, the more money the woman made. Luisa proudly recalled, 'We had a chart with names, how many requests, how many juices you got. I was number one every day!' The bodies of entertainers were subject to surveillance and discipline. In Luisa's club, if an entertainer weighed more than fifty kilos, she would suffer a 20 per cent deduction from her salary. Their job also involved a fair amount of emotional work. Luisa had to call her customers on a regular basis. She kept notes of their birthdays, personalities and idiosyncrasies in order to win their loyalty to the club.

I met Luisa in Taipei while she was working as a domestic worker at the age of thirty-eight. While Luisa was telling me about her previous journey in Japan, a Filipina sitting across from us in the churchyard looked at her with a suspicious look. This reaction is common because the image of *Japayuki* is often conflated with prostitution in both Japan and the Philippines (Tyner 1996, 1997). Another Filipina overheard us and offered the story of her cousin, who also worked in Japan as an entertainer. 'They [the villagers] think she is a bad girl [with] bad thinking,' she commented. Luisa quickly defended herself: 'But I am not like her. I stayed in Japan for many years, but I don't know how to drink, how to smoke. And I had ten years of rosy life.'

After working as an entertainer for six months, Luisa married the club owner and upgraded her status to the cashier/manager in the club. Such a shift of migration route is not unusual. According to Nobue Suzuki (2008), a significant number of Filipina wives met their Japanese husbands while working in Japan as entertainers. Some of the women continue or begin to work as hostesses after marriage in order to augment their family incomes. Suzuki also found that the highly sexualized image of *Japayuki* haunts Filipina migrants as a whole, including those married to Japanese men, whether they previously worked as entertainers or not. Some Filipina wives have attempted to transcend this stereotype by organizing charity events and deploying symbols and images that valorize middle-class womanhood.

Becoming the wife of the club owner brought Luisa material comfort but the marriage was soon on the rocks. The husband had a series of affairs and their quarrels sometimes led to violence. Luisa told me about her 'rosy life' with a mixed sense of humour and sadness: 'That is [how] Japanese husbands [are], you know? Then next day, he said "I am sorry. I hurt you. I will shop you a diamond." Then OK, no more tears when I see the diamond. But, one jewellery is also one cry.'

Luisa finally gave up the marriage and moved back to the Philippines with her two daughters (the son stayed in Japan with his father). She was broke after all her jewellery went to pawnshops. Luisa realized that she had to work abroad to support the family and domestic work would be her only choice since she was then in her late thirties. Single motherhood is a major force that channels many Filipina migrants to work overseas; some are widowed and others are separated (divorce is still not an option in the Philippines), mostly due to the extramarital affairs of their husbands.

In contrast to the occupation of entertainer, in which sexuality is deeply woven into the job script and labour performance, the category of domestic worker is subject to sexualization and desexualization at the same time. The cultural memory of the bondservant as the master's concubine, a legacy of the slavery system in feudal China (Jaschok 1988), continues to shadow the social perception of domestic workers in contemporary times (Ding 2002). Foreign maids, associated with the phenomenon of mail-order brides and sex tourism in South-East Asia, are especially vulnerable to racialized, sexualized images of tropical women (Cheng 2006). Female employers, wary of the presence of foreign maids as potential competitors, often enforce rules like the prohibition of make-up and revealing clothes (Constable 1997). Such management of physical appearances aims to de-feminize and de-sexualize the bodies of migrant women, and simultaneously confirm the class distinction between maid and madam.

Filipina migrant workers like Luisa consider themselves to be class peers of their Taiwanese employers, yet sliding down the status ladder because of personal misfortune and the stagnant economy of their home country. When I asked Luisa if her employer was rich, she bluntly answered, 'I don't think so. They have a simple life. They don't go out. I know that, because I used to be rich.' Having difficulty adjusting to her downward mobility, Luisa chose to disguise her current job from her acquaintances in the Philippines and to conceal her past from her employers in Taiwan.

To perfect her 'maid' performance on the 'front' stage – at work in the employer's presence – Luisa carefully managed the transition from the front to the back stage when going out on her days off. Every Sunday, Luisa left her employer's apartment dressed in her regular 'maid' outfits (T-shirts and jeans or shorts) and brought her jewellery, nice clothes, and make-up kit to change in the church's bathroom. She explained to me about this Sunday ritual: 'When I go out, I want to look smart, fashionable and intelligent. ... In these clothes, I'm like a business manager. Those clothes' – here she pointed at the bag – 'I bought in the market for NT$100 [US$2.99]! I look like a floor manager in those! Before I go home, I change. I take off my make-up. I change my mini-skirt. I look like a totally different person at home. You know, just like Cinderella.'

As Goffman (1959: 113) remarks, 'the passage from the front region to the back region will be kept closed to members of the audience … the entire region will be kept hidden from them'. If the worker failed to maintain segregation between front and backstage settings, her day-off image might shock her employers. Luisa's employer left home early one Sunday. Instead of carrying clothes to change into later, Luisa walked out of her employer's apartment wearing a blouse, make-up and dyed hair. She described what happened and how her employer responded to it:

> My neighbours in the elevator saw me [and] smelled my perfume. And there were rumours in the whole building! They told my employer: 'Luisa goes out like a movie star!' My boss didn't believe it. So the security guard rewound the videotape – they have a video in the elevator – and showed it to my employer. [*How did your employer react?*] She was very surprised! Because I'm not like that on ordinary days. I think she felt insecure after that. She told me: 'I don't have many beautiful dresses, because I don't need them. I am always in the house.

Her employer was sending the implicit message to Luisa that fancy clothes are unnecessary to, and incompatible with, a house-bound maid. The exposure of Luisa's backstage image – stylish, classy and feminine – constituted a symbolic challenge to the class superiority of the employer; more, it stirred the madam's anxiety in gender and sexual terms. As one Filipina commented on Luisa's employer, 'She's afraid you become an attractive woman. Then she will lose her husband!' Luisa thus engaged herself in additional emotional work to comfort the anxious madam: 'I said to my employer: "Tomorrow I will go out, you will have some privacy. You buy a beautiful night-gown!" This kind of words makes her happy. Or, I saw her whitening cream when I cleaned the bathroom. Then I said to her: "Your skin has become whiter, lighter."'

A broken marriage had put Luisa back on the migration trail, but she still desired a new husband to end the hardship of single motherhood and to fulfil her aspiration to romantic intimacy. She had a clear mating preference in mind: 'I don't want to marry a Filipino. They have no money, low salary. What if he says to me: "When will you go back to Taiwan? And send me money?" I will kill him!' In the eyes of Filipina migrants, Filipino men, trapped in the poor homeland, offer little promise of economic security and social mobility. They even run the risk of becoming 'demasculinized' and 'domesticated' husbands who depend on their wives working abroad. Moreover, Luisa was concerned about her disadvantage in the local marriage stakes due to the stigmatized image local people confer on migrant women: 'It's not easy for me to find a Filipino. Because I have worked in Japan, in Taiwan, people think I am a fashionable city girl. They think I must be materialistic, but I am not.'

Luisa turned overseas to look for her prince. Without Internet access in her employer's residence, she asked me to check her personal advertisement posted on the website Heart of Asia. I found smiling faces of Luisa and many other Filipina migrant workers. In their personal profiles, many present themselves with mixed characteristics that accord with the stereotypes of Asian femininities: they wear tightly fitting clothes to reveal their slim bodies and petite figures while describing themselves as religious, God-loving and family-oriented.

Luisa received many responses from men all over the world. Almost every week she read me letters and played audio tapes received from her suitors. Sometimes she also received gifts such as perfume or US twenty-dollar bills. Occasionally, she went on dates with Western expatriates or visitors (pilots and businessmen) whom she met online. It is not uncommon for downwardly mobile Filipina migrants, with fluency in English, to become romantically involved with Western expatriates in Taiwan. Although few of these courtships turn into marriages, these liaisons may temporarily disrupt the schemes of class and racial stratification that position them as lower class and inferior to others in Taiwan. Some Taiwanese employers I interviewed confessed that they felt extremely surprised or even impressed when they found their Filipina maids going on dates with an American teacher or a German engineer.

When I visited Luisa in the Philippines, three years after she left Taiwan, she had just become engaged to an American real estate agent, whom she had met on the Internet. They planned to get married during his next visit. Luisa was hoping to have another child despite her age of forty-two. 'I want a blue-eyed baby,' she happily said. Citizenship regulations across borders have nevertheless complicated the happy ending glimpsed by this global Cinderella. It took years for Luisa to validate her divorce in Japan and her visa application to the US is taking a long time to process. Her American dream is yet to come true.

Santi's story

Santi was born in an East Java village in the early 1980s and finished elementary school education. When she was fifteen, her father was injured in a car accident. To help the family out, she took a job in Jakarta as a live-in domestic helper. In the city, she met a boy who proposed to her but she rejected him for the reason that 'I don't want to get married now. I want to make more money.' She desired a job in the wider world; working overseas also helped her divert the family pressure placed upon Indonesian women to get married at a young age. Santi left for Singapore at the age of eighteen, but her passport carried a forged record of twenty to comply with the minimum age required by Indonesian law.[5]

Working and living in a high-rise building in Singapore was a scary yet exciting experience for Santi. She found the job not only physically exhausting but also emotionally charged because of the risk of sexual harassment. When his wife was not present, the male employer often made sexual advances. Politely avoiding but firmly rejecting the husband, Santi dared not tell the wife for fear of possible repatriation. Shortly after finishing her two-year contract in Singapore, Santi applied to work in Taiwan. For several months, she stayed in a training centre in Indonesia, where potential migrants learned the Chinese language, housework and care skills in order to improve their chances of locating domestic jobs in Taiwan.[6]

Shirlena Huang and Brenda Yeoh (2007) have argued that the paradoxical nature of domestic space – as a private household as well as a public workplace for the live-in maids – exacerbates their vulnerability to sexual harassment and abuse perpetrated by employers. As a public space, the boundaries of home and privacy are not fully controlled by the workers (for instance, some sleep in common areas and some are not provided with keys for their rooms). Yet the private setting could conceal abuse and violence at home from public attention. In contrast to the latent potentiality of sexual exposure at work, the disciplinary rules at the training centre repress the feminine looks of migrant women. Wearing make-up is not allowed and short hair is the required style. Several Indonesian workers I talked to in Taiwan recalled the sad moment when their long hair was cut off upon registration at the centre. Many felt embarrassed at showing me the photographs taken when they first arrived in Taiwan: 'I looked very ugly! Like a boy!'

Santi showed me her photos taken over the years during her stay in Taiwan, and proudly pointed out the drastic transformation in her looks. Gradually, she lost some weight and grew her hair long. She put on make-up, tight jeans and V-neck shirts. She picked up the habit of smoking from her employer. She learned how to use the Internet and email in cyber cafés. She bought her very first mobile phone. And she started dating and experiencing love.

The love and sex lives of migrant workers are often under the constraint of employers. Some employers consider dating a man to be a sign of moral degradation in migrant women, which may lead to pregnancy or 'running away'. Mindful of the criminal acts committed by some migrant domestic workers and their migrant boyfriends, some employers worry about a connection between dating and kidnapping or burglary. Receiving visitors is usually forbidden for both migrant domestics in the employer's house and factory workers in the dormitory.

It has been noted that single youngsters in Taiwan, who mostly live with their parents, feel compelled to conduct their private lives in public space to shield their love and sex lives from the prying eyes of their families (Adrian 2003: 85). The vibrant city landscape is everywhere dotted with love hotels (with rooms by the hour and discreet counter service), KTVs (clubs that offer private karaoke rooms) and MTVs (private movie-viewing rooms). Public gardens, riversides and hilltops are crowded with couples making out in the evenings. For migrant workers with less autonomy, private space and economic resources, the reversed association of the 'public' and 'private' is even more drastic.

In Hong Kong, Taiwan and Singapore, migrant workers have turned public spaces into weekend enclaves for their social and business activities on their days off (Constable 1997; Lan 2006; Yeoh and Huang 1998). These places constitute backstage areas that protect migrants from the surveillance of employers. However, such 'privatized' public space has become a target of media voyeurism in association with the highly sexualized images of ethnic others. For example, a Taiwanese TV programme ran a special report about the Sunday gathering of migrant workers in the park behind Taoyun railway station with the salacious title 'Foreign workers have sex outdoors; X-rated live shows in the park.'[7] It also projected the suspicion that female migrant workers are part-time prostitutes who on their days off provide paid sex service for male migrant workers.

Dance clubs are popular social venues for migrant workers in Taiwan; they are open to the migrant public but hidden in city corners. Many migrant men and women spend Sunday afternoons dancing to electronic music and partying their stress away. These leisure activities create carnival moments in which migrant workers can temporarily escape oppressive relations at work (Wu 1997). They not only deviate from their work routines in the host country but also depart from the ordinary lifestyle in their rural hometown. When I asked my informants if they went dancing in Indonesia, they always laughed at my ignorance: 'There is no disco in the village! And my parents will never let me go to places like this!'

The dimly lit dancing floor is also an important venue to meet potential mates for romance and intimacy. Physical encounters and body movements bridge social distance across gender and ethnic groups and stir sexual energy in the air. The most popular dance music among Indonesian migrant women is *dangdut*, a genre of popular music that combines the sounds of Bollywood with Malay folk music. During my fieldwork in 2003, the controversial pop star Inul Daratista rose to national fame with the gyrating hip motions of her signature 'drilling dance' (*goyang inul* or *ngebor*). Her music videos were widely played in Indonesian delicatessens and general stores in Taiwan. These deterritorialized images constitute a scene of mediascape and ideoscape (Appadurai 1996) which not only embodies a link to the pop culture of the homeland but also echoes a sense of liberation in the sojourning lifestyle.

Intimate liaisons across ethnic groups and extramarital affairs are common in the migrant community. Santi, for instance, was involved with a married Indonesian man and later had a Thai boyfriend. The courtship between Thai men and Indonesian women is a result of the uneven gender ratios of these two migrant groups in Taiwan. Some Indonesians, who speak relatively fluent Chinese, also develop relationships with Taiwanese men. Local men try to attract migrant women not only with the potential of marriage and residency, but also by showcasing their relative monetary advantage through gifts, especially mobile phones.

Few of these relationships end in marriage. Migrant workers have coined terms to describe ephemeral courtship in their transient stay: FTO (For Taiwan Only) and TLA (Taiwan Love Affair). The recruitment of rural-to-urban migrant women in China is mostly mediated by social networks; their behaviour in the city is thus under the surveillance of relatives and acquaintances (Ma and Cheng 2005). By contrast, South-East Asian migrants in Taiwan are mostly recruited through brokers; this commercial intermediation contributes to the alienation and loneliness of migrant workers. Yet, at the same time, a sense of anonymity in the community frees migrant women from parental control and village gossip. In addition, the city provides space that shelters sexual activities from the judgement of moral norms. The owners of love hotels in urban Taiwan have quickly noticed the potential of migrant customers and offer them discount prices on Sunday afternoons.

What happens after these global Cinderellas return home? In my book I argue that the transnational social space composed of both home and host countries constitutes another set of front/backstage distinctions in the lives of migrant workers. In front of the audience back home – their family, relatives and villagers – migrant workers are cast in the role of 'overseas heroes' who are assumed to have achieved material gains and undertaken a pilgrimage to global modernity. The dark secrets of overseas work are often hidden backstage and shared only with migrants in the host country. Santi is no exception. During the first few days of her return, she was busy delivering gifts to family and friends and shopping for modern household appliances, including a large television and refrigerator.

There is yet another performance Santi has to conduct in front of her parents. She needs to play the role of 'modest daughter' and prove to her parents that she still abides by their moral lessons and has not gone astray in the course of her overseas journey. During her first few days home, she constantly chewed candy to fight her craving for cigarettes. She told me she hid her last pack of Virginia Slims somewhere in the closet, but she simply did not know where she could sneak out to smoke without being spotted by someone in her small village.

Indonesian migrant women, mostly in their early twenties, are generally not too worried about their marriage prospects in the future. Actually, many are concerned that they will be pressured to get married once they finish the contract and return home. Marriage is not on Santi's current agenda either. Becoming the major breadwinner in the family, she has earned some autonomy from parental pressure to conform to the local norms of womanhood. She plans to work overseas again, and this time she wishes to save some money for herself. Fellow villagers often associate returned migrant women with wealth and rich dowries. Santi is thus worried that money may become a barrier to true love. A young man in the village proposed to her after she returned home for a week. Flattered and confused, she said to me, 'How could he fall in love with me so soon? Do you think he likes me or he just likes my money?'

Conclusion

This chapter has drawn on two narratives of migrant worker lives to demonstrate the migratory trajectories and lived experiences of global Cinderellas. In conclusion, I summarize how sexuality matters in framing the social positions and agency of migrant women and in reproducing or reconfiguring inequalities in the power geometry of global mobility.

First, sexuality constitutes a major driving force and structural mechanism that contributes to the feminization of migration. The patriarchal economy of pleasure and desire has supported a continually growing sex industry (as broadly defined) located domestically and internationally. In wealthy East Asian countries, the industry employs a substantial number of migrant women, largely from South-East Asia and mainland China. In general, young women gain privileged access to certain niches of migration where femininity and sexuality are essential components of labour performance. Yet, since the value of their bodily capital tends to depreciate over the years, their journeys are forced to end or change routes due to age discrimination imposed by state regulation or market demand. In the private realm, cross-border marriages between East Asian men and South-East Asian women have greatly expanded in recent decades. Women's moves as workers often lead to marriage migration; some consciously seek overseas marriages to end the journey of labour migration (Constable 2003a; McKay 2003).

Second, sexuality serves as a conduit of power and a marker of differences in the sojourn of migrant women. Xenophobic discourses in host countries tend to sexualize the bodies of migrant women as a signifier of ethnic differences. The image of migrant women as a whole, across job categories and migration paths, is shadowed by the stigma of prostitution. They are viewed as either tropical others with sexually aggressive natures or poverty-driven victims with few options. The vulnerability of foreign maids to sexual harassment and abuse perpetrated by employers is a result of grossly unequal power relations based on class subordination and citizenship exclusion. The desexualization of migrant women in terms of physical appearance and dress codes, conducted by both brokers and female employers, is another means to confirm the class distinction between maid and madam.

Third, sexuality constitutes various forms of social imagery that shape the ways people think about and act toward migration. The ideoscapes of liberated sex and 'free love', as a result of either corporeal migration of people or virtual circulation of images and information, influence how people contemplate and pursue emigration (Pessar and Mahler 2003: 830). Some women seek labour or marriage migration to escape less than ideal marital opportunities at home while hoping to experience love and sex matching their imagined ideas of global modernity (Constable 2003b). Beside, the images attached to overseas lifestyles can also stigmatize returned migrant women in the village and push them to stay abroad, voluntarily or reluctantly.

Finally, sexualities are situational practices in which migrant women assert agency to negotiate given constraints across social settings. Migrant domestics may carefully manage their physical appearance and body language on the work front, but emerged transformed to play a different role on the back stage of Sundays, outside the reach of employers. Living overseas, they may gain some liberation and freedom from parental control and conservative norms at home, but they have to seek reintegration and approval once they return to their home towns and face the moral suspicion attached to migrant women. Meanwhile, the economic assets and discursive resources accumulated overseas can help migrant women challenge local norms regarding marriage, gender and sex, and reposition themselves in the power geometry of globalization.

Notes

1 This chapter is partly based on my book *Global Cinderellas: Migrant Domestics and Newly Rich Employers in Taiwan*, Durham, NC: Duke University Press, 2006.

2 See Mahler and Pessar (2006) for a review of recent studies about gender and migration.

3 The Council of Labour Affairs in Taiwan has adopted a quota system and point system to control the quantity of migrant workers and their distribution. The qualification for employers to hire a foreign domestic helper or a foreign caretaker is based on the 'urgent need' for care as measured by the number and ages of children or the medical condition of the ward.

4 Statistics released by Bureau of Employment and Vocational Training, Council of Labour Affairs, Executive Yuan, Republic of China, <http://www.evta. gov.tw/files/57/72307.pdf>, accessed on 16 October 2007.

5 Nana Oishi (2005) argues that in Asia the emigration policies for female migrants such as the minimum age regulation are driven by social values and moral concerns with the aim of 'protecting' women from potential harms such as rape and abuse in overseas employment.

6 Amy Sim (2006) has noticed that these training centres, due to their population density and single-sex setting, often become a breeding ground for lesbian relationships, which denote female same-sex romantic friendships, whether or not physical expressions of sex are involved.

7 'The Pioneer Combat Cops' (*zhan-jinh-ji-xian-feng*), 1 May 2003.

References

Adrian, Bonnie (2003) *Framing the Bride: Globalizing Beauty and Romance in Taiwan's Bridal Industry*. Berkeley, CA: University of California Press.

Appadurai, Arjun (1996) *Modernity at Large: Cultural Dimensions of Globalization*. Minneapolis, MN: University of Minnesota Press.

Battistella, Graziano (2002) *Unauthorized Migrants as Global Workers in ASENA*. Scalabrini Migration Center, Philippines.

Cheng, Shu-Ju Ada (2006) *Serving the Household and the Nation: Filipina Domestics and the Politics of Identity in Taiwan*. Lanham, MD: Lexington Books.

Constable, Nicole (1997) 'Sexuality and discipline among Filipina domestic workers in Hong Kong', *American Ethnologies*, 24 (3): 539–58.

———— (2003a) 'A transnational perspective on divorce and marriage: Filipina wives and workers', *Identities: Global Studies in Culture and Power*, 10: 163–80.

———— (2003b) *Romance on a Global Stage: Pen Pals, Virtual Ethnography, and 'Mail-Order' Marriages*. Berkeley, CA: University of California Press.

Ding Naifei [丁乃非] (2002) 看不見疊影－家務與性工作的婢妾 影 ['Seeing double, or domestic and sex work in the shade of the bondmaid-concubine'], 台灣社會研究季刊 [*Taiwan: A Radical Quarterly in Social Studies*], 48: 135–68.

Goffman, Erving (1959) *The Presentation of Self in Everyday Life*. New York: Doubleday, Anchor Books.

Gregson, Nicky and Gillian Rose (2000) 'Taking Butler elsewhere: performativities, spatialities and subjectivities', *Environment and Planning D: Society and Space*, 18: 433–53.

Groves, Julian McAllister and Kimberley A. Chang (2000) 'Neither "saints" nor "prostitutes": sexual discourse in the Filipina domestic worker community in Hong Kong', *Women's Studies International Forum*, 23 (1): 73–87.

Huang, Shirlena and Brenda Yeoh (2007) 'Emotional labour and transnational domestic work: the moving geographies of 'maid abuse' in Singapore', *Mobilities* 2 (2): 196–217.

Jacka, Tamara and Arianne M. Gaetano (2004) 'Introduction: focusing on migrant women' in A. M. Gaetano and T. Jacka (eds), *On the Move: Women and Rural-to-Urban Migration in Contemporary China*. New York: Columbia University Press, pp. 1–38.

Jaschok, Maria (1988) *Concubines and Bondservants: the Social History of a Chinese Custom*. London: Zed Books.

Lan, Pei-Chia (2006) *Global Cinderellas: Migrant Domestics and Newly Rich Employers in Taiwan*. Durham, NC: Duke University Press.

———— (2008) 'Migrant women's bodies as boundary makers: reproductive crisis and sexual control in the ethnic frontier of Taiwan', *Signs: Journal of Women in Culture and Society*, 33 (4): 833–61.

Ma, Eric and Hau Ling 'Helen' Cheng (2005) '"Naked" bodies: experimenting with intimate relations among migrant workers in South China', *International*

Journal of Cultural Studies, 8 (3): 307–28.

Mackie, Vera (1998) 'Japayuki Cinderella girls: containing the immigrant other', *Japanese Studies*, 18 (1): 45–63.

Mahler, Sarah J. and Patricia R. Pessar (2006) 'Gender matters: ethnographers bringing gender from the periphery toward the core of migration studies', *International Migration Review*, 40 (1): 27–63.

Manalansan, Martin (2006) 'Queer intersections: sexuality and gender in migration studies', *International Migration Review*, 49 (1): 224–49.

Massey, Doreen. 1994. 'A Global Sense of Place,' in *Space, Place and Gender*, 146–56. Cambridge: Polity Press.

Massey, D., G. Hugo, J. Arango, A. Kouaouci, A. Pellegrino and J. Taylor (eds) (1998) *Worlds in Motion: Understanding International Migration at the End of the Millennium*. Oxford: Clarendon Press.

McKay, Deirdre (2003) 'Filipinas in Canada – de-skilling as a push toward marriage' in Nicola Piper and Mina Roces (eds), *Wife or Worker? Asian Women and Migration*. Lanham, MD: Rowman and Littlefield Publishers, pp. 23–52.

Oishi, Nana (2005) *Women in Motion: Globalization, State Politics, and Labor Migration in Asia*. Stanford, CA: Stanford University Press.

Ong, Aihwa (1999) *Flexible Citizenship: the Cultural Logics of Transnationality*. Durham, NC: Duke University Press.

Pessar, Patricia R. and Sarah J. Mahler (2003) 'Transnational migration: bringing gender in', *International Migration Review*, 37 (3): 812–46.

Povinelli, Elizabeth A. and George Chauncey (1999) 'Thinking sexuality transnationally: an introduction', *GLQ*, 5 (4): 439–50.

Pun Ngai (2005) *Made in China: Women Factory Workers in a Global Workplace*. Durham, NC: Duke University Press.

Schein, Luisa (2000) 'Introduction: East Asian sexualities', *East Asia: an International Quarterly*, 18 (4): 4–10.

Sim, Amy (2006) 'The sexual economy of desire: girlfriends, boyfriends and babies among Indonesian women migrants in Hong Kong', paper presented at the International Workshop on Sexuality and Migration in Asia, Asian MetaCentre, National University of Singapore, 10–12 April 2006.

Suzuki, Nobue (2008) 'Between two shores: transnational projects and Filipina wives in/from Japan' in David Blake Willis and Stephen Murphy-Shigematsu (eds), *Transcultural Japan: at the Borderlands of Race, Gender, and Identity*. London: Routledge. In press.

Tyner, James. A (1996) 'Construction of Filipina migrant entertainers', *Gender, Place and Culture*, 3 (1): 77–93.

——— (1997) 'Constructing images, constructing policy: the case of Filipina migrant performing artists', *Gender, Place and Culture*, 4 (1): 19–35.

Wimmer, Andreas and Nina Glick Schiller (2002) 'Methodological nationalism and beyond: nation-state building, migration and the social sciences', *Global Networks: a Journal of Transnational Affairs*, 2 (4): 301–4.

Wu Ting-Fong [吳挺鋒] (1997) 『外勞』休閒生活的文化鬥爭 ['Cultural

struggles in the leisure life of "foreign workers"'], 東海大學社會學研究所碩士論文 [MA thesis, National Tung Hai University], Taichung, Taiwan.

Yamanaka, Keiko, and Nicola Piper (2003) 'An Introductory Overview.' *Asia and Pacific Migration Journal* 12(1–2): 1–19.

—— (2004) 'Feminised cross-border migration, entitlements and civil action in East and South-East Asia'. Unpublished paper for the United Nations Research Institute for Social Development.

Yeoh, Brenda and Shirlena Huang (1998) 'Negotiating public space: strategies and styles of migrant female domestic workers in Singapore', *Urban Studies*, 35 (3): 583–602.

2 The Making of *Sekuhara:* Sexual Harassment in Japanese Culture

MUTA KAZUE

Among stereotyped images of Asian women, Japanese women predominate, portrayed as Madame Butterfly: obedient, modest, chaste and doll-like. As with all myths, however, such images have never reflected the reality of Japanese women, and contemporary Japanese women conform less and less to the stereotype.

One of the most rapid changes in recent years is the increase in sexual activity of young women. Among high school students, more girls than boys are sexually active: 26.6 per cent of boys and 30 per cent of girls in 2005, compared to 1999 measures of 26.5 and 23.7 per cent, respectively. The increase is even more dramatic compared to 1974 statistics of 10.2 per cent (boys) and 5.2 per cent (girls).[1] High school students are not unique in this respect. Women have become more accepting of sex among unmarried persons and more tolerant of divorce over the last thirty years.[2] Women have also become more active in other areas. Their workforce participation has been growing since the 1960s, with women comprising 41 per cent of those employed in 2007.[3] The enactment of the Equal Employment Opportunity Law in 1986 has not only brought more women into the workforce but also expanded the range of fields in which they work.

Yet transnational statistics show that Japanese women hold only 10 per cent of managerial positions in their country's economy, a surprisingly small percentage compared to 58 per cent in the Philippines and 43 per cent in the United States, to name only two examples. Female representation is also low in the political arena at both the national and local levels. As a result, Japan is ranked 54th among 93 countries by the Gender Empowerment Measure (GEM) of the United Nations Development Programme (in its Human Development Report for 2007/2008). This ranking reflects the low level of women's participation and decision making in political and economic matters, as well as their powerlessness over Japan's economic resources.

In such conditions, sexual harassment in the office is a critical problem because it is reinforced by the power imbalance between the sexes and enabled by the popular attitude towards sexuality. In fact, the very rapidity with which awareness of the concept of sexual harassment has spread in Japan reflects the impact of this problem on the society.

This chapter begins with an exploration of how the concept of sexual harassment was introduced and spread in Japan in the late 1980s. It led to the coining of a new Japanese word, *sekuhara*, which in turn helped to popularize the concept. The impact of this word has been so great that most Japanese are now quite familiar with it, if unaware of its origin. I argue for the importance of the problematization of sexual harassment in a Japanese corporate culture that valorizes the group ethos in a way that makes women more vulnerable to and silent about what they experience. I go on to explore the conceptual development of sexual harassment in Japanese society. Interestingly, *sekuhara* does not carry exactly the same meaning as 'sexual harassment' but has a broader connotation. In fact, it is sometimes so ambiguous that the word serves as a euphemism that hides the reality of sexual oppression and abuse perpetrated against women, contrary to the original function of the concept of sexual harassment. Finally, I argue that the vagueness and ambiguity of *sekuhara* reflects precisely the reality of women and sexuality in Japan. Though de-radicalized and de-politicized, *sekuhara* broadened its scope and became more usable for powerless women exactly because of its less confrontational implication. *Sekuhara*, whether immature or fully developed, is a unique adoption and adaptation of the term 'sexual harassment' that reflects sex and sexuality in Japan. In conclusion, therefore, I shall make some suggestions as to why sexual harassment is important to understanding sexuality in contemporary Japan.

Sexual harassment: before and after

Sexual harassment came to general attention as a problem in Japan in the late 1980s when a female worker in Fukuoka, a city in southern Japan, brought the first sexual harassment case to court in August 1989. The origin of the problem, however, stretches back at least to the beginning of Japanese modernization and industrialization in the late nineteenth and early twentieth centuries. In fact, *Joko-aishi* (*The Plight of Female Factory Workers*), a well-known, classic piece of reportage written by Hosoi Wakizo in 1925, contained documented incidents of rape, forced intercourse, and unwelcome sexual advances by a factory manager towards workers – although this part of the book drew less attention at the time. Or one could look further back,[4] even before industrialization, for examples. However, the term and concept 'sexual harassment' did not exist in Japan until 1989. Before that, there was no way to discuss the issue.

The Fukuoka case was the turning point. It turned on the male senior editor's verbal abuse of the female plaintiff. He spread false rumours about this employee to her co-workers and outsiders. When he ignored her request to stop, she went to the editor's supervisor. Although he knew his subordinate was to blame, the supervisor told her that she could not protest, as the senior editor was a man and she was a woman. Ignoring his 'advice', she continued to complain to him and to the president of the company. Then she was fired for causing trouble.

The plaintiff sued for three million yen (US$25,000) arguing that the editor and the company had violated civil law[5] and the Constitution,[6] and characterizing the violations as constitutive of sexual harassment. In April 1992, after a two-and-a-half-year trial, the court decided in her favour, ruling that the company and the editor had violated the woman's rights on almost all of the above counts, although it decreased the compensatory sum to 1.5 million yen.

Initially, when the case was brought to court in 1989, it was reported by the press and television news nation-wide, although some forms of media such as tabloids and entertainment TV programmes trivialized the issue.[7] This media coverage made the term and concept of sexual harassment very popular in a short time, and the word '*sekuhara*', clearly drawn from the English '*sexual harassment*', was coined. At the end of 1989, the year the Fukuoka case went to court, the word *sekuhara* won the 'most trendy word' prize for the year. Although knowledge about sexual harassment was so superficial that confusion and misunderstanding of the problem was widespread, it was remarkable that the word itself diffused so quickly.

The rapidity of this diffusion reveals that although the word and concept were new, many women were aware of the reality of sexual harassment. The word *sekuhara* touched their unnamed but genuine feelings and their various experiences of suffering in the workplace. A questionnaire survey of 6,500 women conducted in 1989, just after the Fukuoka case went to court, revealed that 59.7 per cent of the women had experienced sexual harassment at work,[8] in the forms of unwelcome sexual talk, physical touching, exposure to nude posters or pornography, unwelcome advances, and even rape, attempted rape, or forced intercourse.[9] It is astounding that so many women experienced sexual harassment; and it is also impressive that so many women finally obtained the means to express their unpleasant or even sickening experiences through the survey. Before the concept of sexual harassment spread throughout Japan, such research had never been conducted. Women's experiences with sexual harassment and their revulsion had never come out in the open, but remained hidden. Thus, some women might have thought they were just unfortunate; some thought it was too trivial to mention. Others blamed themselves for the experience, thinking that they could have or should have been able to escape from it. As a result of learning and owning the word *sekuhara*, women who had experienced sexual harassment realized that these experiences were not their fault, that they did not have to endure such behaviour, and that they had the right to speak out against it.

As MacKinnon writes, 'Sexual harassment, the event, was not invented by feminists; the perpetrator did that with no help from us. Sexual harassment, the legal claim – the idea that the law should see it in the way its victims see it – is definitely a feminist invention' (MacKinnon 1987: 103). This quote makes it clear that the problematization and awareness of sexual harassment together denote a radical change of perspective. For Japanese women especially, the concept transformed the way they see their daily life experiences. I would say that Japanese women realized that 'the personal is political' through the recognition of sexual harassment.

Feminist activism played an important role in creating the new perspective. First of all, the case could not have been brought to court without the commitment of feminists. The plaintiff had consulted other law firms in vain before she met a pair of feminist lawyers who had just opened their office, The Law Firm for Women, in the spring of 1989. It was the first law firm dedicated to working for the feminist cause in Fukuoka. They took the plaintiff's case seriously as a sex discrimination case, while other lawyers thought it too trivial to bring to court (Shiensurukai 1992: Chapter 1).

In cooperation with the lawyers, several feminist activists organized a nation-wide support group (*Shokuba deno seiteki iyagarase to tatakau saibanwo siensuru kai*; hereafter, Shiensurukai) in order to support the plaintiff. The group played a threefold role. It helped to raise funds for the court battle. Journalists and feminist scholars in the support group contributed to the legal strategy. As this was the first such case in Japan, it was necessary to learn from the literature and legal actions in other countries, especially the United States. Moreover, the support group appealed to the public for recognition that the case was one of sexual harassment and a problem common to all working women. This nation-wide campaign was successful (Shiensurukai 1992: Chapter 2).

Meanwhile another feminist group, Santama-no kai in Tokyo, also contributed a great deal to the case and to raising awareness of the issues. As noted above, the group conducted the first sexual harassment survey in Japan, which was submitted during the Fukuoka case as evidence that many women were suffering from sexual harassment. In addition, the survey was reported in several magazines and national newspapers. Without women's activism and the raised consciousness that resulted, the problem could not have become a social issue.

Sexual harassment and corporate culture

Ten years after the problematization of sexual harassment, Japan's sexual harassment policy was legally enforced in 1999 by an amendment to the Law for Equal Employment Opportunity (Article 21), requiring employers to prevent sexual harassment and establish this requirement in company policy. Equal Employment Opportunity Local Offices, located in each prefecture, opened counselling desks for claims of sexual harassment in the workplace. They have been accepting 7,000 to 9,000 claims annually in recent years.[10]

The impact of the concept of sexual harassment has even wider implications within Japanese culture. It is the power imbalance that exists between the sexes that makes it difficult for a woman to fight against sexual harassment. This can be attributed to the fact that women are likely to be in a subordinate position, while men hold a higher position in the workplace. Furthermore, sexual harassment makes the victim all the more weak and vulnerable. In typical workplace settings, women occupy a place which is distinctly different and structurally inferior to men's. Sexual harassment exploits this structural inferiority to create further power imbalances in the workplace; and sexual exploitation leads to economic exploitation (MacKinnon 1979).

Even though this situation exists throughout the world, the Japanese cultural emphasis on the group ethos, rather than individualism, makes women more vulnerable to sexual harassment and less able to fight against it. In Japan, it is often perceived as impolite to express one's individual wishes and feelings within a group, and this is especially true for women. The strict cultural code that expects Japanese women to be generous, tender, modest, and reserved is alive and well. A 2007 best-seller, *Joseino hinkaku* (*How to Be a Respectable Woman*) by Bando Mariko, a former Director of the Bureau for a Gender Equal Society and now President of a women's university, sings the same song. She writes that women should be very polite and prudent to succeed in business (Bando 2007: 60).

This cultural attitude makes it very difficult for Japanese women to express their revulsion at unpleasant treatment, including speaking out against sexual harassment; they will be punished if they speak out too assertively, even if their remarks are just. Bando advises that it is all right for men to release anger, but never for women to do so. A woman would achieve unending notoriety for her anger, even if she were in the right (Bando 2007: 134). Working women of low status are in the least advantageous position to reject unwelcome advances, and are also the least able to speak out.

Wa, the principle of group harmony, is a key word in everyday life in Japan and especially so in the office environment (see, for example, Whiting 1989). In any company, both employers and employees try hard to maintain good relations among co-workers. It is not uncommon for sexual harassment incidents to occur in the efforts to develop *wa*, but group harmony and *wa* often prevent sexual harassment victims from resolving the problem.

In typical working conditions, male conduct from which women suffer, such as unwelcome sexual jokes, is often perceived as creating harmony in the office. In addition, there are outings, banquets and overnight trips which Japanese companies often arrange for the purpose of developing *wa* among the workforce. On those occasions, drinking is always customary, and somewhat foolish or outlandish behaviour is expected and forgiven. It is not surprising that such behaviour often includes sexual harassment. To the extent that harassment is justified in the name of developing *wa*, it is difficult for women to evade it. Since *wa* is so important, women who complain of sexual harassment are seen as disrupting group harmony. The victim then becomes more of a problem than the harasser, and will be pressured to resign; she may even be fired.

In the Fukuoka case, the primary reason for dismissing the woman was that she complained of the sexual harassment to the president of the company. He acknowledged her complaint, but judged that she was selfish and had caused a breach of harmony (Shiensurukai 1992: Chapter 1). Even the court which decided in her favour deemed her behaviour non-harmonious, and hence reduced the monetary compensation she was awarded. The court felt that the plaintiff shared partial responsibility for the bad relationship with the senior editor (Shiensurukai 1992: Chapter 1).

Corporate culture contributes to the prevalence of sexual harassment in another way. Important business meetings are frequently held over drinks in a bar or nightclub, often accompanied by professional hostesses or geishas. A woman is likely to feel uncomfortable in such a setting, and a working mother encounters the additional impediment of having to leave her family for the evening. But skipping the noctural conferences means missing out on important job information and inevitably hinders career development. The corporate culture reinforces the male bond in business. In that sense, we could say that Japanese corporate culture, by confusing business and sociability after working hours, in and of itself makes for sexual harassment.

Worse than *quid pro quo*

It is well recognized that there are two types of sexual harassment: *quid pro quo*, and hostile environment sexual harassment. *Quid pro quo* sexual harassment occurs when an individual's submission to or rejection of sexual advances or conduct of a sexual nature is used as the basis for employment decisions affecting the individual, or the individual's submission to such conduct is made a term or condition of employment. 'Hostile environment' sexual harassment occurs when verbal or physical conduct of a sexual nature unreasonably interferes with an employee's work or creates an intimidating, hostile, or offensive working environment. *Quid pro quo* sexual harassment became legally recognized prior to the other, hence it is considered to be the most typical and classic sort of sexual harassment.

However, the dichotomous typology does not exactly fit Japan; that is, *quid pro quo* sexual harassment hardly happens in Japanese corporate culture. This is not because bosses are too good-natured to make such demands, nor is it that Japanese working women are autonomous enough in the office to prevent such harassment. The fact is that a direct superior would indeed make unwelcome sexual advances and oblige his subordinate to comply with his wishes, but would hardly have the managerial power to offer a favour to her in exchange for her compliance. In the Japanese office personnel management is usually centralized, so that a boss has no direct power over hiring, promotion and pay rises for his subordinates. A boss cannot give a substantial favour in exchange for sexual advances, unless he is at the top of the company. This does not mean, however, that a boss has no power to affect the working conditions of a subordinate. If she refuses his sexual advances, he can retaliate with bullying or subtle abuse until she quits her job.

It goes without saying that *quid pro quo* harassment is problematic even when the victim/subject is treated favourably in return for her compliance. The point is that Japanese women in the workplace are virtually certain to suffer from sexual harassment, because it happens to affect the working conditions of women only for the worse but never for the better in the Japanese office.[11]

Women are not immune from sexual harassment outside the office. As mentioned above, many women revealed that they experienced sexual harassment while commuting. In big cities commuter trains are extremely crowded during rush hours so that Japanese working women and schoolgirls are often the targets of molestation. In some cases a molested woman reports the perpetrator to the transportation police but, by and large, women do not raise their voices but just endure it. A woman feels too embarrassed to speak out in public, and she recognizes that molestation is often taken to be a trivial matter, although local by-laws prohibit it and impose a minor penalty.

Women also feel harassed on trains during the less crowded hours. Newspapers and magazines sold in the train station sometimes convey sexually explicit representations and sex industry advertisements. A man would never bring such publications home to his family, but he does not hesitate to open and read them on the train. A woman has no choice but to face such images when a passenger beside her opens the paper. She feels not only embarrassed but also sexually objectified and threatened. These are disgusting or even sickening experiences which many Japanese women have suffered, and they are ubiquitous in everyday life. Now women have come to realize that these conditions are also *sekuhara*, and constitute unfair behaviour towards women.

Sekuhara as a wild card: its impact and ambiguity

We cannot overemphasize how important it was for Japanese women to discover the word *sekuhara* to express their experiences in and out of the office. The word immediately became 'trendy' precisely because it captured the reality of so many women. As the word *sekuhara* has become more and more popular, however, it has grown into a sort of wild card. Almost all instances of inappropriate behaviour and language have come to be considered as *sekuhara*: even sexual crimes are now included in *sekuhara*'s remit. Does the enlarged meaning of the word signify its strength or not?

Compared to the United States, the definition of sexual harassment in Japan covers a wider scope of behaviour. In 1999, the National Personnel Authority (Jinji-in), the office which controls personnel matters affecting all governmental employees, promulgated a new statute, Rule 10-10, to prevent sexual harassment. The components of its definition of sexual harassment are as follows: (1) sexual speech or behaviour which causes unpleasantness for the other person; and (2) the occurrence of such acts in the workplace, or between employees.

In other words, according to the National Personnel Authority rule, virtually any behaviour or speech in the workplace that displeases a person constitutes sexual harassment. This definition is extremely broad and vague, but as it is the National Personnel Authority rule, it can be considered the most official definition of *sekuhara* in Japan. The breadth of this definition stands out, especially compared to the United States. The Equal Employment Opportunity Commission (EEOC) is the US federal agency responsible for enforcing Title VII of the Civil Rights Act of 1964, which prohibits discrimination based on race, sex and other factors. The EEOC Guidelines, 29 CFR Section 1604.11, provide the following definition of sexual harassment:

Unwelcome sexual advances, requests for sexual favors, and other verbal or physical conduct of a sexual nature constitute sexual harassment when (1) submission to such conduct is made either explicitly or implicitly a term or condition of an individual's employment, (2) submission to or rejection of such conduct by an individual is used as the basis for employment decisions affecting such individual, or (3) such conduct has the purpose or effect of unreasonably interfering with an individual's work performance or creating an intimidating, hostile or offensive working environment.

In contrast, the Japanese definition might seem peculiarly imprecise, but the broadness and vagueness of the definition reflects the general usage of the word among Japanese people. Since the word and concept of sexual harassment emerged in Japan in 1989, and the word grew to popularity before the concept became established as a legal term, it was inevitable that it would take on a broad and vague meaning. In fact, one feminist proposed that we should label every 'unofficial sexual injury', including elevator eyes or unpleasant comments in private, as *sekuhara* (Nagata 1997: 66).

Eventually the terminology was extended to imply non-sexual matters. An educational video produced in 1992[12] for the prevention of sexual harassment groups various behaviours as such, including favouritism based upon the looks of female employees, or asking them to run a private errand. Interestingly, the video also portrays men smoking, a big sneeze, and even body odour as not only unacceptable behaviour for female employees, but as sexual harassment as well. That is, in this illustration, anything that makes the woman employee feel that the atmosphere is 'unpleasant' is given identical weight, regardless of the presence or absence of a sexual element. The video is fifteen years old, but such terminology survives today in numerous handbooks or leaflets on sexual harassment in the workplace and on campus. In these representations, *sekuhara* is just a nuisance, or intrusive behaviour. There is no recognition that sexual harassment is a matter of discrimination or human rights.

We can see another extension of the usage of the word: discrimination against women in terms of wage, promotion and hiring are often called *sekuhara*. It goes without saying that a woman feels angry or displeased if she experiences discrimination and unfair treatment. However, employment discrimination is not identical to sexual harassment and requires different remedies. A claim of job discrimination that relies on the popular connotations of *sekuhara* is unlikely to be taken seriously. As we can see, the terminology of *sekuhara* has extended this far, almost to reverse effect.

On the other hand, some sexual crimes such as rape, obscenity or molestation are often grouped inclusively as *sekuhara*. This is a more problematic extension of the terminology. We can find an example of this usage in a well-known incident from 1999. Yokoyama Nokku, then Governor of Osaka Prefecture, a former Senator and a famous comedian, was running for re-election for the governorship. He committed a sexual assault against a member of his campaign staff who was also a college student, by groping her private parts through her underwear while in a campaign van. She was too terrified to say no at the time, but came out publicly the following day. The governor denied the charge at first, but later was found guilty on an obscenity charge and resigned from office. His celebrity status, and the hideous nature of the crime itself, attracted a huge amount of media attention. Television and newspapers widely publicized the crime as '*sekuhara*'. So did the victim herself when she later published a memoir of the incident under the pseudonym Moe Tanaka and titled it *My Struggle against the Governor's Sekuhara*. In this case, a repugnant sexual crime was toned down by calling it *sekuhara*.

In cases of child sexual abuse, such a euphemism creates more serious problems. Since the 1990s, many cases of sexual abuse by teachers in schools have been reported,[13] and many of them have been labelled *sekuhara*. In fact, in an effort at prevention, the phrase 'school *sekuhara*' was coined around 1995.[14] Nowadays, local educational boards officially use the word.

One of them, the Oita prefecture Educational Board, delivered a statement in March 2003 on the prevention of sexual harassment in school ('Guideline for prevention of school sexual harassment'). This defined 'school *sekuhara*' as a behaviour by teachers which makes a pupil or a student sexually uncomfortable. Examples illustrated are indecent assault, molestation, peeping, or rape, as well as unnecessary touching, unwelcome photographing, or words of a sexual nature. It is an important development that schools and educational boards have come to acknowledge the problem and begun to take preventative measures. But it is highly inappropriate to refer to child sexual abuse as *sekuhara*.

Why such euphemisms or ambiguity regarding *sekuhara*? What are the consequences? At first glance, euphemizing seems to work against preventing sexual harassment and treating sexual crimes appropriately. Mixing up sexual harassment with sex crimes could lead to obscuring the atrocity of the crime. Furthermore, sex discrimination should be treated and redressed for what it is, without being confused with sexual harassment.

If we recall that the concept of sexual harassment grew alongside the consciousness-raising process among women and the recognition of their long-term sexual oppression, such euphemisms seem only to be turning back the clock. On the other hand, the broad usage of the word *sekuhara* can be seen as part of the process of women's empowerment and the fight against sexual crime.

Certainly it is improper for sex crimes, especially child sexual abuse, to be included in sexual harassment. Still, it is very important to recognize that the victims probably would not have come forward without using the word *sekuhara*. Nor would the female employee have raised her voice against unfair treatment over wages if not claiming it as *sekuhara*. Unvarnished terminology such as sex crime, sexual abuse, or even sex discrimination still seems alien to most Japanese women.

Furthermore, the restrictions on expression by women of sexual concerns, which is grounded in traditional Confucian ethics and modern gender role education,[15] have not slackened. However accurate words such as indecent assault (*kyosei waisetsu*) or rape (*gokan*) may be, their judicial or strong 'feminist' connotation makes ordinary women feel alienated. Women do not feel that those frank words represent their personal reality. But *sekuhara* has captured their feelings, precisely because the word carries vague implications. The word *sekuhara* is an easy tool, but also a meaningful one for women.

As for child sexual abuse, we have never had a word for it. It has been called *itazura*, meaning mischief, which even sounds innocuous. In spite of the serious problems with the usage of the word *sekuhara,* it still represents a big step for Japanese women and girls.

Crucial advancement or a façade?

Sexual harassment policy has been developing as a part of a governmental endeavour to promote gender equality at both the national and local levels. I have mentioned the legal enforcement of sexual harassment policy through an amendment to the Law for Equal Employment Opportunity in 1999. From the time that the Basic Law for a Gender

Equal Society (hereafter, 'Basic Law') was enacted in the same year, governmental efforts have grown apace. The Basic Law describes what to do to prevent sexual harassment, and all local by-laws for a gender-equal society, without exception, include a corresponding article on prevention. Many cities and prefectures have even opened their own counselling desks for sexual harassment claims.

It goes without saying that sexual harassment policy is important and necessary for women, but we have to be prudent and examine whether the developments are working to advance women's rights as a whole. Paradoxically enough, in fact, the development of sexual harassment policies reflects a lag in the amelioration of women's working conditions. Despite enforcement of the Basic Law, women's status in the workforce has not changed much. As mentioned in the first part of this chapter, the number of women in managerial positions in offices remains low. The government platform aims to increase the proportion to 30 per cent by 2010, but no one expects that goal to be fulfilled easily.

This is not surprising. Although the Basic Law aims in principle to provide equal opportunities for both sexes in public and private areas, it does not create effective tools in practice. Affirmative action in employment is included in the law, but remains only nominal – a concession to the opposition mounted by the industrial sector at the time of legislation. In fact, more and more women, far from climbing the corporate ladder to managerial positions, have been thrown into the peripheral job market generated by the globalized economy in recent years.[16] The Basic Law, at both the national and local levels, has little power to enforce its principles, such as pay increases and job stability for women, on private companies. Addressing only sexual harassment, then, is a convenient way for both companies and governments to exercise the principle of the Basic Law. It costs much less for companies to establish a sexual harassment policy than to ameliorate substantially the working conditions of their huge numbers of female employees; officials charged with enforcing the Basic Law and by-laws also find it easier to work effectively with companies by dealing with sexual harassment issues rather than with other areas of employment.

In sum, the sexual harassment policy can be seen as a façade obscuring the lag in improving working conditions for women. Moreover, it is doubtful that sexual harassment is seen as an issue of women's rights, or that the legal sexual harassment policy is based on a consideration of women's rights. Rather, I would say, conservative politicians and employers were eager to establish the law and policy because they saw sexual harassment disrupting morale and order in the workplace, and thus doing harm to 'innocent' and weak women. Workplaces should be free from sexual harassment not because it violates women's rights, but because workplaces should be free from obscenities. And as long as women are innocent, weak and obedient, and refrain from insisting on autonomy or independence, they deserve protection under the law. In other words, the sexual harassment policy was smoothly legislated because women were seen as victims rather than autonomous subjects. Some feminists in the United States warned that sexual harassment and date rape regulation can lead to 'sanitation' or control over sex in the workplace and on campus (Roiphe 1993; Gallop 1997). This is true for Japan.

The politics of *sekuhara*

The development of Japan's sexual harassment policy and the pervasiveness of the concept are to be understood not simply as advancements, but also as problematic ones. The ambiguity of *sekuhara* has de-radicalized or de-politicized it as well as broadening its scope, making it more palatable to Japanese corporations. Yet, at the same time, this has made it potentially more usable and handy for Japanese women than a more confrontational concept might be: this underlines women's relative powerlessness within corporate culture. By the same token, traditional oppressive attitudes about sexuality contributed to the euphemistic usage of *sekuhara* as a vague term for sexual crimes. It also, however, helped victims and their families to overcome oppressive attitudes to the damage and to speak out – precisely because the euphemism made this easier. In this sense, I would like to suggest that the development of the concept *sekuhara* reflects the reality of Japanese women and illustrates the politics of sex and power in Japanese society.

Sexual harassment, then, is a key aspect of understanding sexuality and gender in Japan. Along with other East Asian countries such as Korea, Japan has been experiencing rapid change in prevailing sex and gender norms. Old norms are no longer dominant and contemporary values are diverse, or, to be more precise, are confusing. Lack of a religious code on sex exacerbates the confusion in Japan's case. Sexual harassment is emblematic of such confusion. It is not easy to figure out what the line is between acceptable or not, and blameworthy or not, especially because sexual harassment crosses the border between the public and private realms as it occurs in offices or educational institutions. Through sexual harassment cases, people learn the transforming rules of sex and gender. Sexual harassment, in a sense, provides a textbook for deciphering sexuality in contemporary Japan.

Notes

1 Surveyed by日本性教育協会, the Japanese Association of Sex Education, in 2005.
2 The 13th Basic Research on Population by the National Institute of Population and Social Security Research, 2006.
3 The Bureau for Gender Equal Society, *The 2007 White Paper for a Gender Equal Society*, Tokyo.
4 *The Tale of Genji*, the world's oldest novel, written in the eleventh century by Murasaki Shikibu, can be read as a sexual harassment story. Hikaru Genji, the handsome and noble protagonist, falls in love with women one after another in and around the court. He is depicted as so gorgeous and gentle that women could hardly resist his advances and fell to him happily in the story, but what choice did they have as long as he was a son of the Emperor and they were working in the court? The story is fiction, but it was probably based on fact, as the author had experience as a court maid.
5 Article 709: torts; Article 715: responsibilities of employers.
6 Article 13: Human Rights, and 15: Prohibition of discrimination by gender.
7 Even some pornographic videos were released to feature and ridicule sexual harassment in that year.
8 The survey was carried out and published in 1991 as a book titled *Onnatachi no shogen* (*Testimony of 6,500 Women*) by Santama-no kai, the grassroots women's group which will be mentioned below.
9 The first official survey on sexual harassment in the workplace was conducted by a research group in the Ministry of Labour (present Ministry of Labour and Welfare) in 1992, a little after the Santama-no-kai survey. In the published report, out of 992 women in 173 companies, 25.7 per cent reported 'sexually unwelcome and offensive experience' in the previous two years. This includes sexual talk, physical touching, social advances, exposure to pornography/being stared at, sexual advances, and sexual letters or phone calls, in decreasing order of occurrence. The harassers are supervisors, colleagues, and clients, in order of occurrence. (Rôdôshô Joseikyoku, 1993)
10 Ministry of Health, Labour and Welfare, <http://www.mhlw.go.jp/general/seido/koyou/danjokintou/kigyou01.html> (1 January 2008).
11 Sexual harassment in academic settings tells a different story. A professor has direct authoritative power over his students, especially graduate students.

Numbers of *quid pro quo* sexual harassment cases concerning professors and graduate students went to court. Well-known among them is the Tohoku University case in 1999 in which a male professor coerced a female student working on her master's thesis into a sexual relationship with him, threatening her that she would fail in her thesis and lose her future career as a scholar if she quit the relationship. She filed lawsuits and the court required the professor to pay seven and a half million yen compensation, which was then the highest sum awarded in a sexual harassment suit.

12 *Joseishain no munenouchi* (*The Heart of Female Employees*), Kyoei Seimei insurance company.

13 In 2004, 139 teachers admitted to committing sexual harassment or indecent assault (*waisetsu koi*) and were fired or suspended from their jobs. About half of them (48.8 per cent) are high school teachers, 31.9 per cent middle school, and 15.7 per cent elementary school teachers. The Ministry of Education and Science, 「教職員のわいせつ行為等に係る懲戒処分事案の具体的状況について」<http://www.mext.go.jp/b_menu/houdou/17/08/05081202/006.pdf>.

14 Kodomo Seigyakutai Boshi network Osaka, 'White paper on sexual harassment', 2001.

15 In pre-modern Japan, Confucian sexual restriction was enforced in the samurai warrior class but was not so rigid among commoners. After modernization, schools began gender-specific education nation-wide to teach women to be chaste in order to be good wives.

16 More than half (52 per cent) of the female workforce are in peripheral job markets as part-time workers or temporary staff (according to a 2005 workforce survey by the Ministry of Internal Affairs). The number has been increasing since the 1990s. Most 'part-time' workers and temporary staffers are working nearly as long as full-time workers but earn less than a third in wages, without substantial fringe benefits such as social insurance.

References

Bando Mariko [坂東真理子] (2007) 女性の品格 [*How to Be a Respectable Woman*]. Tokyo: PHP [出版].

Gallop, Jane (1997) *Feminist Accused of Sexual Harassment*. Durham, NC: Duke University Press.

Hosoi Wakizo [細井和喜蔵] ([1925] 1980) 女工哀史 [*The Plight of Female Factory Workers*]. Tokyo: 岩波書店 [Iwanami Shoten Publishers].

MacKinnon, Catharine (1979) *Sexual Harassment of Working Women*. New Haven, CT: Yale University Press.

—— (1987) *Feminism Unmodified: Discourses on Life and Law*. Cambridge, MA: Harvard University Press.

Muta Kazue [牟田和恵] (2004) 縮減される意味と問題 ['Trivialization of the sexual harassment problem'], フォーラム現代社会学 [*Sociology Forum*], 3: 29–41.

—— (2005) セクシユアル ハラスメント と ソーシヤルコント ロー ['Sexual harassment and social control'] in Hôgetsu Makoto and Shindô Yûzô (eds), 社会的コント ロールの現在 [*On Contemporary Social Control*]. Kyoto: 世界思想社 [Sekai Shisô-sha Publishers].

Nagata Eriko (永田えり子). (1997) 道徳派フェミニスト宣言 [Feminism and Ethics], Tokyo: 勁草書房

Rôdôshô Joseikyoku [労働省女性局] [Bureau for Female Workers, Ministry of Labour] (1993) 女子雇用管理とコミュニケーションギャップに関する報告書 [*Report on personnel management of female workers*]. Tokyo: Nijuisseiki shokugyô zaidan [21世紀職業財団].

Roiphe, Kate (1993) *The Morning After: Sex, Fear, and Feminism on Campus*. New York: Little, Brown.

Santama-no kai [三多摩の会] (1991) 女たちの証言 [*Testimony of 6,500 Women*]. Tokyo: 学陽書房 [Gakuyô shobô Publishing].

Shiensurukai [職場での性的嫌がらせとたたかう裁判を支援する会] (1992) 職場の常識が変わる [*Challenging 'Common Sense' in the Workplace*]. Tokyo: インパクト出版会 [Inpakuto shuppankai Publishing].

Tanaka, Moe (pseudonym) [田中萌] (2001) 知事のセクハラ、私の闘い [*My Struggle against the Governor's Sekuhara*]. Tokyo: 角川書店 [Kadokawa Group Publishing].

UNDP (United Nations Development Programme) (2008) *Human Development Report 2007/8*. New York: UNDP. Available at http://hdr.undp.org/en/

Whiting, Robert (1989) *You Got Have Wa*. New York: Macmillan.

3 The Office Party: Corporate Sexual Culture and Sexual Harassment in the South Korean Workplace

LEE SUNG-EUN

This chapter takes the office party as exemplifying Korean organizational leisure culture and relates it to the practice of sexual harassment. My data derive from qualitative interviews with 28 female clerical workers in Seoul, South Korea, but have wider implications in illustrating how the sexual victimization of women is embedded within oppressive features of heterosexuality and male-dominated organizational culture. In order to demonstrate this, I begin by discussing organizational culture in general and in the Korean context before going on to discuss the office party in detail. I highlight the role of the heterosexual culture in promoting and sustaining sexual harassment in Korea and show how its specificities are intrinsically related to male-dominated organizational culture.[1]

Organizational culture

Organizational culture has been defined 'in terms of shared symbols, language, practices and deeply embedded beliefs and values' (Newman 1996: 11). A number of feminist scholars have noted that sexual harassment is closely associated with both gender and sexual culture within organizations (Cockburn 1991: 143; Adkins 1995: 3; Hearn and Parkin 2001: 3). Some have focused primarily upon the subject of gender within organizations. Itzin defines gender culture in the context of organization as hierarchical, patriarchal and sex-segregated (Itzin 1996: 52). Acker outlines a number of gendered features of organizations: first, the gender segregation of work is partly produced by organizational practice; second, this gender segregation is related

69

to the unequal income and status between men and women within organizational processes; third, widespread cultural images of gender are produced and reproduced within organizations; fourth, individual gender identities, such as masculinity, are also outcomes of organizational processes and pressures (Acker 1990: 140). While such studies are indicative of the gendered culture underlying sexual harassment in organizations, they overlook the issue of sexuality. For example, Itzin defines sexual harassment as solely a feature of gender culture, without considering how sexuality itself figures within organizations. I argue that an adequate analysis of organizational culture and its relations to sexual harassment should address gender and sexuality as analytically distinct but interrelated aspects of social life.

Other feminists, however, have considered the relationship between sexuality and the structure of organizations. Pringle, in analysing the services secretaries provide, identifies the relationship between sexuality and work. She suggests that:

> the boss–secretary relation need not be seen as an anomalous piece of traditionalism or an incursion of the private sphere, but rather a site of strategies of power in which sexuality is an important though by no means the only dimension. Far from being marginal to the workplace, sexuality is everywhere. (Pringle 1989: 90)

Pringle also explains how coercive forms of power and control operate through less coercive constructions of heterosexuality such as sexual joking and game playing between men and women at work (Pringle 1989: 92–3).

Oerton also sees heterosexuality as integral to hierarchical organizations:

> The dominance of heterosexuality is not restricted to incidents and events within the life of an organisation, but is constitutive of the hierarchical power relations upon which organisations are based. ... [L]ess heterosexual/patriarchal processes and practices of power and control are more likely to be constitutive of less- or non-hierarchical organisation, whereas hierarchical organisations are inevitably 'contaminated' by heterosexuality. (Oerton 1996: 65)

Adkins similarly emphasizes the close relationship between the gendered relations of production and the sexualization of female workers within the labour market, arguing that 'sexual harassment and the sexualisation of women at work is the outcome of the organisation of gendered relations of production' (Adkins 1995: 155). Hearn and Parkin (2001) draw attention to the gender-sexuality-violation complex within organizations, and emphasize the interconnection between the gendered features of organizations and heterosexuality. Sexual harassment is hence defined as a representative practice of organizational heterosexuality (Hearn and Parkin 2001: 9–12). These feminist works suggest that organizational culture is integrated with not only gendered power but also (hetero)sexuality. In particular, incidents of sexual harassment are displayed as gendered and heterosexual practices within organizations.

Gender, sexuality and organizational culture in Korea

This chapter is centrally concerned with the leisure culture of organizations, since in the Korean context leisure plays an important role in the production and incidence of sexual harassment. In particular, I will investigate how the male-dominated and military-centred drinking culture acts to further sexualize female workers.[2] In order to set this in context I will first explain more about the conditions of women's corporate employment in Korea and how the social ordering of gender and sexuality in the workplace impacts upon women. I draw upon interviews with seventeen female workers from five conglomerates; three female secretaries from a public institution; four female workers from financial companies; and four women from small companies.

The five conglomerates are the largest companies in Korea – huge corporations involved in various industries.[3] For example, 'conglomerate S' owns diverse types of affiliated companies such as electronics industries, machinery and heavy industries, chemical industries and financial services. Furthermore, most large firms are managed directly by their owners. Lee, a Korean management scholar, has observed that the main feature of this culture is its bureaucratic, tough, macho mode of operation.[4] All companies share this culture, but it is modified in relation to the style and belief of each owner (Lee, H. J. 1997: 61). A further defining characteristic of these organizational cultures is the influence of Confucianism, which values loyalty and obedience to one's seniors, and women's deference to men. Thus hierarchy and obedience become the most important factors within Korean organizations (Lee, H. J. 1997: 107). Consequently, female workers have had to obey male workers in an organizational culture characterized by patriarchal modes of behaviour, in which the ideals of the owners have permeated the minds of the more junior staff.

Korean organizations are highly gendered, governed by male workers both quantitatively and qualitatively. According to the annual survey of the economically active population by the Korean National Statistical Office, 58.7 per cent of the workforce is male and 41.3 per cent female. Men overwhelmingly dominate top jobs: only 4.9 per cent of the higher positions − such as legislators, senior officials and managers − are occupied by women. Not only do men outnumber women in the workplace, but they are also entrusted with the principal duties, with most women being assigned minor, supportive tasks. This gendered hierarchy is related to the incidence of sexual harassment. According to the Women Link's survey, 40.7 per cent of women clerical workers indicated that the main factor in sexual harassment is the male-dominated and hierarchical organizational climate, and 28.1 per cent said that the main reason why they are sexually harassed is because of their lower status within the workplace. Sexual harassment, then, takes place within a male-dominated and sex-discriminatory organizational environment.

Itzin points out that the gender culture in organizations is characterized by a number of distinct and interrelated features − patriarchal hierarchy, sex segregation, sexual divisions of labour, sex stereotyping, sex discrimination, a sexualized environment, sexual harassment, sexism, misogyny, resistance to change and gendered power (Itzin 1996: 49–51). In a similar fashion, Korean feminists criticize the various forms of sex discrimination in workplaces. For example, Cho notes that Korean women find it more difficult to obtain a job after they graduate from a higher education institution than do Korean men with similar qualifications (Cho, J. A. 1993: 18). Another feminist scholar criticizes the common practice whereby Korean companies prefer to employ women workers according to a standard of attractiveness (defined as measuring over 160 centimetres in height and under 50 kg in weight) (Cho, S. K. 1994: 29). These are some obvious indications of sex discrimination and, in particular, of the sexualization of female bodies within these organizations. A further example is the dress code for female workers. Until the economic crisis of 1997, it was common for corporations to insist that their female employees wore uniforms, seen as symbolic of the company image. This practice has declined as companies were forced to limit their expenditures. But many women I interviewed recalled their feelings about the uniform, which usually comprised a short skirt and tight jacket. It was described as 'so uncomfortable' (Yoo-Jin), and 'not suitable for work . . . too tight' (Mi-Ja).

There are a number of other features of organizational culture that cannot be discussed in detail here, such as inequality of opportunity, sex discrimination in income and promotion, instances of sex discrimination towards married female workers, and, finally, the unstable nature of employment for female workers since introduction of the IMF system.[5] Nevertheless, most women workers do not actively resist discrimination, but generally accept it despite their recognition of its existence. The main reason for their submission is the endemic job insecurity they have faced since the advent of the IMF strictures, which makes them fear that any complaint will be met with the threat of dismissal. Furthermore, women find it difficult to believe that, even if they do resist their office culture, they will succeed in reforming it. The highly gendered and male-dominated Korean organizational culture seems impervious to attempts by female employees to improve their working conditions. Thus women also find it difficult to combat sexual harassment, which is embedded in office culture and particularly evident in the sexualized forms of leisure activity that flourish in Korea. An examination of this facet of work practices will uncover additional factors, which will allow us to understand precisely how this environment is sexualized; and how the construction of leisure activities contributes to the nature and incidence of sexual harassment.

Leisure culture and the office party

Leisure plays an important part in the culture of Korean companies. In outlining the key features of this leisure culture, Sean notes that employers attempt to instil a spirit of cooperation in their employees and emphasize the importance of togetherness by organizing various events including picnics, workshops, athletic meetings and office parties. By these means, leisure activities are defined as not merely opportunities for enjoyment, but also an extension of one's daily work and a demonstration of loyalty. Sean also observes that the leisure programme replicates the hierarchical, male-dominated working relationships within the organization. Staff members are pressured into participating in an event they would rather avoid, and the specific schedule is organized around the interests of the male workers: in particular, the heavy consumption of alcohol (Sean 1997: 192). By the same token, the needs of female workers are neglected, and this tends to isolate them. Within the specific context of the office party, moreover, the women are blatantly construed as sexual objects. I intend to explore this particular event in greater detail, because it is the most common, and popular, type of corporate leisure activity, and one which generates a considerable number of complaints from women. The office party entails the consumption of large quantities of alcohol within the sexualized environment of a 'room salon',[6] where men are served and entertained by female hostesses. I explore the features and problems of these events on the basis of the accounts of several female employees, considering the importance of alcohol, the rationale for drinking, the sexualized environment and the patterns of behaviour typical of these events. Finally I consider briefly other forms of leisure, and whether women have found these to be equally male-centred.

The cultural importance of drinking

The 'drinking culture' is characterized by extremely heavy and rash alcohol consumption. For example, Korean men drink various kinds of alcohol for extensive periods of time and often throughout the night. It thus becomes a daily habit. If men reject these practices, they are excluded from mainstream male culture and therefore many male workers also suffer greatly as a consequence of this enforced regime (Beon 1997: 234). As Beon points out, many male workers believe a 'drinking culture' is a means of maintaining good relationships with their colleagues, cementing business alliances and clinching deals. Drinking is therefore central to the Korean way of organizing workplace and business relationships.

Most Korean companies require that their employees are able to cope with the consumption of large amounts of alcohol, and that they are familiar with the conventions of a business meeting accompanied by drinking. Therefore, some companies will interview candidates for employment and demand that they drink alcohol throughout their oral examination. Many employers believe that a person's job capability is directly connected to their ability to remain unaffected by alcohol (Sean 1997: 195). Korean companies often have an individual known as a 'Sool-Sangmoo' – a term that might be translated as 'drinking manager' or 'drinks monitor', indicating that the 'drinking culture' is not located only within the spheres of entertainment and leisure, but is also an important aid to business. Ha-Jin has identified the structural bases of the 'drinking culture'.

> In this society, people think that the ability to form a good personal relationship with a colleague is more important than the ability necessary for success in a job. Therefore, people try to form an intimate relationship as soon as possible, by meeting over a drink. After all, in order to have an intimate relationship with their co-workers, drinking entertainments and prostitutes are necessary. If we buy newspaper reporters drinks in an expensive bar, for example, they write a favourable article about this company, so we have to meet for drinks with our co-workers. (Ha-Jin)

Ha-Jin's job is to collect information about other companies, government policy and judicial affairs. She indicates that if she wants to get important information, she will need to arrange a drinking meeting with the person who can provide her with the data. This belief is reinforced by the myth, strongly endorsed in Korea, that when people are drunk they are liable to speak truly and frankly. As Beon notes, Korean men in particular associate alcohol with intimacy. Most men believe that drinking with someone encourages both persons to relax, and thus talk more freely about business and other issues (Beon 1997: 233). As a result, Korean people think that they can become friendly with each other relatively fast by means of a drinking meeting, and that they will talk very honestly. In this context, if they want to get something from co-workers, they will arrange a full-scale party with entertainment for these colleagues. The drinking culture is thus based on traditional and ingrained habits of mind, which make drinking seem essential to doing business.

Hyun-Jeong, however, suggests another reason for the persistence of the 'drinking culture': that it is a consequence of the personal stress which is generated by work pressures. 'The drinking culture is the dominant culture at S Insurance. As the job of insurance sales is a very stressful profession, many people like to drink very much.' According to Hyun-Jeong, workers in the insurance business drink to remedy their stress, because they have no idea how to alleviate it. In comparison to Western countries, Koreans have little time for personal enjoyment. They have come to believe that alcohol is the easiest means of achieving relaxation after their daily work is over. This belief has become thoroughly ingrained in the dominant culture.

A further explanation offered for the ubiquity of drinking culture among Korean men is the influence of compulsory military service. Military culture inevitably influences the ethos of all other organizations, because the majority of staff members are men and most of them have experienced military service. Cho, a Korean feminist researcher, notes that men who experience army service are initiated into the norms of male-dominated culture, the logic underlying traditional power relations, violence, and the objectification of women. They are isolated from society and live only with men for two years within a violent and hierarchical system. Thus they attempt to seek relaxation through the purchase of sex, pornographic films and magazines (Cho, S. S. 1997: 155–7).

When Yeon-Joo started her job, she was pressured into drinking alcohol: 'When I was a new recruit, we had a welcoming party for all the new recruits; at that time, I was made to drink a lot of alcohol. Seniors praised me. I thought that they harassed me.' This requirement is part of a traditional ceremony for new employees in Korean companies. It is a tradition which has been influenced by military culture. When men join the army they experience a similar ceremony characterized by heavy drinking. Conversely, female workers, who have not experienced such a regime, feel deeply uncomfortable.

Women may also simply feel bored by and excluded from men's drunken reminiscing about their army life. As Ju-Mi said: 'In the bar, some male workers often talk about their army experiences. During these times, I feel isolated and angry.' This male-dominated drinking culture is, in general, resented by women workers who are forced to participate in it. Hyun-Jae enjoys drinking with her colleagues, but she feels that the office party is merely an extension of daily work: 'When I drink with my colleagues, I am relaxed and comfortable, but when we have to have an office party with our seniors or boss, it is a kind of duty.' Thus the event signified for them not an enjoyable occasion, but a tiresome obligation. Jeong-Mi said that her seniors force women staff members to drink, in order to facilitate the creation of a harmonious environment: 'After dinner, we usually drink, but three female workers of our team do not like to drink wine and some seniors have forced them to join in by saying, "Why don't you drink? Can't you drink to create a harmonious environment?"' I asked her what a 'harmonious environment' is. It seems to mean that even if female workers do not want to drink alcohol, they must do so in order to preserve, and implicitly show approval of, the prevailing atmosphere. But this environment is clearly created for the benefit of the male and senior members of the staff, rather than for their women colleagues. Thus even if the senior's order is unreasonable, the female workers must obey it.

Through the statements of the two interviewees below, we can construct an image of a typical office party.

When we have an office party or a picnic, most activities are related to drinking alcohol from opening to closing time. Sometimes, we sing a song or play a game. (Hae-Ja)

Our culture is one of pretence. When we drink with our seniors, some male workers pretend to be loyal. For example, drinking from a big glass signifies loyalty to the boss. (Soon-Ju)

Hae-Ja's account indicates that drinking is the dominant entertainment within the organizational leisure culture, though she criticizes the foolishness and hypocrisy of its rituals. The content of these rituals, such as drinking to show loyalty to one's boss, clearly illustrates the hierarchical and male-centred origins of this culture.

One of the consequences of this widespread 'drinking culture' is violence towards female workers. When excessive alcohol consumption is combined with a sexualized environment, female workers are often seen as sexual objects, while the hierarchical ordering of this work-related leisure makes it difficult for them to resist the harassment they experience.

A sexualized environment

The office party generally takes place in a room salon where men are served and entertained by sex workers. When people go to drink in a room salon, they occupy a closed room and expect to receive sexual services from a young woman. Any kind of sexual behaviour is permitted here except sexual intercourse. Jeong- Mi and Ha-Jin talked about the behaviour of men in room salons.

> I know that when men go to drinking bars or room salons, they play with the hostess and touch her body. I asked the married male seniors, 'Even though they are Christians, they behave like this?' But if they want to be regarded as a normal and sociable person, they need to accept, and to participate in, this leisure culture. (Jeong-Mi)

> Because of the nature of my duties, I often go to the room salon with male workers. I think that although Korean men get married, they still want to enjoy sexual freedom. They enjoy other women, and they are proud of having an affair. (Ha-Jin)

According to Jeong-Mi, Korean men who are defined by their peers as 'normal' and 'sociable' often 'play' with room salon hostesses. The 'play' includes strip shows, dancing, singing and petting. The hostesses have to do anything that their customers require. Moreover, as Ha-Jin indicates, it is acceptable for married men to engage in these activities. Within this sexual environment, many male workers apparently find it difficult to distinguish between their female co-workers and the hostesses, regarding both as similarly sexualized objects (Beon 1997: 233). Consequently, their female colleagues often find that they are the targets of unwanted sexual advances.

Even when this does not happen, women can be made to feel uncomfortable, as is clear from Soo-Won's and Soo-Hee's accounts of men's behaviour in the room salon.

> I was really shocked. In the room salon, my male colleagues and senior engaged in explicitly sexual behaviour with the hostesses in front of me. After that, I did not go there anymore. (Soo-Won)

> When I was a new recruit, I went to a room salon. At that time, female hostesses served male seniors and workers. I was not surprised, but I was interested in the situation. However, after that, I was so upset and I did not want to go there anymore. One day, I asked my senior, 'If I was not there at that moment, how would you have behaved with the hostess?' He said, 'Because of you, we had to control our needs, but if you had not been there, we could have enjoyed the hostess more fully and sexually.' (Soo-Hee)

Both Soo-Won and Soo-Hee expressed discomfort at the way their male colleagues behave with hostesses. Soo-Won was 'shocked' at the behaviour of her male co-workers and said that she experienced feelings of personal humiliation because, as a woman, she felt aligned with the hostesses. Soo-Hee expressed similar opinions. She was deeply concerned by the observation that men would behave in a more sexually explicit way with the hostesses if there was no female colleague present.

Boo-Young and Yoo-Jin indicate that they were made to feel like hostesses at their office parties: 'When I was twenty years old, some seniors told us at the office party, "You have to sit between male workers", but now they do not force me' (Boo-Young). 'When we have an office party, I have to sit beside the head of the department' (Yoo-Jin). Ji-Hae also experiences such a situation:

> There are two female workers in this department. When we have an office party, if we sit side by side, a senior asks us 'Why do you sit side by side? Sit between your male colleagues.' Sometimes, the seats between the head and boss are empty. It means we have to sit there. Depending on the nature of the situation, I decline or agree to sit there. (Ji-Hae)

'To sit beside male seniors' is actually a euphemism for serving food and wine to these men. In such a situation, women feel themselves to be occupying the role of hostess and are often deeply uncomfortable and unhappy; but they find it difficult to resist their seniors' demands because this behaviour is widespread and has become normalized. The compulsory nature of this female service can be defined as a type of sexual harassment. For example, drunken male workers try to touch the woman's body, and the woman has little power to resist, for any complaint will be met with an accusation that she is spoiling the 'harmonious atmosphere'. Hence, women are placed in 'dual roles' at the office party: colleagues and sex objects.

In addition, the 'drinking culture' plays a role in the imposition of force and violence. Korean women are inculcated with the belief that a woman should not drink to excess, and we have already noted that they often avoid drinking when possible. However, they are frequently expected to drink at university and at company functions: 'Male workers say, "We cannot refuse to drink, so why can female workers refuse to drink?" They wish female workers would drink a lot and play with them cheerfully at office parties. However, when they are drunk, we are not drunk and we do not want to be distracted' (Min-Hee). Min-Hee states that she cannot be cheerful and engage in horseplay with drunken men; she cannot drink very much and does not enjoy being in this environment.

Yeon-Joo's account demonstrates starkly why it is impossible for female workers to enjoy the 'drinking culture': 'When I go to the drinking bar where hostesses are serving, I am so confused and upset. The screen shows a type of pornography. Therefore, I cannot stay in the situation because I feel so uncomfortable and humiliated.' In recent years, many Korean women have begun to drink more alcohol, but this 'female drinking culture' is very different from the male equivalent. For example, women drink together as a means of establishing a greater degree of communication with each other. However, most men simply enjoy drinking as a sensory stimulant: at an office party, they do not talk about their opinions and experiences, but only seek pleasure from the pornographic material. There is thus an implicit relationship between men's drinking and their sexual behaviour and needs. This often results in the humiliation of women.

One of the activities at the office party which female workers dislike the most is unwanted close dancing. According to Women Link statistics, 39.2 per cent of women have had this experience, making it the most common form of physical sexual harassment. Women workers prefer not to dance, but it is usually enforced. They particularly wish to avoid dancing with old, and frequently drunken, seniors, who often indulge in unpleasant touching. However, like Kyung-Ae, the majority of female workers cannot reject their advances.

> Enforced dancing is very common at the office party. It is not a new situation. Male seniors want young female workers to serve them drinks in the bar and dance with them. When I was a new recruit, I did. If an old senior wants to dance with me, I am really upset. However, if he has power in the company, I accept him, but if he does not have any authority, I just reject him. (Kyung-Ae)

Kyung-Ae could not reject the requirement of unwanted close dancing because older seniors possess institutional power, which they could invoke to fire her; alternatively, they could promote her career opportunities. Therefore, female workers feel obliged to undertake the duties of hostesses, which include serving wine and dancing with their bosses. None of the female workers quoted below want to dance with male workers and seniors, but feel they cannot avoid it.

When we have an office party, we have to dance with seniors. I don't like dancing with them. I do not know how I should respond to it. (Hyun-Jae)

When we have an office party in a nightclub or karaoke bar, my senior asks to dance with me or touch my body. Even though I do not want to dance with him, I have to. (Jeong-Hee)

When we go to a nightclub, male colleagues or seniors force me to dance with them. I do not really like dancing. (Ji-Hae)

The main reason why these women wish to avoid their male colleagues in this context is because dancing is merely a pretext for sexual opportunism. They cannot actively resist, however, because of the power disparity between themselves and their male co-workers and the particular situation of a party. Thus, if they voice a complaint, they will be accused of spoiling the prevailing mood of enjoyment and relaxation. Therefore, as Eun-Soon reported, when female workers do not want to dance with seniors, they seek the only available refuge:

If someone touches a female worker, other people also touch her, even though she does not like the physical contact. And, female workers do not like dancing with male colleagues and seniors in the nightclub, so some female workers escape to the toilet.

In a male-centred drinking environment within which unwanted dancing is experienced as sexual harassment, the office party is an unpleasant rather than an enjoyable situation for women workers.

Mee-Soon, who has worked for H Insurance for twelve years, emphasized the unchanging duties of female workers at the office party: 'Still we need to serve a glass of wine for male workers at the office party and even though we do not want to dance with them, we have to do so.' Even though she is married and occupies a senior position, Mee-Soon is still required to serve wine to her male colleagues.

Other forms of corporate leisure activities should be mentioned briefly. These events are also male-centred and male-dominated, and lead to similar effects of female isolation. They perpetuate the 'office wife' syndrome in the context of Korean workplaces. Female workers need not only to do mundane chores (cleaning the office or making a cup of coffee) but also prepare food for the picnic – another popular form of corporate leisure. Therefore, the picnic does not represent leisure time but further domestic labour for the female staff: 'When we go to a picnic, female workers have to cook the meal' (Hae-Ja). Therefore, female workers prefer to avoid taking part in the picnic, which is a regular event in most companies. They never enjoy themselves, because they have to serve men as if they were their wives rather than their colleagues. It is a further manifestation of the rigid and hierarchical division of sex roles, and thus constitutes another form of sex discrimination.

To conclude, one can assert that the office party is a material and representative example of the ethos of Korean organizational leisure culture. The main features of this event align it closely to the 'drinking culture', which acts to isolate and objectify the female workers and encourage male behaviour towards them that can be defined as sexual harassment. This culture remains remarkably resistant to change, because it is rooted in structural and ideological features of Korean society, which are long-standing and widespread. Consequently, women employees have encountered extreme difficulty in voicing, let alone attempting to change, the iniquities of their situation.

Conclusion

I have examined the relationship between sexual harassment and organizational leisure culture, which seemed to highlight the specific relationship between gender and sexuality in Korean companies. The main form that this leisure activity takes is that of drinking within the institution of the 'office party'. This drinking culture is in turn deeply influenced by the ethos of military service. Both cultures are male-centred and male-dominated, so most female workers are forced into sexual and service roles. The entrenched belief that one must always obey one's senior, and the commercialization of sex in bars, are other important factors. The consequent sexual objectification of women employees within a leisure setting fosters a climate in which sexual harassment can flourish, and be perceived as normal male behaviour. Therefore, I believe that the various forms of sex discrimination are all closely related to the phenomenon of sexual harassment. They all tend towards the perception that the female worker is a sexual object and that her body, and the nature of her sexuality, are to be defined and controlled by men.

Notes

1 This chapter is based on my PhD thesis (Lee Sung-Eun 2002).

2 I use the term 'drinking culture' to indicate the centrality of alcohol consumption in work-related leisure.

3 Whitley suggests that 'In South Korea the economy is dominated by enormous family-controlled conglomerates, or *"chaebol"*. Korean *chaebol* are vertically integrated and centrally control a variety of functions and activities' (Whitley 1990: 47).

4 Lee's ideas are not derived from a feminist perspective, but his thorough research into Korean organizational culture since the 1980s provide useful insights.

5 The 'IMF system' is used in Korea as a convenient shorthand for the economic strictures placed on Korea by the International Monetary Fund as a result of the 1997 economic crisis.

6 Koreans have adopted these European words into their own language to describe this kind of bar. Since the legislation on preventing the selling of sex in 2005, Korean public organizations and conglomerates officially prohibit staff attendance at room salons for business meetings, and therefore the culture of the room salon has gradually become less evident – on the surface, at least.

7 Editors' note: there is no direct translation for this term. Literally, *sool* means alcohol and *sangmoo* is a supervisory or junior management position. A 'sool-sangmoo', however, is not a formal occupational status but an informal social role and the term has slightly humorous connotations. A man given this role will be one who 'drinks well', who can cope with heavy drinking and facilitate sociable interaction.

References

Acker, Joan (1990) 'Hierarchies, jobs, bodies: a theory of gendered organisations', *Gender and Society*, 4 (2): 139–58.

Adkins, Lisa (1995) *Gendered Work: Sexuality, Family and the Labour Market*. Buckingham and Philadelphia, PA: Open University Press.

Beon Hwa-Soon [변화순] (1997) 남성의 사회적 연결망 ['The social network of men'] in 여성한국사회연구회 [Women's Institution of Korean Society] (ed.), 남성과 한국사회 [*Men and Korean Society*]. 서울: 사회문화연구소 [Seoul: Sa-Hae-Mun-Hwa Yeon-Gu-So].

Cho Jeong-Ah [조정아] (1993) 대졸 사무직 여성의 노동과 좌절 ['The difficulties and obstacles in the employment of the higher educated women']. Unpublished MA dissertation, 이화여자대학교 [Ewha Woman's University].

Cho Soon-Kyung [조순경] (1994) 성희롱 왜 고용 상의 차별인가? ['Why is sexual harassment defined as a form of sex-discrimination in employment?']. Paper presented at 고용평등을 위한 교수 모임 공청회 [The Workshop on Equal Opportunities for Employment], Committee of Feminist Researchers for Equal Opportunities, Seoul.

Cho Sung-Sook [조성숙] (1997) 군대문화와 남성 ['The military culture and men'] in 여성한국사회연구회 [Women's Institution of Korean Society] (ed.), 남성과 한국사회 [*Men and Korean Society*]. 서울: 사회문화연구소 [Seoul: Sa-Hae-Mun-Hwa Yeon-Gu-So].

Cockburn, Cynthia (1991) *In the Way of Women: Men's Resistance to Sex Equality in Organisations*. London: Macmillan.

—— (2001) *Gender, Sexuality and Violence in Organisations*. London: Sage.

Hearn, Jeff and Parkin, Wendy (2001) *Gender, Sexuality and Violence in Organizations: The Unspoken Forces of Organization Violations*. London: Sage.

Itzin, C. (1996) 'The gender culture in organizations' in C. Itzin and J. Newman (eds), *Gender, Culture and Organizational Change*. London: Routledge.

Lee Hak-Jong [이학종] (1997) 한국 기업의 문화적 특성과 새 기업 문화의 개발 [*The Cultural Feature of Korean Companies and the Transformation of New Organizational Culture*], 서울 박영사 [Seoul: Park-Young-Sa].

Lee Sung-Eun (2002) 'Sexual harassment in Korean organizations', PhD thesis, Department of Women's Studies, University of York.

Newman, Janet (1996) 'Gender and cultural change' in C. Itzin and J. Newman (eds), *Gender, Culture and Organizational Change*. London: Routledge.

Oerton, S. (1996) *Beyond Hierarchy: Gender, Sexuality and the Social Economy*. London: Taylor and Francis.

Pringle, R. (1989) *Secretaries Talk: Sexuality, Power and Work*. London: Verso.

Sean Seoung-Young [손승영] (1997) 기업과 남성 ['Men within Korean companies'] in 여성한국사회연구회 [Women's Institution of Korean Society] (ed.), 남성과 한국사회 [*Men and Korean Society*]. 서울: 사회문화연구소 [Seoul: Sa-Hae-Mun-Hwa Yeon-Gu-So].

Whitley, R. (1990), 'The comparative analysis of business recipes', Working Paper 191, Manchester Business School.

4 Sexualized Labour? 'White-collar Beauties' in Provincial China

LIU JIEYU

The high participation rate of women's employment in socialist China has sometimes misled scholars into believing that Chinese women enjoyed gender equality at work. However, quantity does not necessarily guarantee quality. Western and Chinese feminist scholars have demonstrated that in the Maoist era, owing to the absence of a revolution in the domestic sphere, women workers suffered from the double burden (Honig and Hershatter 1988; Wolf 1985). My own study of the micro-processes involved in Chinese workplaces prior to the 1990s found that the work allocated to women tended to be low-grade and that they were excluded from resources and power; gender was integral to organizational control (Liu 2007a). The recent large-scale economic reform has been viewed as an opportunity to raise the status of women in the labour market. However, studies show that gender is once again becoming the marker of the newly formed labour regimes. Older urban women workers have been thrown out of their former workplace and pushed into the informal labour market (Liu 2007b). Migrant women workers are mainly occupied in factories in the free economic zones and service sectors in urban areas (Jacka 2006). Young, less-educated women were drawn into 'youth occupations', service sector jobs such as waitress or flight attendant, for which physical attractiveness is required (Wang Zheng 2000).

The change in women's employment is accompanied by a rising discourse re-emphasizing women's femininity and a growing market consumption of women's bodies. In the 1980s, as a result of the rejection of the practice of erasing gender differences during the Cultural Revolution, feminine figures and womanly virtues such as being a good mother were reconfigured as appropriate to a woman. As

85

the economy progressed in the 1990s, the deployment of a sexualized femininity has appeared in the market domain. The beauty economy is booming: commercial companies employ models to advertise their products and many local governments have sponsored beauty contests to boost local tourism (Xu and Feiner 2007). The sex industry has also proliferated as a result of the emergent consumerism, catering to the demands of the increasing numbers of wealthy businessmen (Jeffreys 2004). This re-sexualization of women makes it imperative to reconsider the existing framework within which gender and work in China have been analysed. In the broader context of sexual commodification and sexual consumption, how are women in paid employment affected? Is sexuality[1] at play in work? How do women negotiate the sexual politics in their working environment?

Many studies of migrant workers have documented the emerging sex work in China (see Ding and Ho, Chapter 6 in this volume; Zheng 2006). In terms of sexuality at work, the few available studies have focused mostly upon women employees at the lower level of the hierarchy in the labour market (see, for example, Hanser's 2005 study of the less-educated service workers). By contrast, this chapter focuses on highly educated young professional women, widely hailed in the Chinese media as 'white-collar beauties'. They are depicted as living an enviable lifestyle, earning high incomes and buying luxury products. They are considered to be at the front line of a pioneering modernity, a position to which many university women students aspire. However, despite the glamour associated with their occupations, I argue that there are drawbacks as well as advantages to their situation. In this chapter, I aim to explore the gendered practices these young professional women experience at work; how they are affected by sexual politics by comparison with their counterparts in low-level service work; and how they deal with the growing sexual consumerism in China's transition to a market economy.

Sexuality at work: the feminist literature

Western feminist scholars have developed critiques of mainstream organization studies for overlooking the issue of sexuality. Like gender, rather than being irrelevant to organizational life, sexuality is an integral part of work relations and the organization provides an arena for the performance of powerful sexual politics (Burrell and Hearn 1989). One explicit norm of sexuality in organizations is the requirement that everyone should present himself/herself as heterosexual (Martin and Collinson 1999). As sexual relations are constructed in conditions of gender inequality (Connell 1999), men and women experience sexuality differently in the organizational setting. For example, male workers develop predatory sexual discourses and shopfloor cultures that derogate women (Collinson 1992); male bosses tell sex jokes and exploit boss–secretary relationships (Pringle 1989); and women who enter non-traditional occupations such as insurance sales companies are subjected to greater sexual harassment (Collinson and Collinson 1996). However, women workers also actively engage in sexual politics: Pringle (1989) found that women secretaries flirt with their male managers in order to have fun or gain concessions.

In Western Europe, the recent move from manufacturing to a service- or consumption-based economy has seen an emerging demand on women to perform emotional, aesthetic and sexual labour (Black 2004). For example, jobs are often designed to incorporate sexual appeal with a view to attracting male customers (Adkins 1995). Women in traditional women's jobs such as receptionists and salespersons were encouraged to draw upon their sexual skills to facilitate the operation of the enterprise (Hearn and Parkin 1996). Hochschild (1983) showed that the sexy looks and manners of an airline's cabin crew were partly an achievement of corporate management. On the other hand, Collinson and Collinson (1996) also found that the customer-centred requirements of service-sector employment rendered women more vulnerable to sexual harassment.

This feminist literature on sexuality at work will inform my analysis of Chinese professional women's working experiences. However, these studies are grounded in a discourse of sexuality markedly different from that in China. Formerly, gender equality in China was pursued mainly through the desexualization of women. Opening up the economy has resexualized women but in a context in which the continuance of past restrictions on sexual expression and discussion provides them with little or no opportunity for sexual autonomy. China has not experienced anything comparable to the 'sexual revolution' of the 1960s and 1970s in the West, and Chinese feminists have seldom addressed issues of women's sexual desire and autonomy. This makes any sexual politics that these young professional women have to negotiate particularly problematic. This chapter will thus explore sexual politics in the business culture and examine the gendered and sexualized practices in Chinese companies, and the experiences of professional women in this environment. It aims to reveal the situation facing highly educated women who have had to learn how to negotiate a sexualized business culture in a society where women's sexuality is strictly moralized and rarely discussed.

The study

This chapter is based upon my in-depth interviews conducted with twenty Chinese professional women and a focus group with four professional men in Nanjing during two field trips in 2003 and 2007.[2] All of the participants held a bachelor's degree. They were aged from 24 to 35, and were working in sales departments as managers or representatives of their companies. Their organizations were Chinese state-owned or privately owned companies covering a wide range of industries: finance, trade, medicine, stock exchange, real estate, insurance, car manufacturing, telecommunications and information technology (IT). The women interviewees who were over 30 years of age were mostly married with a child; those who were under 30 were mostly partnered with a boyfriend or about to get married. The four men were aged from 28 to 30 years, and worked in finance and telecommunications companies. Two were single and two were partnered with a girlfriend.

'Being pretty but not sexy'

All my women interviewees were strikingly pretty women. Some of the interviewees had themselves served on recruitment committees and pointed out that the sales section of their own company would not recruit people with an unattractive physical appearance, because sales people are a company's 'front door'. However, the criterion of beauty is both arbitrary and gendered. The implicit consensus is that women who have fair skin and a slim figure with symmetrical facial features are pretty. But when I asked the recruiters what type of men were good-looking, they simply said 'tall men',[3] but added that 'since not many men are tall, if they look smart and clean, that's acceptable'. Indeed, to my eyes none of the four male professionals in the focus group were either 'tall' or smart. It seems that the women's physical appearance was under particular scrutiny; it was regarded as a commercial resource to be commodified and developed by business organizations. Accordingly, aware of the importance of their physical capital, these highly educated women paid special attention to the maintenance of their figure and appearance. For example, one interview was conducted at the interviewee's home; during the whole interview, she was wearing a special face cream to boost the level of moisture of her skin. Another was conducted during lunchtime so I was invited to join the interviewee for a work lunch: each of us was issued with a lunchbox but she stopped after eating only a quarter of hers and claimed to be on a diet despite the fact that she already looked very slim. By contrast, the only grooming men professionals described was concerned with matters of hygiene such as shaving, keeping their hair short and presenting a clean appearance.

Women had to make a double effort to maintain their aesthetic self-image. When presenting themselves in the work environment, they had gone through further careful management of gender display. As doing femininity involves 'doing heterosexuality', which is looking 'sexy' in heterosexist ways (Connell 1999), a gender display carries sexual connotations. Therefore, these women professionals, while trying to look pretty, expressed a desire not to be associated with appearing sexy. The common understanding of the dress code is that neither revealing clothes nor mini-skirts should be worn at work. According to these women, this restriction on the display of overt sexuality was partly required by the company management. Like their Western counterparts (see Tancred-Sheriff 1989), Chinese organizations view sexual display at work as deviant and likely to disrupt organizational authority.[4] At the same time, this desexualization of their self-presentation was actively deployed by professional women themselves. Aware of the wider context of sexual consumption in the market economy, some women emphasized the need to desexualize themselves at work. As a woman sales representative in insurance (aged 28) joked: 'If I were to wear those revealing clothes at work, I'd have been in the same boat with a street walker.' Therefore, this carefully managed gender and asexual display has become an important means for the professional women to distinguish themselves from 'decadent'[5] women. The women also felt that it was important in their work environment to make their professional status very clear. As one sales manager in medicine (aged 31) put it, 'If you dress very sexy and wear very revealing clothes, it will inevitably excite others' visual sense. Others think that you are only a woman so that they can do anything to you. They will forget about the fact that you are a sales manager or sales representative.' Her strategy of desexualization seemed to have two aims. First, desexualization helped to minimize any potential suggestions of eroticism and thus acted as a protective mechanism against sexual harassment by clients – commonly experienced by these women, as we shall see later. However, what she implied here was that women's sexualized appearance was the cause of the harassment. Second, she expressed a desire not to be perceived in a sexualized way in order to be respected and taken seriously. Managers in China are still linked with a masculine identity, so desexualizing herself and thereby destabilizing her gender display was her way of trying to 'blend in' (Sheppard 1989) with the existing organizational setting.

In contrast to the women, their male counterparts were not faced with the need carefully to manage the boundary between gender and sexuality. First, the traditional concept of masculinity fits well with the male-defined set of norms and culture within the organizational setting. Second, their gender is rarely sexualized. Pre-modern China had long established the tradition that women were consumed as sexual commodities, and the recent economic reforms have resurrected this practice. However, there was no link made between being masculine and being sexy in the past; nor, as yet, has this association emerged in contemporary Chinese society.[6] Therefore, the male professionals had no need to worry about being perceived in any sexualized way at work. When I asked the men in the focus group if they thought that they looked sexy, or were perceived to be so by the women in their workplace, they all expressed confusion at my question and were unable to make any connection between this idea and their experiences.

Sexualized encounters in the company offices

Paradoxically, while women expressed the desire to desexualize themselves at work, they told another story when I asked about their encounters with the clients in the office. When I asked what were the advantages of working in the sales profession as a woman, a common response was: 'Women were more likely to persuade the clients as most clients are men. The principle that the opposite sex appeals works well.' Their replies reflected the vertical segregation by sex in the business world as well as the 'selling of sexuality' (Hearn and Parkin 1987) by women sales professionals. A woman sales representative (aged 28) provided a detailed example: 'Women have the advantage: during the negotiation, women could *sajiao* [act like a spoiled and naughty child], pestering the client. But for men, he can't do this – neither to a female client nor to a male customer – otherwise it will be disgusting.' The word *sajiao* is used to describe playful children and women. When used to describe a woman, it has the connotation that she displays feminine and sexual charms. This quote shows that women can use their sex appeal to gain interactional power over their clients in order to complete the deal. As the income of sales professionals was closely linked to the quantity of sales,[7] these women recognized the value of being able to play on men's sexual susceptibility. There is a contradiction between the seriously desexualized image presented by their clothing and their use of 'feminine' wiles in the sales pitch. When I asked them how they reconcile the contradiction, they emphasized the importance of they subtle in the latter situation. In the focus group, the male professionals were aware of their female counterparts' gendered advantage, but they rationalized the disparity by saying that 'This is their advantage but is also their sadness.' Here the men deployed the conventional and moral view that reputable women should not use sexuality for financial ends; secretly they despised the women who worked in these sales jobs.

On the surface, these women had a financial incentive to deploy their sexual skills during encounters with clients, even though this might jeopardize their sexual reputations. However, what were advantages *for them* as women working in sales were also advantages *for the company* employing sales women. The capital accumulation of such enterprises loomed behind their behaviour. All the participants commented that the sales department was the core of their company, because only if the products were sold could the company make a profit. No matter what method sales people used, as long as the deals were made the company was happy. In fact, the organizations deliberately created a competitive atmosphere in the sales department. In privately owned companies, several women mentioned the practice of ranking all the sales people on a blackboard according to their sales results monthly.

The first three would be given a bonus but the bottom three would be punished by a deduction from their basic wage until the next list went up. If a person had been among the bottom three for three months, he/she would face the possibility of being sacked. Sales staff were put under great pressure in these organizations and suffered considerable anxiety as a result. Therefore, in the absence of other incentives with which they could cajole their clients, women had to fall back on a personal resource, their sexual charm, in order to outdo their peers and gain the approval of the management. Although these Chinese companies had imposed restrictions on overt sexual display in the organizational setting, the guidelines about the interactions of sales staff with clients were vague and could even be seen as encouraging the 'selling' of women's implicit sexuality during these encounters.

Three-step socializing outside the organizational setting

I now move to their encounters with clients in settings outside the organization and examine the ways in which Chinese businesses utilize the facilities offered by the entertainment and leisure sector to cultivate relationships with clients[8] (such activities are common to other East Asian societies: see Muta on Japan and Lee on Korea in chapters 2 and 3 of this volume). I will show that the selling of women's sexuality in the extra-organizational setting is institutionalized and deliberately deployed by the management.

Social connections (*guānxi*) play a very important role in everyday transactions in China. Therefore, Chinese companies pay special attention to the development and maintenance of relationships with their clients; after-hours socializing with clients accordingly becomes an important part of the work of sales professionals. My interviewees described a three-step entertainment activity common to most Chinese companies. The first step is banqueting. Despite its more dignified name, it is in fact a drinking event.[9] Usually, the general manager would take a few sales staff to meet the client, who would also be accompanied by a few of his/her employees. During the socializing, men were the main actors; however, rather than being excluded, women also played a particular role on these occasions. As a woman sales representative (aged 27) in the stock exchange put it:

> Have you found any banquet that is made up of male guests only? There

is no point in all the men drinking together. Chinese men are like this: they always feel that if there are some girls there, the atmosphere will be better. We women are like the dressing in a dish.

Simply being present at the banqueting table did not suffice: women were also expected to participate in the drinking activity. In the Chinese business drinking culture,[10] the host is expected to make a toast to the guest. Therefore, as members of the host company, the sales staff are expected to take the initiative and offer a toast to the client and his staff. Such a toasting exercise would last several rounds until the end of the banquet. As traditionally drinking was a male activity, making women drink had become a form of entertainment at the table. As one woman (aged 26) in the telecommunications industry explained:

> If a woman claimed that she could not drink, some male client became excited, deliberately claiming that she was lying and she must be able to drink, and then insisted on her drinking something. Or some male clients tried to entice women to drink by saying 'Little girl, if you drink one glass, I will drink three glasses.'

The male professionals in the focus group also noticed the special effect upon clients of women drinking, commenting: 'When a man makes a toast to you, you will take it for granted, but if it is a girl who does this, you will pay special attention to her. So the manager liked the idea of women participating in our drinking.'

Although some women claimed that they were naturally good at drinking, many complained about being compelled to drink at such events. One woman (aged 26) in finance explained: 'If I didn't drink, I'd have been considered as cramping the style. The manager always sent signals at the table implying that I should make the toast. I had no choice but to drink. Otherwise, the next day I'd definitely get a scolding from the manager.' In the face of pressure to drink, the interviewees had found ways of coping. Some women had started drinking at home or during their own socializing events in order to develop their drinking capacity. Others had devised ways to control the level of their own intake. A woman sales representative (aged 29) summarized her tactics: 'Since we are the hosts, we will be able to control the bottle. I will pour some liquid into his glass before the client notices. Sometimes I will swap the spirits with water or spill the alcohol into a small towel.' However, many interviewees emphasized that care had to be taken over such ploys; if they were found out, it would be considered rude to the clients. Ill-health, though, was an acceptable excuse for abstinence. One interviewee had experienced bleeding in her stomach after a drinking event and had thereafter been excused from drinking.

Alongside excessive drinking is the talking at the table. In fact, in conversation the formal business topic was hardly ever mentioned: the main aim was to strengthen the relationship. Therefore, in order to 'enliven' the atmosphere, telling sex jokes had become a common practice. One sales woman (aged 27) in a stock exchange company complained: 'Nowadays the society is really open. Men tell sex jokes freely whether women are present or not. We are forced to listen, just like second-hand smoking.' This sexual bantering was indeed a particularly disturbing form of harassment for the female audience. On many occasions, the people implicated in the sex jokes are the persons present; women reported that a young single woman was most likely to be the target of such jokes, as had been the experience of many interviewees. The common strategies were to play the fool, pretending not to hear the joke, or to laugh it off. As one woman working in banking remarked: 'As a woman, what can I do about these comments? They are all about sexual relations. Pretending to be a fool is the wisest.' The women were forced to listen; but they were not in a position to participate and manipulate the situation, unlike some of their Western counterparts (Loe 1996). This is because in China's market economy, men have open access to various versions of sexual discourse whereas the restrictions on women's autonomy in sexual discourse have barely been lifted. Thus the wisest and safest strategy for morally reputable women is to keep quiet and play dumb.

After drinking, the next step is to go to karaoke bars. Again, these women professionals were expected to accompany the clients in singing and dancing. One woman (aged 27) in an insurance company described the occasion:

> We had to be there too. And if you didn't sing, the manager would point at you specifically, saying: 'Someone [the interviewee's name], why not sing a duet with the guest?' Then if the client wants to dance, I have to accompany him too. After all, the boardroom dances are like walking. I just walk along with them. But sometimes if you bump into some men whose action was a bit inappropriate, that's really unlucky.

Together with the banqueting, these two-step socializing activities usually lasted from 6 pm until midnight or 2 am. Indeed, five interviewees had rescheduled the interview because of their socializing duties. One interview actually took place at 11 pm after the interviewee had slipped out of a karaoke bar. After karaoke, the final event was going to a sauna. However, the descriptions given of the third step differed sharply. The majority of the women claimed that they would go home after the karaoke bar and leave the male professionals to accompany the clients to the sauna. Only four admitted that they went along with the clients to the sauna. However, they emphasized that there were two types of saunas – with sexual services or without – and that they only went to the latter. They said that men and women usually had their sauna in separate cubicles; but afterwards they went to the resting hall where men and women could chat together. They took great care to dissociate themselves from any places offering sexual services; but they all mentioned that they had heard from their friends that male customers sometimes went to saunas where the services of sex workers were available.

This long-drawn-out sequence of entertainment was not only exhausting; the sexist and sexual content of such interactions was extremely stressful for the women. For one of them it felt like 'serving in prison' (a sales woman in insurance, aged 26, single).[11] The women's narratives reflect a masculine business culture where men were able to consolidate their domination and create a climate of sexual exploitation. The sexuality of the women forced to participate in that culture has become a public commodity to be consumed by the male guests, a practice which has been deliberately initiated and developed by management. One representative working in car sales expressed her confusion as to why women had to attend such events: 'I feel that it seems whenever there are men, women are there too. Chinese feel the need to have women accompany men. This explanation seems a bit extreme, inappropriate. But in fact it is like this. I don't know how to explain it more clearly.' I suggest that her use of 'inappropriate' arose out of a realization that she had almost grouped herself together with 'decadent' women, the sex workers who worked in those entertainment settings. Her difficulty in finding a suitable explanation may reflect an awareness that there were similarities between the sexualized labour women like her were forced to perform and the sexual services provided by sex workers.

However, overtly to acknowledge that association was to run the risk of damaging the image of professional women in everyone's eyes by recognizing the threat to their sexual respectability. She might not have been able to find the words to express the situation or she might have been refusing to consider the connotations.

Sexual harassment was another practice often arising from these sexualized social activities. The women reported incidents of unwanted touching, hugging, kissing and sexual advances. However, they were left to cope on their own, with no organizational regulation or protection from harassment.[12] At the same time, they had internalized the expectation that they should be self-reliant; and some suggested that women themselves were to blame if they were harassed. A woman sales manager in medicine (aged 34) commented:

> Some of my clients also gave me hugs occasionally. I just laughed it off. Men always have such a habit. You should look at it positively, taking it as a compliment. No need to take it as harassment. Look, in Western countries hugs and kisses are local custom. So there is no need to consider it as sexual harassment. Don't over-stimulate the situation. The more you are sensitive, the more he is likely to have those ideas. If you take it casually, he will probably do nothing to you.

Later, when she mentioned her colleague's experiences of harassment, she blamed her for being sluttish and misleading the clients. As she was the manager of the Nanjing branch of her company, I asked her if she had passed on any suggestions to her employee. She replied: 'If she couldn't take this light-heartedly, I'd advise her not to stay in this occupation.' Like many of her Western counterparts, this manager blamed the victim and normalized the men's behaviour; she, too, saw harassment as a '*rite de passage* – a gendered test to assess women's ability' to deal with the added pressure of working in a sexist business world (Collinson and Collinson 1996: 51). Resignation became the only option for women who could not deal with harassment. One woman (aged 24) who had recently graduated suffered from harassment. She found her job extremely stressful and sighed:

> Having just entered society, I felt lost. Nobody taught me how to survive in society. I wish when I was at university, the teacher had explained what society really was. But now I had to explore and tried to understand everything on my own. It is very easy to make mistakes.

Negotiating the sexualized business culture

My data suggest that these professional women were expected to perform sexualized labour during socializing activities. However, because the restrictions on women's autonomy in sexual relations are still strong and women's sexuality is highly moralized, their frequent contact with male clients has caused problems for women professionals and thrown doubt upon the morality of women who work in professional occupations that require them to provide emotional, aesthetic and sexual labour services. For example, one woman manager (aged 29) in real estate said:

I am aware of the importance of business networks but I know what I am supposed to do, how to be sensible. For example, I often attend those conferences where there are many big developers. But as a woman, it's not convenient for me to approach these men. If other men don't talk to me first, I can't take the initiative to approach them. Because I am a woman, I need to behave myself. Be careful; I don't want any unnecessary things. At the conferences, women are a minority so a lot of attention is already on you. If I were a man, I'd definitely go to talk to these big developers because they are important business resources.

Being a woman was not the only cause of her difficulties.[13] It was her awareness of the implications arising from the gendered and sexual nature of social relations that made her extremely careful of her behaviour. Like the older generation of Chinese women (see Liu 2007a), she had internalized the view that women were responsible for their sexual reputations. This double standard of sexual control disadvantaged her in terms of career development: to be a reputable woman she was constrained not to initiate contact with a businessman and thus she lost access to the important resources embedded in social networks. She also referred to other difficulties that relationships with clients could present. Recalling her sales experiences, she offered this summary: 'It's easy for a woman to know a client quickly but it's hard for a woman to know the client well and deepen the relationship. At the most, you can only take them for tea or a meal; how could you take him to a sauna like other male sales professionals?'

The majority of the interviewees commented that being a woman gave them advantages but at the same time disadvantaged them. Several other women had tried to avoid attending socializing events[14] for the sake of their sexual reputations, but they also expressed regret that they thus lost access to important networks and had to resort to other strategies to maintain the business relationship. For example, they had been extra-careful in providing products and services after making a sale, had extended care to the client's family members, and had been ready to fulfil other requests (such as finding a doctor for a client). In addition to those women who tactically withdrew from business leisure activities, there was a minority who said that, as long as they knew they were morally acceptable, they would continue to engage in such socializing activities. They claimed that the business networks were too important to lose, so they simply put up with knowing that they were the butt of sexual gossip. For all of the women interviewees, another reason for maintaining ties with clients was their concern about the devaluation of their physical capital as they grew older. As an interviewee in trade (aged 28) put it, 'In China, women over 35 are considered old. So I feel we sales women are also like those in youth occupations. Face and figure are very important. But I also find that clients are important social resources. For example, if I choose to move to another company, I'll take my own groups of clients with me. The company will be keen on my experiences as well as on the resources I will bring in.' (Indeed, she had rejected job offers from several companies and was intending to open her own company by drawing on the resources of her existing clients.)

Despite the various strategies these women adopted in face of the sexualized business culture, their occupation had in one way or another impacted upon their private lives. Their long working hours and close contact with male clients sometimes drew suspicion and resentment from boyfriends or husbands. For example, the telephone calls or text messages a woman received would sometimes lead to misunderstandings. Indeed, the male professionals in the focus group preferred not to find a girlfriend in a sales occupation on precisely such grounds. Moreover, if a partner did not earn more than his wife or girlfriend, he would feel threatened by their career achievements and especially their larger salaries. Many male partners had suggested that the women change jobs but none had followed this advice because they were clearly aware of the link between paid employment, financial independence and bargaining power in the family. When they spoke of responsibilities for domestic work, these women did not mention struggles and difficulties like the older generation of women in my earlier study (Liu 2007a). On the contrary, having been the only child of their parents many of them took it for granted that their mothers and mothers-in-law would take over their domestic duties so that they could devote themselves to a working life. Thus, the release of these professional women from the double burden was dependent on their exploitation of senior generations of women.

Conclusion

In this chapter, I have examined the working lives of some young professional women in China and outlined the new forms of inequality in the Chinese workplace. Drawing upon interviews with 'white-collar beauties', most of whom worked in sales departments of Chinese companies, I have shown that in their interactions with clients – both within the workplace and in social locations to which they had to accompany clients – they were expected to engage in aesthetic and sexualized labour more commonly associated with women workers in service industries. In particular, the sexualized aspects of Chinese business culture subjected professional women to sexual exploitation and made them vulnerable to sexual harassment. Women's sexuality had become a commercial resource deliberately initiated and developed by their organizations.

With China's transition to a market economy, the selling of sexuality demanded of these professional sales women parallels in many ways the experience of their Western counterparts in service-based or consumption-based economies (see for example Adkins 1995; Collinson and Collinson 1996; Hearn and Parkin 1996). However, the wider social discourse of sexuality in China differs considerably from that in many Western countries, where the idea of sexual liberation has circulated since the 1960s and where sexuality is constantly discussed in public arenas. Despite the resexualization of Chinese women brought about by the market economy, the past restrictions on sexual expression and discussion have given women little or no opportunity for sexual autonomy. While men happily consume women's sexuality, women who are actively engaged in sexual activities are considered decadent; women's sexuality is still strictly moralized. This has created challenges for these Chinese professional women as they attempt to negotiate the sexualized work culture within which their occupations are embedded. In the studies examining sexualized labour performed by women employees in Western countries, there is hardly any documentation of employees' concern with their sexual reputations in working in those settings. By contrast, this kind of concern constantly emerged from my interviews. To be a reputable woman as well as to excel in a sexualized business world created a critical dilemma for them. For example, socializing with clients was considered crucial for building business connections; yet, paradoxically, frequent contact with male clients threw doubts upon the women's sexual morality and had negative consequences for their career prospects and their marital relationships. Some women withdrew from the after-hours socializing in order to retain their reputation as respectable women. A few brave ones ignored the sexual gossip about them and maintained contact with clients as part of a career plan. In view of the restrictions on women's sexual autonomy, it seemed impossible for them to achieve one goal without jeopardizing the other. By examining the situation facing educated women who had to negotiate a sexualized work culture in a society where women's sexuality was strictly moralized and rarely discussed, I hope this chapter has illuminated the sexual politics inherent in the operations of commercial companies in China's new market economy, and enhanced knowledge of the position of professional women in the new labour market in East Asia.

Notes

1 Here I follow the social constructionists' definition of sexuality and consider sexuality as socially organized through the institutions of society and sustained by a variety of discourses, scripts and everyday practices.

2 This chapter is based upon a pilot study for my current research project exploring the impact of China's economic development and globalization upon young Chinese women.

3 In East China, the commonly understood height of 'tall' men is 1.78 metres and above.

4 In fact, women reported that various companies have regulations which discouraged office romances. If two staff in one office get married, one (usually the woman) has to be transferred to another section.

5 The word 'decadent' is widely used to describe the moral implications of the behaviour of sex workers. It has a specifically sexualized connotation.

6 In recent years, images of Western men as 'sexy' have begun to appear in the media – in perfume advertisements, for example.

7 Their monthly income consists of a basic wage and commission. Sometimes,

either quarterly or yearly, they will be given a bonus depending upon the profits of the company. Their basic wage is about 800–1,000 yuan, equal to half the average salary of a university-educated graduate in an administrative job (about 2,000 yuan). The commission depends upon the quantity of their sales. According to these professionals, sometimes they could take home up to 20,000 yuan of commission each month.

8   See Zhang's paper (2001) on *goudui* in south-western China for a discussion of the similar ways in which private entrepreneurs dealt with government officials.

9   Male professionals in the focus group complained that they could not eat well during 'banqueting' and had to eat again when they arrived home.

10 Women reported that at the table people often drank spirits as well as white and red wine. The choice of alcohol depended upon the guests' preferences. However, it was expected that when making a toast to an important guest, drinking spirits was the ultimate in politeness. According to the male professionals in the focus group, 'the higher the degree of the spirits, the better to enliven the atmosphere at the table'.

11 Male professionals in the focus group did not talk about stress. The main concern they had was the impact of excessive drinking upon their health.

12 The issue of sexual harassment at work has only been openly acknowledged as a problem in the last five years, and it has not yet been formally recognized in labour legislation.

13 After telling me her viewpoint, she claimed her attitude was a conservative one. However, by examining her work history, I found that her special caution seemed to be a result of a past experience involving a relationship with a colleague in her company. A male section manager (aged 40) in her office became jealous when she was promoted over his head and had her secretly followed in the evenings. At that time she often went to saunas with another sales manager, thinking of it as 'normal socializing'. The jealous manager claimed that she had inappropriate sexual relationships and reported her to the general manager at the Beijing headquarters, who scolded her without asking for her side of the story. She felt extremely wronged and in the end quit her job.

14 Women sometimes used the excuse of family emergency (the illness of family members, for example) to get out of socializing without being sanctioned by their companies. But they tended to be the older ones in their departments.

References

Adkins, L. (1995) *Gendered Work: Sexuality, Family and the Labour Market*. Buckingham: Open University Press.

Black, P. (2004) *The Beauty Industry*. London: Routledge.

Burrell, G. and J. Hearn (1989) 'The sexuality of organization' in J. Hearn, D. L. Sheppard, P. Tancred-Sheriff and G. Burrell (eds), *The Sexuality of Organization*. London: Sage, pp. 1–28.

Collinson, D. L. (1992) *Managing the Shopfloor: Subjectivity, Masculinity and Workplace Culture*. Berlin: Walter de Gruyter.

Collinson, D. and M. Collinson (1996) '"It's only dick": the sexual harassment of women managers in insurance sales', *Work, Employment and Society*, 10 (1): 21–56.

Connell, B. (1999) 'Making gendered people: bodies, identities, sexualities' in M. M. Ferree, J. Lorber and B. B. Hess (eds), *Revisioning Gender*. Thousand Oaks, CA: Sage, pp. 416–48.

Hanser, A. (2005) 'The gendered rice bowl: the sexual politics of service work in urban China', *Gender and Society*, 19: 581–600.

Hearn, J. and W. Parkin (1987) *Sex at Work: the Power and Paradox of Organization Sexuality*. New York: St Martin's Press.

—— (1996) *'Sex' at 'Work': the Power and Paradox of Organisation Sexuality* (revised edition). London: Prentice Hall.

Hochschild, A. R. (1983) *The Managed Heart: Commercialization of Human Feeling*. Berkeley, CA and London: University of California Press.

Honig, E. and G. Hershatter (1988). *Personal Voices: Chinese Women in the 1980s*. Stanford, CA: Stanford University Press.

Jacka, T. (2006) *Rural Women in Urban China: Gender, Migration, and Social Change*. Armonk, NY and London: M. E. Sharpe.

Jeffreys, E. (2004) *China, Sex and Prostitution*. London: Routledge Curzon.

Liu Jieyu (2007a) *Gender and Work in Urban China: Women Workers of the Unlucky Generation*. London: Routledge.

—— (2007b) 'Gender dynamics and redundancy in urban China', *Feminist Economics*, 13 (3–4): 91–124.

Loe, M. (1996) 'Working for men – at the intersection of power, gender and sexuality', *Sociological Inquiry*, 66: 399–421.

Martin, P. Y. and D. L. Collinson (1999) 'Gender, sexuality and organization' in M. M. Ferree, J. Lorber and B. B. Hess (eds), *Revisioning Gender*. Thousand Oaks, CA: Sage, pp. 285–340.

Pringle, R. (1989) *Secretaries Talk: Sexuality, Power and Work*. London: Verso.

Sheppard, D. L. (1989) 'Organizations, power and sexuality: the image and self-image of women managers' in J. Hearn, D. L. Sheppard, P. Tancred-Sheriff and G. Burrell (eds), *The Sexuality of Organization*. London: Sage, pp. 139–57.

Tancred-Sheriff, P. (1989) 'Gender, sexuality and the labour process' in J. Hearn, D. L. Sheppard, P. Tancred-Sheriff and G. Burrell (eds), *The Sexuality of Organization*. London: Sage, pp. 45–55.

Wang Zheng (2000) 'Gender, employment and women's resistance' in E. Perry and M. Selden (eds), *Chinese Society: Change, Conflict, and Resistance*. London: Routledge Curzon.

Wolf, M. (1985) *Revolution Postponed: Women in Contemporary China*. Stanford, CA: Stanford University Press.

Xu, G. and S. Feiner (2007) 'Meinü Jingji/China's beauty economy: buying looks, shifting value, and changing place', *Feminist Economics*, 13 (3–4): 307–23.

Zhang, Everett Yuehong (2001) '*Goudui* and the state: constructing entrepreneurial masculinity in two cosmopolitan areas of post-socialist China' in D. Hodgson (ed.), *Gendered Modernities: Ethnographic Perspectives*. Basingstoke: Palgrave.

Zheng, Tiantian (2006) 'Cool masculinity: male clients' sex consumption and business alliance in urban China's sex industry', *Journal of Contemporary China*, 15 (46): 161–82.

5 Sex and Work in Sex Work: Negotiating Sex and Work among Taiwanese Sex Workers

CHEN MEI-HUA

In the past four decades, feminists in the West and in Taiwan have developed two divergent perspectives on commercial sex. The first theorizes prostitution in terms of gender oppression, focusing on the sexual exploitation of women through men's appropriation and commodification of their bodies and their consequent loss of self (Barry 1995; Pateman 1988; Hwang 1996). The second focuses on how sexual oppression shapes the ways we understand commercial sex, citing Gayle Rubin's (1993 [1984]) idea of 'sex hierarchy' to argue that the stigma of sex prevents us from seeing sex work as just work while also suppressing individual sexual expression (see, for example, Ho 1998). The former position, in focusing on gender oppression, makes sexuality central; the latter, in focusing on sexual oppression, seeks to decentre sex in discussions of prostitution in favour of work, while at the same time promoting sexual freedom.

Prostitutes' rights groups and advocates tend to support the latter position, emphasizing that 'the sex industry is not the only industry which is male-dominated and degrades women' (Lopez-Jones 1988: 273) and that sex work is just like any other job (Wang and Ku 1998: 153) – except that its illegal or marginal status makes it harder for prostitutes to defend their jobs. This approach recognizes prostitution as work, and prostitutes as workers, but sidelines the sexual aspect of the work. This tendency can be identified in Josephine Ho's writing (Ho 1998). She analyses sex work in the light of the historical transformation of labour in a capitalist market. She explains that sexual labour, like other productive and reproductive labour that was once carried out in private, is now integrated into the capitalist market through the commodification of labour. According to Ho:

As a work in public, sex work implies a possible future of sexuality, where sex will not be involved with unacceptable manipulation of affection, and it will not be the only criterion for love and intimacy. Most of all, since sex is a form of work, sex will not function as the only criterion to measure women. (Ho 1998: 223, my translation)

This is an optimistic attitude towards the commodification of sex, which envisages the possibility of women's sexual liberation by freeing sex from intimacy. Nonetheless, whether sexual liberation is gained at the cost of working-class women's involvement in commercial sex is left unconsidered. In addition, she does not clarify how sex workers understand the sex acts provided in commercial sex. Are they labour or sex? If they are labour, what is the nature of the labour involved? Moreover, even if these sex acts are labour, it does not guarantee that sex workers are free contract workers.

The either-sex-or-work approach constitutes a barrier to an intelligent feminist account of how sexuality and labour are intertwined in sex work. It seems that once we take the sexual side of prostitution seriously, we fail to deal with its labour dimensions. Once we analyse it as work, we fail to identify the sexual. Both sides fail to analyse sex work as a sequence of labour tasks that have strong sexual connotations, and to see sex workers as simultaneously waged workers and sexual subjects.

This chapter tries to fill the gap and to analyse how sex and work are intertwined in sex work. Drawing on interviews with 18 Taiwanese sex workers, I suggest that they are usually expected to undertake several forms of labour, such as aesthetic labour, explicit sexual labour and embodied emotional labour. In addition, sex workers perform labours differently due to the varying organization of sex work. Moreover, I will argue that being able to perform these labours signifies sex workers' professionalism. It is the ability to exercise the technique of 'role distance' (Goffman 1961) that makes sex workers able to differentiate the situated role they perform from their sense of self. I will draw on interview data to show how women use diverse strategies to maintain the boundary between the work role and their senses of self, and how they differentiate commercial sex from intimate sex. Nonetheless, the effort to manage the boundary signals the danger of blurring it.

Forms of labour in the Taiwanese sex industry

O'Connell Davidson's (1998) research indicates that the employment status of sex workers and the nature of the sexual contract between clients and sex workers are the major factors that influence Western sex workers' working conditions. The same could be said of the Taiwanese sex industry. Taiwanese prostitution can be classified roughly into two traditional sectors: *mai shen* (body selling) and *mai xiao* (pleasure selling). The body-selling sector (such as brothels, massage parlours, organized call-girl services or streetwalking) provides explicit sexual services to clients and thus the relations between sex workers and clients are relatively standardized or commercialized. In the pleasure-selling sector, there is a whole range of more personalized sexual and entertainment services and relations catering to clients' diverse demands (from karaoke bars to traditional tearooms), in which sex is not necessarily involved. Above all, the two sectors differ from each other in terms of legal status. As body selling makes the exchange of money for sex explicit, it is directly targeted by prostitution laws which criminalize those (women) who sell sex while tolerating those (men) who buy sex.[1] In the name of urban hedonism, pleasure selling occurs in legal, modern, urban entertainment venues which serve to justify men's sexual consumption. Usually, sex workers who work in the body-selling sector suffer more from police raids and harassment.

Furthermore, the conditions under which women perform sex work are also affected by the degree to which commercial sex is institutionalized. Those who work in highly organized or hierarchic sexual establishments (such as karaoke bars or call-girl stations) are usually subject to the surveillance of a third party and have less control over their work – but are better protected from police raids and thus face lower risks. The other extreme is independent streetwalking, where women control the whole process of the sexual transaction and keep all the earnings, but are most vulnerable to police harassment. The labour sex workers actually perform is varied and diverse. to avoid falsely homogenizing sex work(ers) I interviewed sex workers who worked in different settings.[2]

The labour dimensions of sex work

By seeing prostitution as selling sex, mainstream discourse in Taiwan tends to see sex work as something any woman could do and as therefore lacking professionalism. Hwang Shu-ling (1996: 142) wrote that 'when any female aged 8 to 68 can get high pay from the sex industry, it is a job that needs no talent or skill. It thus cannot be professional' (my translation). This comment not only neglects variation in sex workers' incomes, but also fails to recognize the fact that sex workers' 'high pay' is in sharp contrast to many female workers' inadequate wages in the formal labour market. It also fails to unveil various labour dimensions of sex work, and how they are performed differently in different sex industry locations.

Dressing like a whore
'Dressing like a whore' is identified as the first step to performing the role of whore. Interviewees reported that they knew they would have to 'dress for that job' before they got involved in it. Young girls, mainly casual call girls, reported that their bosses or 'companies' would demand that they dress in a particular style (typically mini-skirts, tiny tight vests, and high heels) to 'present female beauty' and 'show off their good figures'.

This dress code draws attention to gender as performance. Performing femininity is rarely considered or appreciated as a kind of labour, mainly because women are generally expected to be feminine and sexually desirable both in private and in public. Pan-pan, the only lesbian interviewee, always bound her breasts and wore jeans when she was not working, but reported that for work: '[I] would pay attention to my clothes . . . because clients would be scared, if I looked more masculine.' 'Dressing like a whore' became a task of negotiating the boundary between maintaining her gendered sexual identity of being a 'very masculine tomboy' and being a feminine and sexually desirable whore.

Performing femininity is not confined to sex work, but is common in the service economy. Adkins suggests that service work creates 'a new sovereignty of appearance, image, and style at work' (2002: 61) and thus excludes some specific workers. Witz et al. (2003) argue that interactive service work involves aesthetic labour in which workers' embodied dispositions are mobilized, developed, and commercialized by employers of service occupations. It is no surprise that the performance of aesthetic labour is strongly demanded in sex work: uniformed bar girls offer an excellent example.

Pretty Girls is a *jyh fwu diann* (uniformed bar) where bar girls' uniform comprises three pieces (and cost them NT$4,000, about £80, at the time they were interviewed): a well-decorated bra that clearly shows off the girls' 'big breasts', which are augmented by padded sponge, a tiny piece of mini-skirt which opens in a slit to the waist, and a silk robe which has to be taken off when seeing clients. Moreover, each bar girl is required to wear a G-string for clients' sexual pleasure. Moreover, doing 'body work' is an important daily routine, which includes skin care, putting on (subtle) make-up, wearing designer perfume and fashionable hair styles. Echoing Witz et al. (2003), the uniform and girls' 'body work' signify the bar: they embody the image of the bar and present it as a more 'stylish' or 'refined' sexual establishment. The workers' embodied dispositions are thus successfully mobilized by the bar, put on sale, and transferred into economic capital for the bar owners. Moreover, the emphasis on the 'refinement' of the bar also serves the girls' interests and self-identity: it indicates that they work in a unique bar that makes them different from other working women who are seen as vulgar in their dress and speech.

Just 'doing that thing'
Whether in high-class or low-class locations, sexual acts are central to what sex workers do. Apart from a few interviewees who could clearly report this aspect of their job content, most when asked about it replied that they are 'just doing that thing' or 'doing something that people would do with their boyfriends'. At first glance, 'that thing' seems self-evident. However, 'that thing' not only includes diverse sexual practices, but is also deeply embedded in workers' various working settings.

> We simply did what ordinary lovers do to each other. . . . I charged NT$5,000 per hour, but clients were only allowed to do it once in an hour. Usually [we] let them come in ten minutes. After they finished it, we would just leave. (Wei-wei, 18, six months as an [independent] call girl)

By posting small advertisements on the Internet, Wei-wei organized her call-girl services independently. She therefore controlled all the details of her work, such as deciding what services to provide, keeping all the earnings and insisting on using condoms. Her account, however, does not unveil the secrecy of the sexual services or labour she provides. Sue-lian, one of the few interviewees who explicitly described the sequence of turning a trick, offers a fuller account:

> Usually a man came in and lay down on the bed. I would rub his dick. He then got a hard-on and then I let him penetrate. That's it. So, I didn't have many clients. (Sue-lian, 41, ex-licensed sex worker, in prostitution for 28 years)

Commercial sex here is so standardized that male sexuality is considered as nothing but a series of stimulus-response bodily reflexes. Ho (2000) pointed out that this standardized service indeed functions to save labour and desexualize the sexual encounter. These sexual services were desexualized to the extent that Sue-lian could completely ignore the existence of her clients:

> Sometimes I even kept knitting a sweater when a man was fucking me. (*Laughs.*) Yes, it's true. . . . Sometimes I would read a comic when clients were fucking me. But, you know what, he was moving on my body all the time, so the comic would jump up-and-down in front of my eyes. That really tired my eyes. (*Giggles.*) It's true. I did. (Sue-lian)

If this was a 'sexual' encounter, it was an alienated one. The scene described above is more like a postmodern parody than an erotic sexual encounter. It offers perhaps an extreme example of why so many clients complain about sex workers' bad performances or blame them for being cool or heartless (Høigård and Finstad 1992; O'Connell Davidson 1995). It is precisely the desexualization of these encounters that opens up a space for working women to differentiate 'sex as work' and 'sex for fun'. Many sex workers, however, are expected to mask this distancing by performing emotional labour.

Embodied emotional labour

Hochschild (1983) argues that emotional labour is in high demand in service occupations. As performing emotional labour deeply involves people's feelings and inner self, she concludes that workers who have to perform emotional labour might develop particular strategies to construct their self. She also mentions that prostitution is one of the few working-class jobs which involves meaning making and/or feeling management (1979: 570). Western literature on the subject indeed shows that emotional labour plays an important role in sex work, which includes talking and flirting with clients (Chapkis 1997;

McIntosh 1996). In my study, interviewees from both body-selling and pleasure-selling sectors expected to perform emotional labour to different degrees. The demand for emotional labour could be identified easily when they were asked if there is any professional skill in doing sex work:

> No, I didn't think so. You simply need a good temper. (Mei-yun, 61, ex-licensed sex worker, in prostitution for 17 years)

> Professional [skills] . . . no, I don't think so. You just need to be able to please clients and . . . be able to drink. And . . . you should be highly cooperative. There is nothing professional. Anyhow, you need to please clients and . . . umm, don't show a bad temper. (Fung-fung, 29, three years as a bar girl)

While these women deny having professional skills, I would argue that these accounts mark out the ways in which women's emotional work is taken for granted and devalued both in public and in private (Meerabeau and Page 1998; Duncombe and Marsden 1998).

Young call girls talked about the paradox of 'professionalism' in sex work, when asked the same question:

> Clients would be more fond of you, if you didn't have much sexual skills. Because he could teach you and that turns him on. (Xin-xin, 16, casual call girl)

> If you looked very (sexually) experienced, he would feel that 'Oh, you are a . . . .' So, it's better to make yourself look not so experienced. For example, you could shyly ask that 'Is it all right?' [smiles] before he did something to you. Umm, pretending to be pure. . . . Tut, I don't know . . . because if you looked too pure, they knew that you was faking [laughs] . . . . (Wei-wei, 18, six months as an independent call girl)

Performing femininity here is both sexual and very much embodied: shyly ask . . . '*Is it all right?*' and *smile* at the same time. The performance turns the men on because Taiwanese clients tend to eroticize sexually inexperienced young girls. Paradoxically, the phrase 'Oh, you are a . . .' highlights the embodied performance of femininity demanded here. The missing word in the phrase is, no doubt, *ji nu* (whore). It suggests that the performance of embodied femininity is a balancing act in which 'professional' working women should present themselves as not 'real whores' in order to turn on clients!

Furthermore, the embodied emotional labour is extremely sexualized: many interviewees reported that they had to 'sound sexy' and 'act high' and fake orgasms:

> Even though you didn't have an orgasm, you would pretend you did. Umm, if I didn't have an orgasm, I still would pretend I have one. Making a noise like, 'ah, ah…' [smiles]. Umm, I mean . . . pretending you are extremely high. That turns men on. You just need to make an effort to make noises [giggles]. (Wei-wei, 18, six months as an independent call girl)

'Men make a mess; women make a noise' (Jackson and Scott 2001: 107) sums up the gendered performance of orgasm in heterosexual relationships. Faking an orgasm is not only a matter of 'making noises' mechanically. These noises, as Pan-pan put it, should 'sound sexy or feminine'. In order to perform a living orgasm, one should 'sound sexy' and 'look high'. This performance nonetheless is very exhausting and/or annoying, hence some interviewees do not want to be bothered with it. Again, whether sex workers perform orgasm relates to the ways their work is organized. Call girls in this study frequently reported they made a great effort to 'make noises' mainly because their work was controlled and organized by a third party.

It is worth noting that performing embodied emotional labour does not mean that sex workers are helpless victims or that they lose their 'authentic self'. Many did emotional labour not only on bosses' demand, but also as a means of investing in business in the long term. Bar girls who strongly emphasized mobilizing *shoou wan* (social skills) to woo clients actually were keen to create an illusion of 'falling in love' with clients in order to keep business going.

Doing sex work therefore does not necessarily destroy sex workers' bodies and self as Pateman (1988) suggested. On the contrary, as Chapkis (1997) argues, the ability to perform emotional labour makes sex workers able to differentiate their self in work from their sense of self in private life. Here Goffman's performance theory and his concept of 'role distance' are helpful in explaining a complex situation. As Goffman argued:

> one can afford to try to fit into the situation as an act that can be styled to show that one is somewhat out of place. One enters the situation to the degree that one can demonstrate that one does not belong. (1961: 109)

Treating emotional labour as an alienated labour, Hochschild argues that workers may lose their 'authenticity'. However, as workers are consciously aware that they are performing femininity and/or emotional work, they are clearly able to differentiate the 'back stage' from the 'front stage'. For example, many interviewees reported: 'I'm a totally different person when I'm not working.' Sitting in the common room (the 'back stage') of Pretty Girls, I found girls put their legs on tables, made ungraceful noises when eating noodle soup, chatted and yelled loudly when playing cards. They were neither sexy, nor feminine. One way to exercise role distance to differentiate work self from their sense of self is to carefully manage the boundary between sex as sex and sex as work.

Negotiating the boundary between sex as sex and sex as work: the 'boyfriend narrative'

It is widely claimed that prostitutes are badly damaged by their jobs and thus become sexually frigid or indifferent to sex (Davis 1937). Savitz and Rosen's (1988) research on the sexual enjoyment of 46 American prostitutes found that respondents' professional experiences did not appear to interfere with their enjoyment of private sex. Moreover, they claimed that 'the higher the sexual enjoyment in the prostitutes' private sex life, the greater the erotic pleasure reported in their professional realm' (1988: 205). In my study, interviewees hardly ever reported that they 'enjoy' sex during work. They tended to compare their sex with clients and with boyfriends, and differentiate sex as sex and sex as work in what I call the 'boyfriend narrative'. Chen-chen talked about the comparison between sex with clients and with her boyfriend:

> You have more . . . sensual feeling. Having sex with clients . . . it's simply doing work. Job done after you finished it. You have more sensual feeling when you are with your boyfriend. You did it with feeling, so it's much more comfortable. You willingly did it with your boyfriend. *The other is that you feel a bit like you go to make money, you know. Yeah, tan xia zha mou [whore], you feel like that.* (Chen-chen, 17, casual call girl, my emphasis)

This narrative is indeed typical among interviewees. They used phrases such as 'more interesting' and 'feels much better' to describe their private sexual activities, but used 'annoying', 'dirty' and 'wish it would finish quickly' to refer to sex with clients. The importance of the distinction to some extent relates to respondents' (hetero)sexual intimacy and their sense of self. Pan-pan, the only lesbian in this study, reported that doing commercial sex with men 'isn't a big deal, because I have no feeling about men!' Conversely, she felt very 'shy' when seeing female clients, because:

> It's a bit similar to a male and a female [encounter]. Yeah, like, I'm a boy, and she's a girl. You more or less would feel a bit . . . shy . . . Umm, [I] felt a bit shy. I mean, she's a girl after all, and it's the first time to do it with her. If you have that kind of [sexual] contact for two or three times [with her], you would feel . . . natural or at ease. (Pan-pan, 18, six months as a bar girl and independent call girl)

Feeling shy suggests that Pan-pan saw these sexual encounters as involving her own sexuality. As Morgan (1988: 27), a lesbian sex worker, describes, performing a strip show for lesbians is both 'performing and *playing* with parts of our sexualities' (emphasis in original). Pan-pan enjoyed sexual encounters with female clients; in fact, she only met two female clients and eventually both of them became her girlfriends. I am of course not suggesting that it is easier for lesbians to perform sex work. My point here is to stress the ways in which workers' sexual and gender identities shape their different understandings and experiences of commercial sex, and to highlight the importance of 'boyfriend narrative' in maintaining the boundary between sex and work.

Techniques of boundary management

Marking out the bodily boundary of sex/work
Western literature details many sex workers' taboos in performing sex work – no kissing, no anal sex, no cunnilingus, no penetration without a condom, and so on (see Høigård and Finstad 1992). Ho (2000, 2001) goes further to argue that sex workers use these rituals to mark out the time and space for their work. I would like to add that the organization of sex work might influence the ways sex workers mark out these temporal and spatial boundaries.

Chen-chen, who worked in a call-girl station that demanded

workers provide standardized services to clients (for example, taking a shower, licking his chest, oral sex and intercourse), reported that 'I perform a set of services to clients, and do it differently with my boyfriend.' Ping-ping independently solicited on street corners and usually turned tricks in the room she rented from a hotel. As the room was both for work and her private place, she usually used different bedding to differentiate between her work and her private life. It seems to me that every interviewee, even in the 'body-selling' sector, had an imaginary map of the bodily boundary of sex/work; once clients crossed the border, they might encounter serious resistance. Xin-xin angrily talked about the ways in which she reacted to clients' transgression:

> Some troublesome clients want to kiss you, ask you to lick their penises, or let him to do cunnilingus. Yeah, otherwise they asked for anal sex. . . . Why should we lick him or let him lick us? I think it's very disgusting. Yeah, why should women in this job need to be licked by clients? It's enough to let him penetrate with a condom, isn't it? (Xin-xin, 16, casual call girl)

Many interviewees, just like Xin-xin, tried to maintain the boundaries of their bodies, sexuality and sense of self as a whole in commercial sex; nonetheless, their bargaining power was highly affected by the ways in which their work was organized: for example, call girls and bar girls whose work is controlled by a third party have less bargaining power.

Mobilizing social skills

Marking out the bodily boundary of sex and work is common and helpful in the body-selling sector, but does not work in the pleasure-selling sector. As bar girls commonly argued, it is impossible to tell clients that 'Hey, you cannot touch here or there!' Even in bars that advertise themselves as 'high-class' or 'more stylish', the sexualized bodies of the workers are the main attraction and are available to be touched and fondled as clients please. Fung-fung reported that she had been 'kissed to throw up', and that the vagina of one of her colleagues had been badly hurt by a client. Bar girls frequently reported that sometimes even touching and hugging could be unbearable.

Mobilizing *shoou wan* to manage clients was therefore considered the most important technique in pleasure-selling sectors. Women in the pleasure-selling sector tended to see workers who are only able to make money by selling sex and do not have *shoou wan* as unprofessional. When asked to describe *shoou wan*, they frequently spoke of how to read clients' minds through their words and behaviour, how to let clients feel respected and save face – skills similar to those found in many modern service occupations (see Black 2004, for example). The timing of or occasions on which workers were keen to mobilize *shoou wan* were mainly related to avoiding 'doing S' (offering commercial sex), and to resisting various unpleasant bodily contacts. Usually, bar girls would try everything to keep clients busy and prevent their touching them, such as inviting clients to sing, dance, drink and play all kinds of (sexual) games. In order to avoid unbearable bodily contacts, some women tended to take the lead to 'handle' clients' sexual desire (offering oral sex, for example). Fung-fung talked about why she chose to take the initiative to 'handle' clients:

> If you don't [take the initiative], you will probably get two situations. One is that you will be dismissed. The other is that he will . . . come to touch you. He will then . . . touch you all over, kiss you, suck [your tits], and even dig [your vagina]. He will do everything! In that case, we would prefer to . . . 'handle' him than to be insulted.

Here Fung-fung does not see offering sexual acts to clients as her sex(uality), but as a way to avoid unwanted body-to-body contacts. It is one of the available techniques or strategies that bar girls use to manage the integrity of their bodies, sexuality and sense of self. However, the images of playing, drinking with and offering sex to clients are widely misrepresented in the media as evidence of badly damaged prostitutes.

Dirt management
Performing sex acts is different from other performances partly because it entails body-to-body contact and exchanging bodily fluids, which is considered polluting or dangerous in many cultures (Douglas 2002 [1966]). Dirt management therefore appears to be one of the major themes in sex workers' daily routines. Workers in both body-selling and pleasure-selling sectors make an effort to maintain the boundary between the clean self and the dirty other.

Two interviewees who reported being seduced and trafficked into this job (Yi-ling and Xiao-fan) repeatedly emphasized that they were not 'willing to do it'. The lack of 'free consent' makes them constantly report that '[I]t's dirty!' and that they felt 'spoiled' by clients.

> I felt that I didn't want my body to be touched. . . . It's very dirty. It made me feel very dirty. . . . I felt I was very dirty because . . . too many people touch me. (Xiao-fan, 17, casual call girl)

Similarly, Yi-ling also reported that '[I]f you put it in a more positive way, you are doing sex. But, it's dirty!'

Mary Douglas (2002 [1966]) argues that the dirt is not dirty in itself, but because it transgresses social order. Symbolically, having sex with a boyfriend is pleasurable because it is celebrated by heteronormativity; conversely, doing commercial sex is criminalized and stigmatized. The dirt, nonetheless, is also very much related to hygiene. Former licensed sex workers reported that they tried to avoid exchanging bodily fluids with clients, because that might be the origin of sexually transmitted diseases. As Bai-lan put it:

> Men's dicks are damn foul and you have no idea whether they are healthy or not. To be honest, I was forced to do it [oral sex] when I was trafficked into an illegal brothel. I didn't do it after my graduation [when she was freed from trafficking], no matter how much money clients offered to pay for it. . . . Neither do I want to be kissed. Some men have halitosis. They smelled awful. . . . If clients wanted to do cunnilingus, you better reject them because there are so many germs in people's mouths. (Bai-lan, 41, ex-licensed brothel worker, in prostitution for 18 years)

In the dominant discourse prostitutes are stigmatized as the origin of sexually transmitted diseases, and clients are seen as pure and clean victims. Ironically, clients were considered as the dirty other by many of my interviewees. Their saliva and sperm were treated as potential sources of sexually transmitted diseases that might blur the boundary between healthy self and dirty other. Dirt management, in this sense, highlights sex workers' daily life. The ways interviewees managed the dirt differed according to the diverse organization of sex work. Bai-lan was forced to perform all kinds of sex acts when she was trafficked, but could control what kind of sex she provided as a licensed sex worker. Xiao-van and Yi-ling dealt with the dirt by spending 'more than an hour' to shower or 'using shower gel to brush [my] whole body' after turning a trick. Deep cleaning in a way functions as a ritual to get rid of external dirt or pollution, and reclaim the integrity of the self.

Condoms, of course, create a clear boundary between sex workers and clients, and protect the clean self from the dirty other. Condom usage is widely represented as a way to differentiate sex workers' sexual intimacy from sex work. For younger interviewees, however, using condoms was centred on the very practical concern of avoiding pregnancy. Clients' sperm therefore is considered as both dirty and destructive.

Falling in love with 'real human beings'

Seidman (1991) argues that, in the West, there has been a 'sexualization of love' and 'eroticization of sex' from the nineteenth century onward. Similarly, in Taiwan, having sex in intimate relationships is taken for granted as the *best* way to express love. It is not surprising that most young girls in this study reported that they avoid having sex with their boyfriends and felt that they had betrayed their boyfriends. Yet sex, for some sex workers, is hardly considered as an indicator of love, given that it can be contracted out so easily. The ways Bai-lan talked about the similarities between having sex with clients and her boyfriend shows us a different relationship between sex and intimacy:

> Nothing different, you still got a dick. . . . Gee, sometime he [boyfriend] was fucking me, but I was sleeping. Yes, I did [giggles]. I was very tired, you know. So I had him do it by himself. . . . Of course, we love each other, but it doesn't mean that we should do that thing [sex]. Do you understand? It's not necessary to do that. It's good to respect and take care of each other. It's all right for me that he seeks for a sexual outlet [outside]. Just let him have fun. . . . I was always sloppily dressed, but men still came to see me, you know. They are cheap animals! (Bai-lan, 41, ex-licensed brothel worker, in prostitution for 18 years)

Sex, for Bai-lan, represents a natural drive shared by all kinds of 'cheap animals', it does not even qualify as an expression of love. Thinking in this way, Bai-lan was thus freed from the obsession of sex, and does not bother to monitor her lover's sexual activities. In contrast, mutual respect and care, for Bai-lan, are understood as love or as cornerstones of intimacy. Love is, therefore, desexualized.

The phenomenon of the desexualization of love is quite notable in some interviewees' narratives of how they felt attracted to and even fell in love with some specific clients. It is not difficult to understand that mutual respect and care are so important given that many interviewees reported that they were not respected at all in their job. Indeed, many respondents spent quite a long time describing how 'horrible clients' humiliated them, bargained for a better price, tried to take all kinds of advantage, demanded undesirable sexual services, used verbal and physical violence, and so on. Tolerating or handling 'horrible clients' is an unpleasant daily routine for many interviewees. Therefore, once clients show their respect to sex workers it is very likely that these clients are considered as 'real human beings', rather than 'cheap animals'. It therefore is possible and/or worth it for sex workers to invest emotions in them. In a conversation Fung-fung and Yo-yo discussed how their clients turned out to be their lovers:

> Fung-fung: [Laughs] . . . Usually our boyfriends once were our clients. . . .

> Yo-yo: Basically, men who turned out to be your boyfriends definitely won't touch you. You would feel that . . . He is a real human being. They are human beings; others are animals!

> Fung-fung: Yeah, yeah . . . [laughs].

> Yo-yo: Yes, at least, you need to feel that he is a human being, you know. If a man touched you all over your body, how could you think that he sincerely likes you? In addition, they make us feel that we are respectable. Then we could treat them as friends.

Phoenix's (1999) research on British sex workers also reports that punters are commonly represented as bastards and animals. Here, the metaphor of 'cheap animals' indicates that sex workers are treated badly, simply as a whore, in sexual encounters. 'Cheap animals' only seek sexual satisfaction, thus foreclosing other possibilities, while 'human beings' respect sex workers as persons and, therefore, open up the possibility of creating other intimate relationships – as regular clients, old friends, and even lovers – which are only possible when both parties are treated as equal human beings. In a way, feeling respected as human beings, sex workers might 'feel right' in crossing the boundary and falling in love with their clients.

Conclusion

I have argued that the tendency to frame prostitution either as 'just sex' or as 'just work' is misleading and fails to theorize prostitution adequately. Carefully examining the labour process of sex work, this chapter goes beyond the either-sex-or-work debate. It not only recognizes sex work as work or labour, but also analyses the ways in which sexualization, stigmatization and criminalization of sex work make it impossible for it to be 'just' like some other jobs. In many cases, the stigmatization and criminalization of sex work put sex workers in a risky working situation that makes sex work very different from other work. In terms of sexualization, I argue that Taiwanese sex workers are expected to perform aesthetic labour, alienated sexual labour and embodied emotional labour to different degrees reflecting the diverse ways in which sex work is organized. Furthermore, as the labour demanded in sex work is sexualized to the extent that it is so similar to workers' private sex, interviewees tends to develop different strategies, very much embedded in diverse working settings, to manage the boundary between their sense of self and their work self, and the boundary between sex as sex and sex as work. Hence, sex work is just 'work'; nonetheless, once the boundary is collapsed, it turns out to be 'sex'. Therefore, we should abandon the 'either-sex-or-work' approach and carefully examine when the balance of sex work inclines to sex or work.

Nonetheless, as an instance of feminized work, sex work shares some similarities with other service occupations, such as flight attendants, Taiwanese betel-nut beauties[3] and female clerks in department stores (see Lan 1998). In order to transform workers' labour power into labour, the employers in the service sector design work regimes that demand female workers perform sexualized femininity and embodied emotional labour. With rapid sexualization of female service occupations, analysis of sex work might help us to rethink these female jobs. In fact, it might be interesting to note that sex and work are not exclusive of each other in women's daily lives – as empirical research has shown, heterosexual women are expected to fake orgasms in daily lives. It is thus important for feminists not only to consider the particularity of sex work, but also to examine the ways in which it is related to women's other paid and unpaid labour both in public and private.

Notes

1 The Taiwanese government issued licences to brothels and to prostitutes after 1956. However, licensed prostitution was abolished in September 1997 when Taipei city government decided to criminalize all kinds of commercial sex. This abolition caused 128 former Taipei licensed prostitutes to organize themselves to demand their rights to sex work.

2 These included those who worked as independent call girls and those who worked in organized call-girl centres, those who worked in high-class bars and in lower-class karaoke bars, in tearooms or on the streets, as well as formerly licensed prostitutes (see note 1 above).

3 Betel-nut beauties are young women, often scantily dressed, who sell betel-nut in kiosks by the roadside. They are a common sight on the streets of Taiwan.

References

Adkins, Lisa (2002) *Revisions: Towards a Sociology of Gender and Sexuality in Late Modernity*. Buckingham: Open University Press.

Barry, Kathleen (1995) *The Prostitution of Sexuality*. New York: New York University Press.

Black, Paula (2004) *The Beauty Industry: Gender, Culture, Pleasure*. London: Routledge.

Chapkis, Wendy (1997) *Live Sex Acts: Women Performing Erotic Labour*. London: Cassell.

Davis, Kingsley (1937) 'The sociology of prostitution', *American Sociological Review*, 2: 744–55.

Douglas, Mary (2002 [1966]) *Purity and Danger: an Analysis of Concepts of Pollution and Taboo*. London: Routledge.

Duncombe, Jean and Dennis Marsden (1998) '"Stepford wives" and "hollow men"? Doing emotion work, doing gender and "authenticity" in intimate heterosexual relationships' in Gillian Bendelow and Simon J. Williams (eds), *Emotions in Social Life: Critical Themes and Contemporary Issues*. London: Routledge, pp. 211–27.

Goffman, Erving (1961) 'Role distance' in *Encounters: Two Studies of the Sociology of Interaction*. London: Macmillan, pp. 85–185.

Ho, Josephine Chuen-Juei [何春蕤] (1998) 女性主義的色情／性工作立場 ['Feminists' position on pornography and sex work'] in 何春蕤編性工作：妓權觀點 [Josephine Ho (ed.), *Sex Work: Prostitutes' Rights in Perspective*]. Chungli, Taiwan: 中央性／別研究室 [Center for the Study of Sexualities Press].

—— (2000) 'Self-empowerment and "professionalism": conversations with Taiwanese sex workers', *Inter-Asia Cultural Studies*, 1 (2): 283–99.

—— (2001) 自我培力與專業操演：與台灣性工作者的對話 ['Self-empowerment and professional performativity: conversations with Taiwanese sex workers'], 台灣社會研究季刊 [*Taiwan: A Radical Quarterly in Social Studies*], 41: 1–51.

Hochschild, Arlie R. (1979) 'Emotion work, feeling rules, and social structure', *American Journal of Sociology*, 85 (3): 551–75.

—— (1983) *The Managed Heart: Commercialization of Human Feeling*. Berkeley, CA: University of California Press.

Høigård, Cecilie and Liv Finstad (1992) *Backstreets: Prostitution, Money and Love*. Cambridge: Polity Press.

Hwang Shu-ling [黃淑玲] (1996) 台灣特種行業婦女：受害者？行動者？偏差者？ ['Women in sex industries: victims, agents or deviants?'], 台灣社會研究季刊 [*Taiwan: A Radical Quarterly in Social Studies*], 22 (April): 103–52.

Jackson, Stevi and Sue Scott (2001) 'Embodying orgasm: gendered power relations and sexual pleasure', *Women and Therapy*, 24 (1/2): 99–110.

Lan, Pei-Chia [藍佩嘉] (1998) 銷售女體，女體勞動：百貨專櫃化妝品女銷售員的身體勞動 ['Selling bodies, laboring bodies: bodily labor of department store cosmetics saleswomen'], 台灣社會學研究 [*Taiwanese Sociological Review*], 2: 47–81.

Lopez-Jones, Nina (1988) 'Workers: introducing the English collective of Prostitutes' in Frédérique Delacoste and Priscilla Alexander (eds), *Sex Work: Writings by Women in the Sex Industry*. London: Virago Press, pp. 271–8.

McIntosh, Mary (1996) 'Feminist debates on prostitution' in L. Adkins and V. Merchant (eds), *Sexualizing the Social: Power and the Organization of Sexuality*. London: Macmillan Press, pp. 191–203.

Meerabeau, Liz and Susie Page (1998) '"Getting the job done": emotion management and cardiopulmonary resuscitation in nursing' in Gillian Bendelow and Simon J. Williams (eds), *Emotions in Social Life: Critical Themes and Contemporary Issues*. London: Routledge, pp. 295–312.

Morgan, Peggy (1988) 'Living on the edge' in Frédérique Delacoste and Priscilla Alexander (eds), *Sex Work: Writings by Women in the Sex Industry*. London: Virago Press, pp. 21–8.

O'Connell Davidson, Julia (1995) 'British sex tourists in Thailand' in M. Maynard and J. Purvis (eds), *(Hetero)sexual Politics*. London: Taylor and Francis, pp. 42–64.

—— (1998) *Prostitution, Power, and Freedom*. Cambridge: Polity Press.

Pateman, Carol (1988) *The Sexual Contract*. Cambridge: Polity Press.

Phoenix, Joanna (1999) *Making Sense of Prostitution*. Basingstoke: Palgrave Press.

Rubin, Gayle S. (1993 [1984]) 'Thinking sex: notes for a radical theory of the politics of sexuality' in Henry Abelove, Michele Aina Barale and David M. Halperin (eds), *The Lesbian and Gay Studies Reader*. New York, NY and London: Routledge, pp. 3–44.

Savitz, Leonard, and Lawrence Rosen (1988) 'The sexuality of prostitutes: sexual enjoyment reported by "streetwalkers"', *Journal of Sex Research*, 24: 200–8.

Seidman, Steven (1991) *Romantic Longings: Love in America, 1830–1980*. New York: Routledge.

Wang Fang-ping and Ku Yu-ling (王芳萍、顧玉玲) (1998) 我的工作，我的

尊嚴：性工作就是工作 ['My work is my dignity: sex work is work'] in 春蘋編性工作：妓權觀點 [Josephine Ho (ed.), *Sex Work: Prostitutes' Rights in Perspective*]. Chungli, Taiwan: 中央性／別研究室 [Center for the Study of Sexualities Press].

Witz, Anne, Chris Warhurst and Dennis Nickson (2003) 'The labour of aesthetics and the aesthetics of organization', *Organization*, 10 (2): 33–54.

6 Beyond Sex Work: An Analysis of *Xiaojies'* Understandings of Work in the Pearl River Delta Area, China

DING YU AND HO SIK-YING

The key divide in Western debates on prostitution is between radical feminists who condemn prostitution as a site of male domination and see all women involved as victims (Pateman 1988; MacKinnon and Dworkin 1988; Jeffreys 1997) and 'sex-radical' feminists who praise prostitution for challenging the boundaries of normativity and promoting 'erotic diversity' in the form of 'service work' (Califia 1994; Chapkis 1997; Highleyman 1997). The former insist prostitution be demolished while the latter celebrate the new sexual lifestyle by naming it 'sex work' (Leigh 1997;[1] Brock 1998; Ho 2000, 2001a, 2001b, 2001c; Huang 2004). This continuing heated debate among feminists over the globe on the acceptance of prostitution as a form of work has fuelled the pervasive use of the term 'sex worker' in China (Huang and Pan 2003; Huang 2004; Pan 1997, 2000, 2005b), and there is even a call on the part of some Chinese scholars for prostitution to be decriminalized (Li 2003, 2005).

One of the most popular topics in contemporary Chinese studies of prostitution concerns why and how women entered the sex business.[2] A predominant discourse is that these women are part of the Chinese labour market and their rights should be recognized and acknowledged (Li 2005; Huang and Pan 2003). In some studies, scholars adopt the label 'sex workers' unquestioningly and cite economic motives as the main reason for the women's involvement. In other studies, scholars look at the phenomenon as a 'social problem', or view the women as a group of 'others' that are worthy of attention only because of the proliferation of the sex business and its illegal nature (Xie 2004). HIV/AIDS-control and STD issues are another focus in discussions of this topic (Huang et al. 2004). This literature neglects the multiple realities of women involved in the activity, in that it ignores (1) how these women

123

identify themselves when they become involved in prostitution; (2) other motivations besides economic ones; (3) the stigma attached to the label 'sex worker'; and (4) how the naming issue may actually reflect rural women's desires.

In this context we rethink the label 'sex worker' and choose to call them *xiaojie*,[3] in conformity with common usage in contemporary Chinese. Within the sizzling debates, there have been few efforts to address these women's own understandings of work in relation to their concrete social and cultural backgrounds. This lack may bias our understanding of women's employment and their future aspirations. The discrepancy between the understandings held by academics and by the women themselves may cause further distortion of the 'truer' situation, and thus lead to false views of its social implications. The women's own opinions may inform social services and are an important issue to think about in terms of the broader question of how our feminist position may further a real understanding of the prostitution issue. More important, the term 'sex worker' sometimes seems to express a Western 'academic desire', in which scholars try to impose understandings developed through a Western framework on the reality of these Chinese women: this may lead to 'cultural/academic colonialism' (Doezema 2001; Kapur 2001; Kesler 2002). The present chapter aims to fill the gap between academic discourses and everyday realities by presenting the diversity of this group in the way they identity themselves and how they position themselves in relation to the label 'sex worker'. Moreover, we hope to reflect on the issues of (1) how our everyday realities are shaped by Western ideas and concepts such as urbanization, consumerism, romantic love and marriage; (2) how women's lives are affected and changed by the wave of globalization; and (3) how we should make use of ideas developed within Western cultures such as a tolerance towards prostitution, new understandings of women's work and employment, and women's agency, and 'translate' these ideas into our local languages in order better to understand women's lives and desires in a specific context.

The chapter is based on data drawn from fieldwork in two South China metropolises, Guangzhou and Shenzhen, from 2005 to 2006, in which one of us (Ding Yu) conducted in-depth interviews and ethnographical observations. Guangzhou is the provincial capital of Guangdong and Shenzhen is the border city to Hong Kong. These two cities are among the four most economically developed cities in China, attracting numerous businessmen from all over the world (Liu and Yue 2006). Their economic advancement since China's opening-up in the 1980s has led to the flourishing of tertiary industries. Interviews were conducted with twenty women involved in various types of sex business – streetwalkers, foot massage girls, nightclub girls and home-working women – on topics concerning daily lives, work, love, relationships, family, future plans, past experience and life events. Participant observation was carried out in the hair salons, nightclubs, karaoke houses and night streets where *xiaojies* work, giving insights into how different environments influence their actions and how they react towards different work arrangements. It also entailed visiting their homes, staying with them for a few days from time to time, going with them to shop for groceries or to pay various fees for rented apartments, and exercising with them. These activities reveal much about their lifestyles and how these may affect their understandings of 'work'. The experiences and articulations of the women show a diversity of understandings of the concept of 'work' among them, as only under certain conditions do these women take prostitution to be a kind of work. We argue that the term 'sex worker' over-generalizes their situation as the heterogeneous nature of prostitutes cannot be unified under one category (O'Connell Davidson 1998, 2002; Jeffreys 2004), and suggest using *xiaojie* in the contemporary Chinese sense to capture the subtle meanings that express these women's aspirations.

'Second virginity': from rural wives to urban *xiaojies*

Within the 'prostitution/sex work' debate, one focus is on women's economic conditions – the driving force behind the work must be economic considerations and, since it is a kind of 'work', it must generate income. The argument that sex workers' bottom line is economic need indicates that it is mainly a materially driven activity (O'Neill 2001; Wardlow 2004; Lucas 2005). In the Chinese context, Pan Suiming (2005b: 1), who was the first to take a comprehensive and humanistic look at these women's lives, claimed that *xiaojie* is the equivalent of 'sex worker' in China and thus that these two terms can be used interchangeably. His efforts to depict these people as 'troubled young women' counteract popular as well as official views that are heavily moralistic. He tries to acknowledge their labour rights by calling them 'workers'. However, his overlooking of the naming issue prevents him from seeing these women's lives from 'within' – the many facets of their lives that intertwine to affect their self-perception, which should be put in the context of China's rural–urban migration. The term 'sex work' does offer a broader understanding of the group and opens a way towards legal rights and status, but it fails to represent some women's desires and neglects the non-economic motives involved in these women's decisions to enter the business, especially the motives of married women. We do not argue that women enter sex business without regard to money, but there is something more in the narratives of our informants that brings out deeper desires that may have little to do with money or material interest – to escape unhappy relationships and be young and virginal again. 'Sex worker' does not fully address this aspect, while *xiaojie*, in its literal sense, captures it more vividly.

Regional differences in economic development mean that most *xiaojies* in the areas of Guangzhou and Shenzhen come from Sichuan, Hunan, Guizhou and other inland areas of China. Their migration experiences and ideals of love and intimacy are mutually constituted: their love or marriage experience is one of the driving forces of their emigration, and migration in turn has profoundly influenced their views of and actions in intimate relationships. Studies have shown that migration from rural to urban areas in China is often linked with marriage. Davin (2005) speaks of migration for some women as a way of 'buy[ing] themselves out of a situation in which they are not happy', for example poverty and divorce. It is, therefore, considered as 'promoting female autonomy', especially in the context of a relatively patriarchal rural environment. Beynon (2004) and Tan and Short (2004) point out that migration supports exogamy since many families in rural areas have the tradition of marrying out. Women utilize migration to escape unhappy relationships and seek upward mobility in terms of financial conditions, social status and stability.

For a married woman, rural–urban migration means leaving behind her rural life, her whole family and, more specifically, her dream of depending on a man for a decent life. The sweetness of marriage may soon disappear when she has to face the brutal reality of poverty, child rearing, an uncertain future and in-law relationships. Zhenjie is a 41-year-old 'freelance' *xiaojie* in east Guangzhou. Her husband stays in her hometown Hunan and is said to have 'no ability to earn more money' yet does not give her 'any confirmation and recognition' for what she has done for the family. Property division soon after marriage (*fenjia*), her husband's inability to make life better, the birth of her two children, and the heavy workload all made her disappointed with marital life.

> They never speak of gratification, never mention the emotional bond we have, and even the efforts I have made! They only recognize money. Money, money, money!

She thinks men should be the breadwinners, while the reality causes her to rethink what women can do when men are no longer the main supporters of a family. She thinks of herself as 'clever and nice', not to be wasted in a monogamous relationship with a not-so-desirable husband. When she left the village, she vaguely felt that she not only wanted to earn more money during her urban stay but also wanted to know what she could achieve in the way of love and sexuality. She quickly adapted to urban life and overcame the hurdles on her way to success. Her experience as a *xiaojie* in the cities in a way facilitates her opening up of new possibilities in gender relations. In fact, she keeps trying different forms of 'love consumption', like paying younger men for sex, and enjoys horse racing and beers, while she keeps her marital bond with her rural husband. Now, finding a comfortable way to live and enjoy sex has become her major task:

> Whoever is good, whoever can let me feel happy and feel high, whoever can let me feel comfortable, I can pay him double price, I can play with him. I am also playful! You think only men can play with women? Who says that women cannot fool around with men?! I never think too much.

Wen, 25, and Nana, 23, are sisters who come from Sichuan. They are both married and working in a nightclub in Guangzhou. Wen describes her husband as the 'spoiled' youngest son at home and always quarrelling with her over money and other petty things. He does not have a regular income and is a heavy drinker. She thus worries a lot about their future. When asked the complicated question 'What do you think you want the most in your life?', Wen pondered for a while and said, 'a sense of security', and explained this is why she left home. For her, this meant not only financial security but also a sense of achievement, independence, and personal space in the long run.

Nana seemed to enjoy a sense of popularity more. She always carries her cell phone, sending and reading messages to and from the clients she meets in the nightclub. She enjoys talking about them among her sisters and roommates and gossiping about the possibilities between her and them. Nana keeps herself open to any opportunities and thinks it is good to be able to have more comparisons and choices. She says she wants to try something different since she is still young and does not want to be tied to a small place and only one man, as 'all Sichuan men are like that'. The sisters have an impression that Guangzhou men are better than Sichuan men in that they are more polite, cultured, caring and female-friendly. This is part of the reason they came, in the hope of finding more respect and recognition here.

It is not uncommon that these women's families do not depend solely on their income. Their earnings are mainly spent on maintaining daily lives in the city and buying clothes, cosmetics and other things necessary for their job. They laughed at the label of 'sex worker' when introduced to this idea, saying that it sounds like a closed door – a person that earns her life selling sex, period. By adopting the name *xiaojie*, the women had turned from rural wives to urban *xiaojies*, which symbolizes their 'second virginity' through the subtle Chinese linguistic use – the intrinsic meaning of *xiaojie* as young and unmarried brings them a new image: from rural to urban, from wives to open possibilities, and from married to virgin. This gives them not only a new sense of self but also new ways of doing gender.

New image: from 'country bumpkin' to stylish *xiaojie*

Parent–child conflict was another major driving force of rural–urban migration. This partly reflects what Jacka (2006) has pointed out – different views of chaotic cities, marriage arrangements, and education all contribute to children's leaving home. We hold that conflicts may also involve migrants' urban dreams and their longing for a style of consumption that is both legitimate and 'normal' within China's modernization discourse. Young people in the villages strongly aspire to the idea of consuming and actively seek to be 'urban' in this way or that. Often, when they consciously look up to urban life and reduce it to mere consumption behaviours, they run into conflict with parents who hold different views, as in Lan's case.

Lan's parents had already been working in the cities since she was a child, so she knew well how different city life is from rural life. Lan said she saw 'the shadow of urban life' in the gadgets her mother brought home, like a rice cooker and exhaust fan, which were fashionable in the cities. She began to dream about city life and said she saw it as an 'endless chain of buying and spending, which makes life meaningful'.

> I once had a quarrel with my mom over our own house. They built a three-storey house but I just thought it was not nice enough. I thought the style was outdated . . . and the furniture was outdated. My mom said furiously that she could just achieve this, and if I was more able than she, why not do it myself. . . . They always say that money is earned to build houses, to get married, and to enjoy a secure old age, but I don't like this idea. (May 2006)

The fact that Lan left her village and became a *xiaojie* who 'goes to work' every day in a high-class hotel nightclub further stimulates her desire to live like an urbanite. She sees in this title the glamour of city life. She and her flatmates, who are all *xiaojies*, very much enjoy the daily routine, which involves going to the telecom office to pay phone bills, going to the swimming pool, paying monthly management fees to the estate office, going to the supermarket, using body masks, etcetera. I asked why they enjoy this routine, because it is obviously costly. They said it was not about money, but the feeling that you are actually living in a city, that you now have no distance from an urban lifestyle. One of them commented,

> 'Xiaojie' is a good title for us. We called this kind of women '[people] doing *that*' when we were young. It was not a proper job so we wouldn't mention its name, thinking that it was something that you must hide from people. 'Xiaojie', hmmm . . . it's not that specific although we know what it refers to. There are many people in the city calling each other 'xiaojie', and we also enjoy this 'young' and 'stylish' image as if we were white collars working in the office towers. (Fang, aged 24, June 2006)

China's modernization process is closely connected to a socially constructed urban/rural dichotomy in which a heavily gendered consumption is introduced to mark the advent of a modern urban society (Zhang 2000). The mass media push this tide forward with endless ads in which fashionable, rich, tasteful young urban women become the symbols of China's successful modernization and are admired and imitated by illiterate, backward and eager 'country bumpkins' (Davis 2000; Zheng 2004: 85). Among the scholars working in this field, Zheng (2003, 2004) studied rural–urban migrant bar hostesses in Dalian and argued that consumption is a kind of power operating within the rural–urban apartheid, through which bar hostesses' rural background can be weakened and their new urban identity created and negotiated (2003). Pun Ngai (2003) takes this further, identifying China's market economy as influencing these migrant women's view of consumption. Zheng focuses on a micro level where women's agency is emphasized, while Pun places more emphasis on the macro as in state policy and discourses that encourage consumption as a collective displacement (ibid.: 486). The points we make here to some degree reflect those made by both these writers, but we tend to see *xiaojies'* consumption as impression management tactics, and as a way to express self-esteem and the desire to be urban and modern in its very superficial sense. By saying this, we take up Pun's analysis and see desire as a production machine for further desires, which informs massive rural–urban population movement and consumption based on the collective imaginary of the urban life (ibid.). We argue that *xiaojies* consider consumption as simply a way of becoming urban that is within their reach and that they take up the name '*xiaojie*' as part of their 'urbanization'.

Hui is a massage girl in a Guangzhou leisure centre. The day they got to know each other she mistook Ding Yu for an 'office lady'. She was envious and said, 'You office girls are so lucky, you sit in the office, have air conditioning, face the computer, write and draw and sometimes talk to clients. This is nice.' Her ideal work is office work, because she thinks it is a symbol of 'status', 'quality' and 'fullness of life'. Ding Yu told her that office ladies have their own pressures and they must be very hard-working in order to keep up with this fast-paced world. She said it is just the image of 'office girl' that she finds so beautiful yet far-away. Hui wants to go to evening school one day so she can be one of them, so she can *shangban* (go to work)[4] in those tall office towers and live a life 'that begins at 9 am and finishes at 5 pm'. This concrete timescale of professional life and her delight in high-rise urban buildings have drowned out her other thoughts. One sees the happy faces of *xiaojies* eating McDonald's food, taking taxis to nightclubs and sending text messages to clients, and the proud expressions of those with beautiful make-up and false eyelashes. These are all symbols of an urban way of life – if you are able to manage the impression, the rest does not really matter. It does not matter whether you have an urban residence permit or not; whether you really have the skills and networks for working and living in the cities or not; or whether you have the money to buy good houses or not. It is the self-esteem that they are able to show off to their fellow villagers: a new and broader personal space, and a sense of belonging to an urban environment. '*Xiaojie*' symbolizes all their desires, with a connotation of being wealthy and urban, as in what it originally meant, and becomes a cherished way to identify themselves.

Their migration background deeply influences their way of thinking and what they desire in their lives, and also the way they strive for it. They often adjust their preferences and 'scale down' their aspirations to 'mundane' and 'trivial' things, such as power through small talk, an urban look, the feeling of being 'young' and 'fashionable', the possibility of finding better intimate relationships and so on, rather than the abstract political rights and social status that come with the term 'sex worker'.[5] They do not want to envisage their identity by deliberately calling themselves 'sex workers'. As Hong said, any deliberate fighting against (*duikang*) discrimination by embracing the identity of 'sex worker' is in a sense meaningless. We would like to borrow the concept of 'tactic' from de Certeau (1984) and argue that these *xiaojies'* lived experiences and desires have a tactical nature – they live their lives in a 'spontaneous' way following their own logic, intuition and relationships; their thoughts, behaviours and narratives are gradually formed, shaped and modified with the resources available at hand.

Beyond 'sex' and 'work'

Five *xiaojies* (Hong, Bobo, Mei, Zhenjie and Hui) out of our twenty informants said the term 'sex worker' (*xing gongzuozhe*) is too focused on the aspect of 'sex'. Their initial response upon being introduced to the term was summed up by Hong: 'What I do is not just sex (*xing*), [so] why call me a sex worker (*xing gongzuozhe*)?' For them, the term 'sex worker' not only misrepresents what they do but also increases the stigma attached to them since it shifts all the focus to 'sex' without indicating emotional and social functions that are equally important. On some occasions, more likely in the indoor environment, services like chatting, drinking, dancing and singing are as popular as performing the actual sex, if not more popular. *Xiaojies* all know well how to greet clients in a sweet way, how to please them by playing dice or other little games, how to persuade them to drink more, and how to listen to their stories and express admiration or care at an appropriate time. Bobo and Bing made jokes about these processes as 'very long foreplay', which constitutes a major part of their routine jobs. These are often considered important social skills that contribute to one's sophistication and popularity among both clients and colleagues. Scholars have also discussed the many faces of 'sex work'. For example, flirting becomes 'strategic' and a kind of expenditure of emotional labour for exotic dancers (Deshotels and Forsyth 2006); humour is a strategy for social and psychological distancing (Sanders 2004); 'acting' and 'manufactured identity' are both a self-protecting mechanism and aesthetic and emotional labour involved in female sex work (Sanders 2005). Hence the different perceptions toward 'sex workers' among 'direct' and 'indirect' prostitutes (Harcourt and Donovan 2005). *Xing gongzuo* (sex work), with its focus on sex, to some degree resembles a Chinese term for prostitution in a negative sense, *maiyin* (selling sex/ flesh/body/eroticism), which strongly emphasizes the 'sex/flesh' aspect and is condemned by both the deeply rooted Confucian culture and socialist morality, especially as prostitution is still prohibited under current Chinese legislation. In this situation, the term *xiaojie*, which speaks more euphemistically and richly in context, wins popularity; 'sex work' means a 'sex-focused' dead end that these women emotionally reject.

From the 'work' aspect of the term, we can also see why some *xiaojies* preferred not to be called 'sex workers'. This emphasis does address some aspects of women's desires – empowerment, an equal and tolerant environment to live in, respect for basic rights and self-expression. It is a politics through renaming and also a strategic struggle against social stigma. It is like a campaign with an explicit aim and collective actions (West 2000). However, it is based on a Western framework that exists outside the Chinese context and totalizes the experience of women who may have different understandings of their present lives. Some of them do not see this as a kind of work (*gongzuo*) at all.

In the first place, for some of them, it cannot guarantee a stable income. For those who solicit on the streets like Hong, Ya and Zhenjie, this is an especially acute issue. Those working indoors mainly live on tips from clients, and for each transaction they have to pay a certain amount to the *mama-san*, no matter how much they get from the client. For those who work at home like Mei, income comes in other forms, such as the client's payments towards house rentals and basic living facilities, clothes and make-up, or extra daily expenses. This is by no means a stable income, according to their criteria, as only monthly payments count as such. Second, some feel they have little dignity in this job – as Hong, Bobo, Bing, Zhenjie and Hui pointed out. They have to deliberately create a sense of belonging and pride in themselves, which this work does not provide as naturally as other types of jobs. Third, some feel the absence of a sense of responsibility for what they do. Hui compares her massage job with her former job as a sales person in a department store. She refers to the latter as a job that 'has a basic salary, which imposes pressure' on her; if unable to 'sell that much' to meet the basic salary, she would blame herself. The massage job, on the contrary, brings no such feeling, because if anything goes wrong this is an operational or managerial problem for the boss that has nothing to do with her. Having responsibility would bring a sense of fulfilment, which would make her feel better about herself. Fourth, some of their perceptions of work (*gongzuo*) are closely related to the idea of life goals: this was the case for Hong, Hui, Zhenjie, Juan, Bobo, Bing, Ya and Mei, and was a theme that frequently popped up in our conversations:

> How can this be a kind of work [*gongzuo*]! I even don't know what I am doing. Anyway, I think I am leading an aimless life. I live for nothing. I am just idling my time away. If I have no money, I'll go out (to the street), otherwise I'll just stay home. After I spend it all I go out again. It's like this. It's not meaningful to live on like this. . . . The girls who live with me, they have no goals at all. . . . This is not *gongzuo*, just *wan* [play]. (Hong, aged 26, July 2005)

> I feel like I am just idling my time away day by day, without a clear future, and without money. . . . This is definitely not *gongzuo*. (Hui, aged 24, March 2006)

> Me? I live from day to day. I'm 41, what if I suddenly have no money at all? What if I encounter any difficulty? What if one day I suddenly die? I don't want to live in this world. Why do we need to talk about status and *gongzuo*? I don't want to think too much about it, and I can't. (Zhenjie, aged 41, July 2005)

It was at the point where they linked the concept up with their understanding of what they were doing that we realized how this might complement our construction of the idea of 'work' (*gongzuo*). They very much value a sense of stability, fulfilment and sustainability in their understanding of *gongzuo*. In addition, a clear goal may help decide what they want, which in turn affects their attitudes to what they are doing now. Fifth, and interestingly, they consider it as something other than *gongzuo* – 'just playing' (*wan*), for example, or 'doing business' (*zuo shengyi*), or even a 'lifestyle' (*shenghuo fangshi*). They often use *zuoshi* (doing something), *zuo* (do), or *zuogong* (doing labour), rather than *gongzuo* (work) for their sexual activities. Zhenjie, Wen, Nana and Lan even referred to it as just *chulai* (coming out here) – which tactically utilizes their migration background and the image of a rural woman who jumps from a relatively closed environment to a more open urban space – to illustrate their wanting to break with the underdeveloped, static rural space and traditional consciousness.

Eighteen out of the twenty women who were interviewed showed little interest in finding a long-term stable job (*zhao gongzuo* as well as *dagong*: working for a boss and selling their labour in exchange for wages, as in factory work, hair salon or beauty salon work, and other 'regular' occupations). On the one hand, being 'regular' workers can no longer fulfil their desire of living like a 'decent' urbanite, in terms of social status, citizenship, lifestyle, and, more important, a space of their own where they can explore what they want; and, on the other, they find it possible to articulate their experience and reflection in a social environment that is beginning to value self-support and entrepreneurship. Their priorities are, for women who have been disappointed by their own marriages and relationships, running small businesses of their own; for those who still have hopes for marriage, however vague, marriage or a complete family; and, for women of rural origin like most informants in our study, being urban and modern and getting exposure to a cosmopolitan way of life. Wanting an *anle* life (settled, happy, peaceful, having no undue desire and satisfied) becomes an ideal for many of them.

Conclusion

In this chapter, we argue that the concept of 'sex work' may not work for many prostitute women in the Pearl River Delta Area in China. Sixteen of our twenty informants (80 per cent) do not hold it to be a kind of work at all. First, they recognize a stigma attached to the identification of 'sex worker'; second, in their interaction with clients, they find not only 'sex work' but also love labour and emotional work; third, they may desire something other than political recognition and rights through renaming prostitution as 'sex work'. Married women want to escape the double burden of poverty and patriarchal rural lives, and to be free to earn their own money, as well as to experience 'youth' again. Young rural girls want to leave the boredom of village life, enjoy the image of a modern *xiaojie* and have the ability to consume. Not marrying a rural husband and finding more possibilities in the city become their dream: as women, especially rural women, their economic power is always closely related to marriage. Prostitution gives them opportunities to rearrange their lives, albeit in a 'superficial' sense. It may be a transitional job, a lifestyle, or a means to climb the social ladder. Its different aspects reflect women's different aspirations in a consumption-oriented economy. We also hold that 'sex work' in this context is too homogeneous a category with which to grasp the diverse work and life experience of *xiaojies*. The whole picture is complicated: these women's perceptions of work and life vary with their working environment and the organization of sex business in a specific locale, income levels, motives for engaging in the business, experience, ability to articulate future goals, and so on. These women's own accounts of work and life need to be heard in a rapidly changing economy which has created an unprecedented regional gap and massive rural–urban migration.

Notes

1 The term 'sex work' was first coined, according to Carol Leigh, to 'create an atmosphere of tolerance within and outside the women's movement for women working in the sex industry' (Leigh 1997: 225).
2 In Chinese academic debates over prostitution there are many different proposals concerning why women enter the sex business. At an earlier stage, scholars and politicians alike held a moralistic view that prostitution was a capitalist decadence to be eradicated, otherwise it would erode people's mindsets. Later, attention was diverted to the economic rationale and the regulation of the business. See Pan (2005a) for detailed discussions.
3 Carrying the sense of 'Miss', it had been a respectful way to address wealthy young unmarried women since ancient Chinese times. In rural areas, people addressed women in other ways. The term had been dropped since the founding of New China and during the Cultural Revolution, when it was said to contain a 'capitalist/feudalist tint'. It was brought back to the mainland by Hong Kong/Taiwan business people in the 1980s during the economic reform, however,

with a different 'tint' from the original Chinese meaning – from 'young, well-educated, well-brought-up unmarried woman' (*dajia guixiu*) to virtually any woman in the urban areas (Miss/Ms). Gradually it became a common practice to call prostitute women *xiaojie*, since the businessmen (the majority of clients) who visited entertainment sites were used to referring to women in this way. The term is widely used in the media and daily conversation; for instance, *zuo xiaojie* (literally 'being a *xiaojie*') means being a prostitute, and *zhao xiaojie* (literally 'look for *xiaojie*') means 'go whoring'. However, it is still used to address girls or young women. An interesting thing to note is that women who had been quite used to the term have become very sensitive about it following its pervasive use in recent years to mean prostitutes, so that people have created/picked up other terms to call those who were formerly addressed as *xiaojie*, to avoid offence and embarrassment (*guniang* (girl), *xiaomei* (little sister) and *liangnv* (pretty lady) are among these new usages).

4 *Shangban* means 'going to work'. It usually has the connotation of 'formal' and 'regular' work with a clear and rigid timeline from 9 to 5 and managing rules. In Chinese we have other terms, such as *zuogong* (literally, 'doing labour') and *zuoshi* ('doing business') to refer to other types of jobs. *Xiaojies* working indoors, especially those who are in nightclubs, karaoke houses or massage parlours, always use *shangban* to create a sense of stability and status.

5 See also Travis S. K. Kong (2006). Writing about their 'body politics', he takes the view that prostitute women in Hong Kong are not 'political', but instead tend to use micro-resistance in fighting against social domination.

6 This is the Chinese version of Ho's 2000 paper 'Self-empowerment and professionalism'. However, there are some differences between the two versions so I cite them separately.

References

Beynon, Louise (2004) 'Dilemmas of the heart: rural working women and their hopes' in A. Gaetano and T. Jacka (eds), *On the Move: Women and Rural-to-Urban Migration in Contemporary China*. New York: Columbia University Press.

Brock, Deborah R. (1998) *Making Work, Making Trouble: Prostitution as a Social Problem*. Toronto: University of Toronto Press.

Califia, Pat (1994) *Public Sex: the Culture of Radical Sex*. Pittsburgh, PA: Cleis Press.

Chapkis, Wendy (1997) *Live Sex Acts*. New York: Routledge.

Davin, Dalia (2005) 'Women and migration in contemporary China', *China Report*, 41: 29–38.

Davis, Deborah, S. (ed.) (2000) *The Consumer Revolution in Urban China*. Berkeley, CA: University of California Press.

de Certeau, Michel (1984) *The Practice of Everyday Life* (trans. Steven F. Rendall). Berkeley/Los Angeles, CA: University of California Press.

Deshotels, Tina and Craig J. Forsyth (2006) 'Strategic flirting and the emotional tab of exotic dancing', *Deviant Behavior*, 27 (2): 223–41.

Doezema, Jo (2001) 'Ouch! Western feminists' "wounded attachment" to the "Third World prostitute"', *Feminist Review*, 67: 16–38.

Harcourt, Christine and B. Donovan (2005) 'The many faces of sex work', *Sexually Transmitted Infections*, 81 (3): 201–6.

Highleyman, Liz (1997) 'Professional dominance: power, money and identity' in

Jill Nagle (ed.) (1997) *Whores and Other Feminists*. London: Routledge.

Ho, Josephine Chuen-juei (2000) 'Self-empowerment and professionalism: conversations with Taiwanese sex workers', *InterAsia Cultural Studies*, 2 (August 2000): 283–99.

—— (2001a) 自我培力与专业操演：与台湾性工作者的对话，《台湾社会研究季刊》第41期（2001 年3月）：1–52. This is the Chinese version of Ho's 2000 article 'Self-empowerment and professionalism'. However, there are some differences between the two versions.

—— (2001b) 'A feminist view on sex work and sex trade' in Josephine Chuen-juei Ho (ed.), *Sex World and the World's Prostitutes' Rights Movement* [性工作：妓权观点]. Taipei: Juliu Publishing Company.

—— (ed.) (2001c) *Sex World and the World's Prostitutes' Rights Movement*. Taipei: Juliu Publishing Co.

Huang Yingying (2004) 论小姐的专业化梯度 ['The professionalization of *xiaojies*'] in Zheng Yefu (ed.), 北大清华人大优秀论文选 [*Excellent Dissertations and Theses from Beijing Univeristy, Tsinghua University and People's University*]. 济南：山东人民出版社 [Jinan: Shandong People's Publishing House].

Huang Yingying and Suiming Pan (2003) 'Job mobility of brothel-based female sex workers in current northeast China: the process from *xiagang* worker (lay-offs) to sex worker'. 社会学研究 [*Sociological Research*], 17 (3): 53–65.

Huang Yingying, Gail E. Henderson, Pan Suiming and Myron S. Cohen (2004) 'HIV/AIDS risk among brothel-based female sex workers in China: assessing the terms, content, and knowledge of sex work', *Sexually Transmitted Diseases*, 31 (11): 695–700.

Jacka, Tamara (2006) *Rural Women in Urban China: Gender, Migration, and Social Change*. New York: M. E. Sharpe, Inc.

Jeffreys, Elaine (2004) *China, Sex and Prostitution*. London: RoutledgeCurzon.

Jeffreys, Sheila (1997) *The Idea of Prostitution*. Melbourne: Spinifex.

Kapur, Ratna (2001) 'Post-colonial economies of desire: legal representations of the sexual subaltern', *Denver University Law Review*, 78 (4): 855–85.

Kesler, Kari (2002) 'Is a feminist stance in support of prostitution possible? An exploration of current trends', *Sexualities*, 5 (2): 219–35.

Kong, Travis S. K. (2006) 'What it feels like being a whore: the body politics of women performing erotic labour in Hong Kong', *Gender, Work and Organization*, 13 (5): 409–34.

Leigh, Carol (1997) 'Inventing sex work' in Jill Nagle (ed.), *Whores and Other Feminists*. London: Routledge.

Li Yinhe (2003) 性不应该成为立法的对象 ['Sex should not be the focus of legislation']. <http://new.china-review.com/scholar_person.asp?channel ID=188> (accessed 15 June 2004).

—— (2005) 李银河：应实行卖淫非罪化，根治对性工作者的犯罪 ['Li Yinhe: decriminalize prostitution and eliminate crimes to sex workers']. An interview over the Internet by www.Sohu.com with Li Yinhe, 29 August 2005. <http://text.news.sohu.com/20050829/n226812643.html> (accessed 15 October 2005).

Liu Juhua and Yue Ruifang (2006) 北京上海广州深圳位列中国主要城市总部经济前四强 ['Beijing, Shanghai, Guangzhou and Shenzhen rank top four in economic competitiveness among China's major cities']. <http://news.xinhuanet.com/politics/2006-12/21/content_5517306.htm> [新华网时政快讯 2006 12 21日报道] (accessed 22 August 2007).

Lucas, Ann M. (2005) 'The work of sex work: elite prostitutes' vocational orientations and experiences' *Deviant Behavior*, 26: 513–46.

MacKinnon, Katherine and Andrea Dworkin (1988). *Pornography and Civil Rights: a New Day for Women's Equality*. Minneapolis: Organizing Against Pornography.

O'Connell Davidson, Julia (1998) *Prostitution, Power and Freedom*. Cambridge: Polity Press.

—— (2002) 'The rights and wrongs of prostitution', *Hypatia*, 17 (2): 84–98.

O'Neill, Maggie (2001) *Prostitution and Feminism: Towards a Politics of Feeling*. Cambridge: Polity Press.

Pan Suiming (1997) 存在与荒谬 [*Existing and Absurdity*]. 北京：中国社会科学出版社[Beijing: China Social Sciences Publishing House].

—— (2000) 生存与体验 [*Subsistence and Experience*]. 北京：中国社会科学出版社 [Beijing: China Social Sciences Publishing House].

—— (2005a) 近百年来关于娼妓的研究 ['Research on the prostitution problem in the past hundred years'], 湖南科技学院学报 [*Journal of Hunan University of Science and Engineering*], 26 (3): 74–80.

—— (2005b) 小姐：劳动的权利 [*Female Sex Workers: the Right of Labour*]. 香港：大道出版社 [Hong Kong: Dadao Publishing House].

Pateman, Carole (1988) *The Sexual Contract*. Stanford, CA: Stanford University Press.

Pun Ngai (2003) 'Subsumption or consumption? The phantom of consumer revolution in "Globalizing" China', *Cultural Anthropology*, 18 (4): 469–92.

Sanders, Teela (2004) 'Controllable laughter', *Sociology*, 38 (2): 273–91.

—— (2005) '"It's just acting": Sex workers' strategies for capitalizing on sexuality', *Gender, Work and Organization*. 12 (4): 319–342.

Tan Lin and Susan Short (2004) 'Living as double outsiders: migrant women's experiences of marriage in a county-level city' in A. Gaetano and T. Jacka (eds), *On the Move: Women and Rural-to-Urban Migration in Contemporary China*. New York: Columbia University Press.

Wardlow, Holly (2004) 'Anger, economy, and female agency: problematizing "prostitution" and "sex work" among the Huli of Papua New Guinea', *Signs: Journal of Women in Culture and Society*, 29 (4): 1017–40.

West, Jackie (2000) 'Prostitution: collectives and the politics of regulation', *Gender, Work and Organization*, 7 (2): 106–18.

Xie, Yijuan (2004) 'A study of the present prostitute group in our country'. MA dissertation, Wuhan University, China.

Yan, Hairong (2003) 'Neoliberal governmentality and neohumanism: organizing suzhi/value flow through labour recruitment networks', *Cultural Anthropology*, 18 (4): 493–523.

Zhang, Zhen (2000) 'Mediating time: the "rice bowl of youth" in fin de siècle China', *Popular Culture*, 12 (1): 93–113.

Zheng, Tiantian (2003) 'Consumption, body image and rural–urban apartheid in contemporary China', *City and Society*, 15 (2): 143–63.

—— (2004) 'From peasant women to bar hostesses: gender and modernity in post-Mao Dalian' in A. Gaetano and T. Jacka (eds), *On the Move: Women and Rural-to-Urban Migration in Contemporary China*. New York: Columbia University Press.

Part II

The Politics and Practice
of Intimate Relationships

7 The Sexual Politics of Difference in Post-IMF Korea: Challenges of the Lesbian Rights and Sex Workers' Movements[1]

CHO JOO-HYUN

As Foucault pointed out, sexuality is a social construct, 'a great surface network in which the stimulation of bodies, the intensification of pleasures, the incitement to discourse, the formation of special knowledges, the strengthening of controls and resistances, are linked to one another, in accordance with a few major strategies of knowledge and power' (Foucault 1978: 105). In other words, sexuality is to be regarded as a discursive construct rather than a personal attribute. Though Foucault brought about a transformation of the paradigmatic mode of understanding sexuality, he disregarded the monopolization of the discourse of sexuality by men, women's historical exclusion from it, and thus that sexuality was constructed from a masculine perspective (Snitow 1981: 10).

In the 1990s Korean women started to change their sexual political strategy, breaking their silence through the production of sexual discourses, a move initiated by feminist scholars and activists. They emphasized the gendered sexual identity of the 'pure heterosexual woman', the putative victim of domestic and sexual violence, to organize the movement opposing violence against women (Cho 2000; Min 1999). In mobilizing women under its banner, the Korean women's movement in the 1990s took for granted the normality of pure heterosexual women, positioning others as abnormal. Sexuality was not recognized as independent of gender but was conflated with it. Recently, however, women's sexuality began to unfold in multifarious modes in the intersections of class, family, gender and nation-state policies. That is, women's sexual identities have begun to be constructed in varied forms depending on where women situate themselves or are situated in intersecting networks of diverse systems of domination.

141

I argue that a sexual politics of difference has come to the fore since the IMF crisis in 1997, so that the sexual politics of the Korean women's movement can no longer rely on the 1990s strategy of mobilizing and concentrating women's political power in terms of the 'pure heterosexual woman'. Specifically, I will examine the lacunae in conventional sexual politics revealed by the identity politics practised by the lesbian rights movement, which has found a voice in the last decade, and by the sex workers' movement emerging since the Acts on Prostitution were passed in 2004. I will then analyse the characteristics of the consequent 'crisis' in the women's movement.

These two movements pose a challenge to campaigns opposing violence against women and the assumptions on which they are based. I will examine the issues raised by the lesbian rights movement in terms of the heterosexism it attempts to disrupt and the implications this has for the women's movement. In relation to the sex workers' movement, I will employ the concept of intersectionality (Collins 2000) to analyse how the previous emphasis on prostitution as violence against women has moved into the space of intersections between class, gender, family, sexuality and nation-state policies, and the new discourses and terrain that consequently emerged.

Drawing on my earlier preliminary analysis of sexual politics in Korea (Cho 2005), I argue for two points. First, the 'crisis'[2] in the women's movement originated with deepening differences among women generated as post-IMF Korea was incorporated into globalization. Second, to develop a sexual politics that effectively incorporates the differences between women, the women's movement in Korea should be able to deal with new forms of gender identity and adapt flexibly to each situation and case.

Globalization and the identity 'crisis' of the post-IMF women's movement

In March 2006, activists from most of the progressive NGOs in Korea gathered at a forum to discuss future movement agendas and strategies of alliance. Here activists representing various women's movement organizations had intensive discussions on the characteristics of the 'crisis' in the women's movement and the movement's future directions. They identified such causes of the 'crisis' as the rapid ascension to political power of the Korea Women's Associations United

(KWAU);[3] too close a relation with government; the absence of a coherent standpoint capable of comprehending diverse issues and the consequent failure to create an appropriate agenda; organizational incapacity to reflect rapidly changing cultural environments; and a failure to raise issues close to women's everyday lives.

Though some activists cited legislative and institutional reforms in the past decade as important achievements and suggested that the strategy of maintaining and furthering these achievements was still appropriate, an overwhelming number of participants in the forum saw this emphasis as accelerating the alienation of the movement from women's everyday lives, thus widening the gap between national and local movements and consequently undermining the autonomy of the movement and its critical edge. It was also claimed by some activists that 'progress' should be nobody's monopoly, but should be constructed strategically according to each case and its governing standpoint (Korean Society Forum 2006).

Issues discussed in the Korean Society Forum were later reignited in the colloquium on 'Reflections and Prospects on the Korean Women's Movement' held by the Council for Alliance of the Korean Association of Women's Studies. Kim Kyeong-hee and Yoon Jeong-sook (2006) claimed that the problem of differences emerged as one of the main issues for Korean feminism: 'issues ranging over a wide spectrum such as heterosexism vs. homosexism, prostitution vs sex work, the pros and cons of abortion, the problem of surrogate mothers, the problems of the human egg trade and governmental supports for sterilization, married vs unmarried women, working-class women vs middle-class women, etc. emerged as new problems for the women's movement waiting for a wise solution'. In this colloquium, it was pointed out that a women's movement based only on gender identity is no longer effective, hence the necessity for new discourses able to moderate tensions between gender identity and differences among women, as well as for recognition that differences among women are conditional and dependent on circumstances.

It is somewhat ironic that the finger of blame for the crisis should be pointed at successful legislative and institutional reforms, hailed as the most impressive achievements of the Korean women's movement in the 1990s, and the gender identity that served as the premise for such reforms and as the rallying point for the movement. Behind this irony lie the differences between women. And it was the social-structural transformation of Korean society during the last decade that actually made these differences concrete before our eyes.

After the IMF crisis in 1997, Koreans suffered widespread unemployment and a sense of insecurity about the future. With the collapse of the middle class, a deepening income gap and economic polarization resulted, along with transformations of the terrains of women's work, the family and sexuality (Shin 2004). Women's labour became more polarized into two distinct occupational groups, 'Services and Sales' and 'Professional and Related', and women were beginning to realize that individual economic ability was more essential than ever as the social change triggered by the financial crisis went on (Kim and Kim 2004: 110). Drastic changes in family life, too, can be seen clearly from a glance at a few statistics: the number of divorces per 100 marriages soared from 11.4 in 1990 to 54.8 by 2003; the percentage of women aged 25 to 29 who were single doubled from 20 per cent in 1990 to 40 per cent in 2005, while the percentage who were single between the ages of 30 and 34 nearly quadrupled, from 5.3 to 19 per cent; the fertility rate reached its lowest point in Korean history in 2005; women householders comprised one in five and single people one in seven households (Lee J. 2004: 87–90; Kim S. 2007). In the realms of work, marriage, family and sexuality, women's positions became increasingly diverse, vividly revealing differences between them.

In the meantime, the government sought to save the country from financial crisis through a free labour-market economy and a down-sized state. Accordingly, accelerating globalization and the neo-liberal logic of limitless competition became a part of an increasingly familiar repertoire of social rhetoric. The situation of women who were, voluntarily or not, remaining single for longer in a society dominated by competitive individualism in turn helped to accelerate the desire for sexual intimacy and individualized sexual expression. In a world where love becomes a discourse of salvation and sexuality becomes a project (Kim E. 2006), the sexual politics of a women's movement relying on the fixed identity of 'pure heterosexual women' suddenly finds itself in 'crisis', facing women's resistance by failing to take into account differences between them. In the 2000s, with the new realization that sexuality is socially constituted, movements of lesbians, disabled women and migrant women started to emerge, as did new research issues such as the relation of feminism to lesbians, women's consumption of pornography, masturbation as a form of sexual pleasure, disabled women's bodies and sexual desire, transnational marriage, or migrant women in the sex industry. Thus the content of 'the sexual' in Korean sexual politics gradually became extended and enriched (Byeon 2006).

The realization that 'the sexual' is not essential but socially constructed means acknowledging that women's sexuality cannot be reduced to their gender; rather, it operates independently. Once women could no longer be seen in terms of the single gendered sexual identity of 'pure heterosexual women', and it was realized that the boundary between the normal and the abnormal is never fixed, that boundary could be subjected to scrutiny and diverse forms of women's sexuality could become visible. This situation engendered the 'crisis' within gender politics.

The lesbian rights movement: challenges to feminist gender politics

Beginning with efforts to amend family law, the women's movement in Korea has incessantly criticized and tried to revise the Korean patriarchal family system. In particular, the *hoju* (family-head) system[4] was regarded as one of the main bastions of gender hierarchy (Yang 2000). Its eventual abolition in 2005 is considered one of the cornerstones on which, in the near future, a more egalitarian Korean family system can be built (KWAU 2005).

The critique of gender hierarchy in patriarchal families, however, has proceeded independently of the critique of heterosexuality as an institution, drawing the line at the latter. Gender politics could gain a political voice only in so far as heterosexuality was accepted as the norm. Equality for mothers, wives and daughters within the family could only be claimed on the premise of their pure heterosexuality. By accepting the system of sexuality that categorizes both 'impure' hyper-sexuality and sexuality without heterosexual desire as abnormal or pathological, women with a 'pure sexuality' could secure their rights as the representatives of women in the gender system.

If feminism in Korea is sincere in its desire to represent 'women', it should also accommodate lesbians as 'women' in its gender politics. However, by doing so, it could risk its own hard-earned political voice. It would seem to be asking too much of heterosexual women, for whom heterosexuality might be their only resource for empowerment. Conflicts and discords between the lesbian rights movement, which emerged in the late 1990s, and the women's movement have their origins in this predicament.

In 1994, the first lesbian organization in Korea, called *Kkiri kkiri* (Friends Together), was formed. *Kkiri kkiri* tried to join KWAU in 1997 but was rejected (albeit politely). In 2001, for the first time a paper on lesbianism was presented at the Korean Association of Women's Studies Conference. The paper was critical of lesbian feminists, claiming that lesbianism is biologically determined and that lesbian relationships replicate male and female roles. This argument was rebutted by lesbian rights organizations (Park 2005; Sohn 2001). Attempts to exclude lesbians from the category of 'women' persisted, and in 2004, the Busan Women's Centre, operated by Busan city,[5] barred lesbian activists from participating in its programme for women's movement activists on the grounds that 'lesbian movement organizations do not belong to women's movement organizations' (Kei 2004).[6] Though the Korean lesbian movement has a decade-long history, it has not yet been able to form an alliance with women's movement organizations and has been forced to continue along its own lonely way (Kei 2004).[7]

In November 2004, the Korean Association of Women's Studies held a conference on 'The Sexual Politics of Difference' and invited lesbian rights activists to a session on 'sexual minorities and the politics of difference'. This was the starting point for the politics of inclusion for feminists and lesbian activists. A lesbian activist, Suyeon, who participated in this session, described her experiences of meeting feminists:

> The first thing we had to do was urge them, the feminists and feminist scholars who invited us, to properly recognize our 'differences'. 'Differences' cannot be explained in terms of 'diversity' only; it also means 'discrimination'. . . . We tried to explain that for heterosexual women 'difference' is an experience of 'othering the other', that is, lesbian, whereas for lesbians 'difference' is just experiencing 'discrimination'. However, the responses from the feminists there were not what we had expected. 'Since when did we enjoy vested rights?' 'It seems to me that the discrimination you are talking about is lacking in substance.' 'Why are you so aggressive?' 'Do you have to be so upset? After all, we invited you and were willing to listen.' They treated us

as if we were pigheadedly aggressive toward feminists and indulging in self-victimization. (Suyeon 2005a)

Lesbian activists wished to persuade feminists that 'differences' between homosexual and heterosexual women can mean hierarchical relations between them (Han 2004; Kei 2004; Park 2004). But feminists failed to offer any reconciliatory ground for lesbians by steadfastly holding on to the unitary concept of gender. The remark, 'Since when did we enjoy vested rights?' is an appropriate response for 'women' as a singular oppressed group in the gender system, not for 'heterosexuals' as a dominant group in the sexuality system.

In gender politics, operating under the premise of heterosexism, lesbian feminists are compelled to assimilate into the identity of heterosexual feminists and to keep silent on their homosexual identity. As a consequence, while there is a space where discourses on lesbian identity are allowed to exist in the human rights movement, there is no such space in the feminist movement. Kim Hye-jeong, an activist in the Busan Centre for Women's and Sexual Minority Rights, describes the current political status of the Korean lesbian rights movement:

> There is a certain atmosphere that makes it difficult for lesbians to express their sexual identity freely within women's movement organizations. Due to the homophobic behaviour of women's movement activists, lesbians are discouraged from even coming out in women's organizations, hence a significant number of lesbian activists in women's movement organizations are closeted. Many feminist scholars and activists seem to believe that they know enough about homosexuality and don't need to expend any further attention, at least for the present. Naturally, many lesbian rights activists confess that they feel more comfortable in forming alliances with other human rights organizations than with women's organizations. (Kim H. 2004; in Jeong C. 2004)[8]

Lesbian activists tried to deploy their sexual politics by first forming an alliance with the gay rights movement and the feminist movement (Park 2005). But 'after being isolated between the patriarchal character and arrogance of the gay rights movement and the exclusion of lesbians by the feminist movement' (Park 2004: 2), they finally declared separation from both in May 2005. The Korea Lesbian Rights Movement United, which is an alliance of four lesbian rights organizations, aims 'to protest against the heterosexism and patriarchy of Korean society and pursue an independent movement for lesbian rights based on the reality facing Korean lesbians' (LIL 2005b).

As long as the lesbian identity that they attempt to construct is against 'heterosexism and patriarchy,' they will reject joining the sexual minority/queer movement, which they see as resisting heterosexism, not patriarchy. In fact, they claim that 'as long as we are defined as a 'sexual minority', we will be deprived of our own voices and remain as 'the other' separated forever from 'woman' (Suyeon 2005c), and 'liberation of homosexuals is not in itself lesbian liberation' (Park 2006). In the meantime, though, they believe that feminism is absolutely necessary to construct lesbianism as resisting patriarchy; in their view, the Korean feminist perspective on lesbians is too oriented to Western lesbianism to lend proper consideration to the reality facing Korean lesbians.

> Sexuality in the Western post-modern, post-structural, psychoanalytic feminisms that they had embraced in their college years endowed 'radicalism' to Korean feminists. Some of them were lured into the realm of 'practice' by this 'radicalism'. However, the 'lesbian' of Western theory was not a 'reality' to them, but remained simply a symbol of radicalism. Therefore, they were not interested in real oppression or discrimination experienced by lesbians in Korea. The 'symbolic meaning of lesbian sexuality', 'lesbian as a subversive subject', and 'gender play' are enthusiastically incorporated into their theoretical repertoire, but they consider it boring to raise such questions as 'what kinds of discrimination are Korean lesbians facing?'. Though 'sexual diversity' and 'lesbian' became fashionable keywords among academic feminists, ironically there was no room in this latest academic fashion for the reality of Korean lesbians to find a place. (Suyeon 2005c)

The 'campaign for the prevention of outing' organized by the Korean lesbian rights movement shows the salient characteristics of the movement which is, they say, 'based on the reality facing Korean lesbians' (Suyeon 2005b). The purpose of this campaign is to protect lesbians from having their identities revealed by punishing those who, without permission, disclose or attempt to disclose a woman's lesbianism in her workplace or to her acquaintances. They criticize feminists who encourage lesbians to come out, saying, 'these feminists are just playing conceptual games based on theories, thus ignoring the reality of Korean lesbians and betraying their arrogance' (Suyeon 2005b). Han Chae-yoon (2004) describes the 'conceptual games' of feminists who pressure lesbians to come out:

> They would say, excitedly, 'I met many lesbians when I lived in a foreign country. When they confidently revealed their sexual identity, I was surprised at first but then felt envious. It should be like that in Korea, too. There should be more brave homosexuals coming out.' [However] when asked their opinions on homosexuality, they answer, 'I don't know much about homosexuality, since I have not met any homosexuals. But I don't think they are immoral in any way.' (Han 2004: 7)

Lesbians distanced themselves from those feminists who insist that they come out without realizing the dangers and sacrifices lesbians face by doing so in this utterly homophobic Korean society (Park 2004: 6).

The beginning of a politics of identity among lesbians, who were previously excluded from the normalized gender identity, led to the redefinition of Korean gender politics, which had been focused mainly on heterosexual women. Now, feminism is facing the challenge of incorporating differences in sexual politics into its gender politics. Enabling a space where the coexistence of diverse identities is recognized and the modes of their coexistence are repeatedly contested can destabilize existing gender politics, but it can also open the road to actively politicizing the various positions of women in post-IMF Korean society. The starting point will be recognizing the fluidity of the boundary of feminist sexual politics.

Sex workers' movement: the challenge of agency for gender politics

Since the 'Act on the Punishment of Procuring Prostitution and Associated Acts' and the 'Act on the Prevention of Prostitution and Protections of Victims Thereof'[9] came into force in September 2004, diverse viewpoints on prostitution that were once latent have begun to emerge. These acts replaced the 'Prevention of Prostitution Act', in force since 1961. Though both the new and old acts penalized sex trafficking, feminist scholars see the new acts as significant in three respects. First, by changing the legal term for prostitution from *yullak* (ruining one's body by degrading oneself) to *seong maemae* (buying and selling of sex), the whole context involving buyers and sellers of sex, mediating agents like pimps, the sex industry, and so on, can be scrutinized and questioned rather than, as in the past, merely dismissed by morally stigmatizing women who sell sex. Second, introducing the concept of 'victims of sex trafficking' exempted women who were forced to sell sex from prosecution. Third, defining the act of sex trafficking as involving three persons, including mediating agents, rather than two persons buying and selling sex, made it possible to mete out much tougher punishments to mediating agents (Lee N. 2005; Yang 2004).

The passing of these bills was the result of efforts by the Ministry of Gender Equality (now, the Ministry of Gender Equality and Family), with the participation of Saeumteo[10] and Hansorihoe,[11] two women's organizations that lead the movement against prostitution and had worked with those involved in the sex industry for the past twenty years, and KWAU (Bul-ui domabaem 2001). It also reflected the efforts of the Korean women's movement, which had been striving to prevent violence against women for the previous fifteen years. Movements against violence against women locate women as victims of double sexual standards and of gender hierarchy, and they endeavour to protect women and their rights. In this context, prostitutes are not just regarded as victims of double standards and gender hierarchy, but also as 'poor *eonnis*',[12] 'poor sisters' or victims of the sex industry (Lee N. 2005). This shift in identity from *yullangnyeo* (prostitutes) to 'poor *eonnis*' could be considered the most significant contribution made by these movements.

Behind Korean feminists' support for this new legislation on prostitution lie the post–IMF social changes that caused the growth of the sex industry. Capital unable to find profitable investments flowed into the service sector, which offered high returns with relatively small risks and bloated the entertainment industry, including prostitution agencies. Scarcer job opportunities and harsher working environments for women, and increasing financial responsibility, helped foster their entry into prostitution (Lee Y. 2004: 186). Had the policy of treating prostitution as a crime not been retained, further and, perhaps, uncontrollable expansion of the prostitution industry would have resulted. Unlike the 'streetwalking' and brothels typical of the Western world, the characteristically Asian form of organized sex trade occurs in cooperation with the service industry, for example through hotels and restaurants (Yoo 2007). Therefore Korean feminists adopted the goal of eradicating prostitution: they called for the penalization of men and pimps as culprits and the protection of the human rights of prostitutes, and concentrated their efforts on legislation that would help realize this aim.

However, within a month of the new acts coming into effect, over three thousand prostitutes were demonstrating in the streets. Shouting 'guarantee us the right to live', they demanded that the acts penalizing buyers and sellers of sex be repealed and called on the government to keep its promise to delay the acts' enforcement (Kim M. 2004). Their demonstrations, hunger strikes and suicides brought on by economic difficulties were highlighted by the media, lending support to the stronger voice of men who opposed the prohibition of prostitution.[13]

Feminist scholars are wary of making explicit statements acknowledging the agency of prostitutes because it is so easy for the diverse voices of women to be reduced to conflicts between women, thus serving to maintain the hierarchical gender system. This would be the worst possible consequence that must be avoided at all costs. Therefore, the response of women's movement organizations and the Ministry of Gender Equality was to explain away the demonstrations and hunger strikes by claiming that the prostitutes 'must be confidantes and cronies of pimps or simply so ignorant as to misinterpret the new acts' (Morae 2005). This was more or less inevitable given the strategy of mobilizing women as victims resisting the hierarchical gender system. In fact, Yi Seon-hui, a representative of the Hanteo Women Workers Association that led the demonstrations and hunger strikes, admitted that they had asked pimps and merchants for monetary support for the demonstrations (Morae 2004).

But asking pimps for support and protection in and of itself does not mean that the pimps forced them to demonstrate. Without families, relatives or even boyfriends to help and support them, and considering that they regarded 'women's movement organizations' as 'groups of immature and inexperienced aunties' or 'mouthpieces of the well-to-do', they had no other place to turn (Won 2004). Won Mi-hye interprets their demonstrations as indicative of their increased negotiating power in the sex industry. The original purpose of the new prostitution acts was to free prostitutes from the sex industry, but their enforcement also endowed prostitutes with stronger negotiating power in dealing with customers and pimps. This in turn encouraged recognition of them as beings with agency rather than mere victims, or in other words, as 'sex workers' who are simply doing a different kind of 'work' (Lee N. 2005). Yi Seon-hui explains their work as follows:

> You reporters also earn a salary to make a living and save money for a rainy day. It's the same with us. Asking us to give it all up leaves us completely at a loss as to how to make a living . . . wouldn't you reporters demonstrate, too, if one day you were suddenly asked to drop your cameras and pens and leave your offices? You would be robbed of your means to make a living. Of course you would demonstrate! It's the same with us. We are using different parts of our bodies, I admit, but it's still a job. . . . This is our job. We have been making a living with it, so leave us alone so we can earn money and make our livings. (Morae 2004)

By situating prostitution in the context of 'work', 'making a living', and 'the right to live', they keep their distance from the sexual politics of prostitution as sexual violence. The demonstration that started by demanding the right to live led to the organization of the National Sex Workers United in March 2005 and gave sex workers a voice of their own. They made a 'surprise' intervention in a street demonstration against discrimination against women workers in Seoul and distributed pamphlets announcing the launching of National Sex Workers United with slogans like 'Sex workers are women workers, too! All the women's organizations trying to kill women workers, come to your senses!'

The sex workers' movement constructed their identity as 'workers'. The movement also claimed that, as workers trading in sex, they belonged to a sexual minority group. They claimed that the right to 'sexual self-determination' guaranteed to every human being includes the right to buy and sell, that if 'sexual self-determination' is accepted as a human right, 'sex work' has to be acknowledged as a part of the right to work, thereby merging human rights and the right to work (Guk 2007).

The sex workers' movement continues to construct its identity by constantly opposing itself to the *yeoseong-gye* (all the organization leaders supporting the new acts on prostitution) who have been heading the movement against violence against women. The sex workers criticize members of the *yeoseong-gye* as 'power women' trying to exaggerate their political success by designating sex workers as pitiable 'victimized women' needing protection (statement by National Sex Workers United, 17 October 2006, quoted in Guk 2007).

Last year was a heyday for the power women group to amass wealth and power whereas it was a period of death for sex workers being driven to the edge of life's precipice. You, the 'power women group', do not insult sex workers any more. We are disgusted with the hypocrisy of those in the power women group being well-educated and wealthy. One year after the passing of the new acts on prostitution, we, sex workers, are near death by starvation while you amassed enormous amount of wealth. However, we, sex workers, will not die to satisfy your greed for political power and to create jobs for women's organizations. We will triumph over you by help of just argument and people's power (statement by National Sex Workers United, 22 September 2005, quoted in Guk 2007).

In order not to turn differences between women into exclusion but instead to foster alliances, it will first be necessary to let their diverse voices be heard (Won 2004). In this way, the characteristics of the overdetermined oppression under which these women are subjected must be comprehended. The standpoint of the sex workers' movement in Korea is that they want their prostitution to be designated as 'work', not as 'sexual violence'. In her comparative study of prostitution policies in Korea and Germany, Yoo Sook-ran (2007) reveals a fundamental difference in approach. She explained that, in the gender frame adopted by the women's movement in Korea, prostitution is regarded as violation of human rights, hence as a problem for women in general, whereas in the equality frame adopted in Germany it is not regarded as a problem for women in general, but rather as one form of occupation like any other: hence the problem is just one of improving labour conditions. Thus conflicts between the women's movement and sex workers in Korea could be said to have resulted from the difference in the choice of frame in approaching the problem of prostitution. Which frame will be more productive can be determined only after more sex workers' voices have echoed around in Korea and still more ears have been lent to them, including those of women in the *yeoseong-gye*.

Conclusion

Differences in women's experiences that have recently brought about the 'crisis' of the women's movement in Korea are constructed by the intersections of multiple social systems. As lesbians excluded from the normalized gender identity initiated lesbian identity politics, the politics of the women's movement was reduced to being mainly for heterosexual women. And though gender politics could certainly boast of shifting prostitutes' identity from *yullangnyeo* to 'poor *eonnis*' as a significant achievement, this resulted in the exclusion of prostitutes from gender politics itself by refusing to acknowledge their agency.

If the 'crisis' in the women's movement could be diagnosed as caused by its all too familiar strategy of homogenizing women as victimized women, even though women's experiences had already moved from the realm of gender inequality to that of intersectionality with other systems of dominance, a natural prescription for it would be to start from a close analysis of the process by which these diverse systems intersect to construct women's experiences.

Every woman resides in the intersectionality of class, sex, race, nation-state and cultural systems, hence no woman is only a woman. Naturally gender politics too cannot presuppose that only gender relations count but should be ready to accept that they are constructed within such a nexus. However, if woman is gendered by the intersectionality of these systems, conversely it also follows that gender is a common feature of all these systems. That is, despite all the differences between women, gender still remains a category embracing diverse women (Harding 1991: 181–4). Therefore, for gender politics to sustain women's identity while acknowledging differences between women, it should simultaneously strive to strengthen and transform that identity. Strengthening identity is a requirement for gender politics, whereas transformation of identity leaves the extension of identity open to reflect differences between women (Butler 2003: 18–27).

As the women's movement is based on gender identity, reinforcement of that identity is essential to strengthen its political influence. And the power of influence is a deciding factor in overcoming institutional oppression. However, reinforcing gender identity will eventually exclude or alienate specific women and necessarily introduce a hierarchy among women. This will lead to curtailing the scope of the movement and a loss of its momentum. And, as reactions to exclusion, alienation and hierarchy, diverse women's movements reflecting differences between women will emerge. But a sexual politics vindicating differences will wield little political influence as it starts not by reinforcing but by deconstructing the category of women. Therefore the women's movement in Korea should search for a strategy that can respond flexibly enough to manipulate the seemingly incompatible needs of both strengthening and diversifying gender identity. This will require a new type of collaboration between 'researcher' and 'activist' in Korea. Activists in women's movements need to focus their attention on more specific and concrete issues rather than the broad political ones that were preferred previously. This will allow them more room to cope flexibly with new issues and enable new agendas to emerge. Researchers who were once content to provide rather general and broad cultural and political analysis should now strive to devise more conceptually flexible and practically effective theoretical tools: these are urgently needed by activists in the constantly transforming terrain of Korean sexual politics.

Notes

1 In 1997 Korea suffered a major financial crisis, reflecting ongoing worldwide economic problems, leading her to seek help from the IMF. I will use the term 'post-IMF' to designate the period after the crisis when many social changes occurred following the economic constraints imposed by the IMF.

2 When identity is regarded as fixed, the gender politics of the present day is in crisis. However, when identity is regarded as constituted, it is in the process of reconfiguration and thus not in crisis; hence my quotation marks around this word.

3 A main alliance of progressive women's movement organizations.

4 The *hoju* (family-head) system, formalized in family law as part of the colonial legacy (1910–45), entailed strict patriarchal rules, such as patrilineal succession, patrilocal marriage and patriarchal headship. The part of the Civil Code containing the *hoju* system was finally repealed by the National Assembly in March 2005.

5 A city with a population of nearly 4 million.

6 However, in March 2005, the National Council for Human Rights ruled that 'it is a discriminatory act to exclude organizations for sexual minorities from women's organizations' and recommended that the Mayor of Busan and the head of the Busan Women's Centre prevent further such recurrences (LIL 2005a).

7 http://kirikiri.org/index.php.
8 http://www.ildaro.com/Scripts/news/index.php?menu=ART&sub=View&i
   dx=2004103100014.
9 Hereafter abbreviated as 'new prostitution acts'.
10 *Saeumteo*: a shelter for victims of prostitution.
11 *Hansorihoe*: United Voice (*hansori*) for the Eradication of Prostitution in
   Korea.
12 The term *eonni*, meaning elder sister, is usually used to convey amicable and
   friendly feelings towards a woman.
13 Despite their varied political backgrounds, these men shared in justifying
   men's sexual desires as biological instinct, the result of human evolution,
   and shifted the point at issue from problems of pimps and men to those
   between women, dividing them into prostitutes and 'other women', the latter
   including 'mothers', 'virtuous women' and 'bourgeois women' according to
   the classification schemes based on family, sexuality and class respectively. The
   president of the Korean Council for Men, Yi Gyeong-su, filed a complaint
   to the National Human Rights Commission, claiming that the acts violated
   men's human rights. Congressman Kim Chung-hwan of the Grand National
   Party claimed that young men would 'be deprived of the means to satisfy their
   sexual desires'. The president of the Korean Economic Research Institute said
   that the acts were based on 'the leftist policy that tries to prohibit human sexual
   desires, thus violating human rights', while leftist men of People's Solidarity
   for Social Progress claimed that 'bourgeois women robbed prostitutes of their
   rights to live' (Papermoon 2005).

References

Bul-ui domabaem [불의도마뱀] (2001) 화대월급제? 미아리에선 지금 무
   슨 일이 ['Monthly salaries for prostitutes? What is going on in Miari?], 언
   니네 [*Sisters' Space*]. <http://www.unninet.co.kr/room/column.asp?rlist_
   Idx=1000122&TextCode=6>.
Butler, Judith (2003) 'The question of social transformation' in *Women and Social
   Transformation*. New York: Peter Lang, pp. 1–28.
Byeon Hye-jeong (ed.) [변혜정편] (2006) 섹슈얼리티 강의, 두 번째 [*Lectures on
   Sexuality, Volume II*]. Seoul: Dong-nyeok.
Cho Joo-hyun [조주현] (2000) 여성정체성의 정치학 [*Gender Identity Politics*].
   Seoul: Ttohana-ui munhwa, p. 157.
—— (2005) 'Intersectionality revealed: sexual politics in post-IMF Korea', *Korea
   Journal*, 45 (3): 86–116.
Collins, Patricia Hill (2000) *Black Feminist Thought: Knowledge, Consciousness, and
   the Politics of Empowerment* (second edition). New York, NY: Routledge.
Foucault, Michel (1978) *The History of Sexuality*. Vol. 1. New York, NY:
   Pantheon.
Guk Kyeong-hi [국경희] (2007) 한국 성노동자 운동에 관한 연구 ['A study

on the sex workers' movement in Korea'], 한국여성학회 23차 춘계학술대회 발표문 [*paper presented at the 23rd annual meeting of the Korean Association of Women's Studies*], Seoul, 9 June 2007.

Han Chae-yoon [한채윤] (2004) 이것은 삶의 문제다—과장된 실수, 차이의 허구, 경험의 착각 ['"This is the problem of life" – exaggerated minority, fictionalized difference, and misconceived experience'], 한국여성학회 제20차 추계학술대회 발표문 [paper presented at the 20th annual meeting of the Korean Association of Women's Studies], Seoul, 20 November 2004.

Harding, Sandra (1991) *Whose Science? Whose Knowledge? Thinking from Women's Lives*. New York, NY: Cornell University Press.

Kei [케이] (2004) 한국의 여성학계와 여성 운동계는 한국의 여성 성적 소수자 인권운동을 어떻게 배제시켜왔는가? ['How has the Korean lesbian movement been excluded from both the Korean Feminist Academy and Activism?'], 한국여성학회 제 20차 추계학술대회 발표문 [paper presented at the 20th annual meeting of the Korean Association of Women's Studies], Seoul, 20 November 2004.

Kim Eun-shil [김은실] (2006) 강의를 열며 ['Introduction'] in 섹슈얼리티 강의, 두 번째 [*Lectures on Sexuality, Volume II*]. Seoul: Dong-nyeok, pp. 18–48.

Kim Hae-jeong [김혜정] (2004) 레즈비언 운동과 여성 운동 간의 긴장과 모순 ['Tension and conflicts between the lesbian movement and the feminist movement'], 레즈비언인권연구소,이화여자대학교 대학원 학생회 공동주최 토론회 "'레즈비언 '권리'와 '여성주의'" 발표문 [paper presented at the Conference on 'Lesbian Rights and Feminism' held by the Lesbian Institute for Lesbians (LIL) and the Graduate Students' Association of Ewha Woman's University], Seoul, 29 October 2004. Requoted from Jeong Chun-hi [정춘희] (2004) 여성주의 진영은 동성애 이슈에 대해 배워야 ['The feminist movement has more to learn about lesbian issues'], 일다 [*Waves of Those Women Are Rising*], 31 October 2004. <http://www.ildaro.com/Scripts/news/index.php?menu=ART&sub=View&idx=2004103100014>

Kim Kyeong-hee [김경희] and Yoon Jeong-sook [윤정숙] (2006) 여성운동 의제의 한계와 도전 ['Challenges and limits of the agenda for women's movement'] in 한국여성학회 콜로키움 한국여성운동의 성찰과 전망 [KAWS Colloquium on the Reflections and Prospects of the Korean Women's Movement]. Seoul: Korean Association of Women's Studies, 29 April 2006.

Kim Mi-yeong [김미영] (2004) 직업안정? 쉽게 돈버는 것에 익숙해진 탓 ['Want to be accepted as a job? They have been earning money too easily'], *Hankyoreh Newspaper*, 19 October 2004.

Kim, Seung-kyung and John Finch (2002) 'Living with rhetoric, living against rhetoric: Korean families and the IMF economic crisis,' *Korean Studies*, 26 (1): 120–39.

Kim So-ra [김소라] (2007) 고학력 비혼여성의 독신문화에 관한 연구 ['A study on the single-life culture of highly educated professional unmarried women in Korea'], 한국여성학회 제23차 춘계학술대회 발표문 [paper presented at the 23rd annual meeting of the Korean Association of Women's Studies], Seoul, 9 June 2007.

Kim Yeong-ok [김영옥] and Kim Kyeong-hi [김경희] (2004) 여성노동정책의 한계와 새 패러다임 모색 ['Limits of labor policy for women and search for a new paradigm'] in 한국여성정책의 뉴 패러다임 정립 [*Stance for a New Paradigm for Women's Policies in Korea*]. Seoul: Ministry of Gender Equality, pp. 105–38.

Korean Society Forum [한국사회포럼] (2006) 여성운동, 차이와 소통 그리고 새로운 미래: 나, 여성운동에 할 말 있다 ['Women's movement: differences, understanding, and a new future'] in 한국사회포럼2006자료집 [*Collected Papers of the 2006 Symposium of the Korean Society Forum*]. Seoul: Women's Plaza, 23–25 March 2006. <http://www.demos.or.kr/scholar/viewbody.htm l?category=&code=scholarship&key=&key_re=&keyfield=&keyfield_re=&n umber=9718&txttype=>

KWAU (Korea Women's Associations United) [한국여성단체연합] (2005) 호주제 폐지 민법개정안, 국회 본회의 통과를 환영한다 ['Welcoming statement on the occasion of the abolishment of the *Hoju* registry system'], <http://www.women21.or.kr/news/W_GPDS/GPDS_View.asp?page=1&S earchWord=&SearchGubun=&GB=F&cate=&menu_code=O01&cNo=325 &Rpos=3589>

Lee Jae-kyung [이재경] (2004) 공사영역의 변화와 '가족'을 넘어서는 가족 정책 ['The change of the public/private spheres and family policies beyond "the family"'] in 한국여성정책의 뉴 패러다임 정립 [*Stance for a New Paradigm for Women's Policies in Korea*]. Seoul: Ministry of Gender Equality, pp. 79–104.

Lee Na-yeong [이나영] (2005) 성매매: 여성주의 성 정치학을 위한 시론 ['Prostitution: Introductory remarks on feminist sexual politics'], 한국여성학 [*Korean Journal of Women's Studies*], 21 (1): 41–85.

Lee Yeong-ja [이영자] (2004) 성매매에 관한 정책 패러다임 ['A new paradigm for the policies on prostitution in Korea'] in 한국여성정책의 뉴 패러다임 정립 [*Stance for a New Paradigm for Women's Policies in Korea*]. Seoul: Ministry of Gender Equality, pp. 170–203.

LIL (Lesbian Institute for Lesbians) [레즈비언권리연구소] (2005a) 여성성적소 수자 단체를 배제한 여성단체에 대해 차별행위로 인정, 권고한 국가 인 권위원회의 조치를 환영한다 ['We welcome the decision by the National Human Rights Commission of Korea on the discriminatory action by the Women's Organization], 레즈비언권리연구소 열린기획 [*LIL Open Forum*], No. 9. <http://lesbian.or.kr/htm/m2-3.htm>

—— (2005b) 한국 레즈비언 권리운동연대 발족선언문 ['Inauguration statement of the Korea Lesbian Rights Movement United], 레즈비언권리연 구소 열린기획 [*LIL Open Forum*], No. 11. <http://lesbian.or.kr/htm/m2-3.htm>

Min Gyeong-ja [민경자] (1999) 성폭력 여성운동사 ['The history of the women's movement against sexual violence'] in 한국여성인권운동사 [*The History of the Women's Civil Rights Movement in Korea*]. Seoul: Hanul Press, pp. 17–105.

Morae [모래] (2004) 인물포커스: 성매매 여성이 성매매특별법을 말하다

['Focus on person: a prostitute speaks on the Prostitution Prevention Act'], 언니네 [*Sisters' Space*]. <http://www.unninet.co.kr/monthly/special_view. asp?ca1=8&ca2=241>.

—— (2005) 가려지는 목소리들/드러나는 목소리들 ['Concealed voices/ unveiled voices'], 언니네[*Sisters' Space*]. <http://www.unninet.co.kr/ monthly/special_view.asp?ca1=1&ca2=247&ct_Idx=1893>.

Papermoon [페이퍼문] (2005) 성매매에 대해 말할 자격 ['A right to speak on prostitution'], 언니네 [*Sisters' Space*]. <http://www.unninet.co.kr/monthly/ special_view.asp?ca1=1&ca2=247&ct_Idx=1894>.

Park Tong [박통] (2004) 레즈비언 권리와 여성주의, 어떻게 만나야 하는 가? ['Lesbian rights and feminism: how should they meet?'], 한국여성학회 제20차 추계학술대회 발표문 [*paper presented at the 20th annual meeting of the Korean Association of Women's Studies*], Seoul, 20 November 2004.

—— (2005) 한국레즈비언 권리운동연대의 '도전'과 '실험' ['New challenge and questioning of the Korean Lesbian Rights Movement'], 레즈비언권리연 구소 열린기획 [*LIL Open Forum*], No. 8. <http://lesbian.or.kr/htm/em2-3.htm >.

—— (2006) 레즈비언 정체성의 다양성 ['Diversity in lesbian identities'], 레 즈비언권리연구소 열린기획[*LIL Open Forum*], No. 23. <http://lesbian. or.kr/htm/em2-3.htm>.

Shin Kwang-yeong [신광영] (2004) 한국의 계급과 불평등 [*Class and Class Inequality of Korea*]. Seoul: Eulyoo Press.

Snitow, Ann et al. (1981) 'Introduction' in Ann Snitow, Christine Stansell and Sharon Thompson (eds), *Powers of Desire: The Politics of Sexuality*. New York: Monthly Review Press, pp. 9–50.

Sohn Seung-yeong (2001) 끼리끼리 '한국레즈비언…' 기고에 대한 한국여 성학회의 입장 ['Korean Association of Women's Studies'(KAWS) official position on the contributions by the lesbian group *Kkirikkiri*'], 여성신문 [*Womennews*], 657 (28 December 2001).

Suyeon [수연] (2005a) 레즈비언과 차이의 정치학 ['Lesbians and the politics of difference'], 레즈비언권리연구소 열린기획 [*LIL Open Forum*], No. 7. <http://lesbian.or.kr/htm/m2-3.htm>.

—— (2005b) 여성주의자들에게 띄우는 글 ['A letter to the feminists'], 레 즈비언권리연구소 열린기획 [*LIL Open Forum*], No. 10. <http://lesbian. or.kr/htm/m2-3.htm>.

—— (2005c) 한국의 여성학과 레즈비언의 권리 ['Lesbian Rights Movement and women's studies in Korea'], 2005년 제9회 세계여성학대회 발표문 [paper presented at Women's Worlds 2005: 9th International Interdisciplinary Congress on Women], Seoul, 21 June 2005.

Won Mi-hye [원미혜] (2004) 성매매 여성들의 목소리? '목소리'! ['Voices of prostitutes? Yes, their voices!'], 언니네 [*Sister' Space*]. <http://www.unninet. co.kr/monthly/special_view.asp?ca1=2&ca2=240&ct_Idx=1879>.

Yang Hyeon-ah [양현아] (2000) 호주제도의 젠더정치: 젠더생산을 중심으 로 ['Gender politics in the Korean family-head system: its gender production'], 한국여성학 [*Korean Journal of Women's Studies*], 16 (1): 65–93.

—— (2004) 성매매방지법의 의의와 과제 ['Significance and future agenda of the new Acts on prostitution'], 한국여성학회 성매매방지법 관련 특별 심포지움 발표문 [paper presented at the special symposium by the Korean Association of Women's Studies on the new laws on prostitution], 17 November 2004.

Yoo Sook-ran [유숙란] (2007) 한국과 독일의 성매매정책 결정과정 비교분석 ['A comparative analysis of policy decision process for legislation of prostitution law in South Korea and Germany'], 한국여성학회 제23차 춘계 학술대회 발표문 [paper presented at the 23rd annual meeting of the Korean Association of Women's Studies], Seoul, 9 June 2007.

8 'How Did You Two Meet?' Lesbian Partnerships in Present-day Japan

SAORI KAMANO AND DIANA KHOR

In this chapter we describe how lesbians meet their partners, start and maintain a relationship in the context of present-day Japan, paying special attention to the norms of heterosexuality and the shared experiences of women.[1] We draw on interviews conducted in 2002 with 21 women aged 29 to 51, including nine couples and three individuals, all of whom were in a relationship and the vast majority of whom lived in the Kanto area.

We first sketch the wider context in which lesbians[2] live their lives as 'single/unmarried women' (to society) and as sexual minorities before exploring the issue of lesbian visibility/invisibility and lesbian communities. We then introduce the data on Japanese lesbian women's lives, presenting the material to demonstrate certain themes, including the places where lesbians met their partners, the way they developed the relationship and started living together, and the obstacles they face in society at large.

The wider context: heterosexual norms and lesbian lives

Recent changes in Japanese society suggest a loosening of the norms of heterosexuality with respect to marriage; for lesbians, who may be seen as single women, these changes may be positive in some ways. The trend towards delaying marriage and declining marriage rates among women and men has been in the media limelight in recent years. In 2005, one in three women in their early thirties had never been married, compared to 8 per cent in 1980. The average age of first marriage for women has risen from 25.8 in 1985 to 29.4 in 2005 (National Institute of Population and Social Security Research [NIPSSR] 2007a). In tandem with these changes in behaviour are

161

changes in attitudes towards marriage. For example, survey results show that fewer married women in 2002 than in 1992 thought that 'staying single throughout one's life is not a desirable way of living' (62 and 47 per cent respectively) (NIPSSR 2007b). This is consistent with the findings from qualitative studies showing that women feel that they are not as pressured to marry as their mothers were, or even as much as they themselves were just five to ten years ago (Kamano 2004a).

Although these changes may show a weakening of some core heterosexual norms, other forms of partnership or ways of forming a family, such as cohabitation and lone-parenthood, are not gaining in popularity. Only 10 per cent of people in their late twenties have ever cohabitated. The percentage of cohabiting never-married women has remained stable at 1–2 per cent during the period when the marriage rate declined. Further, despite the apparent acceptance of singlehood, nearly 90 per cent of women and men between 18 and 34 intended to marry, with only 5 per cent explicitly stating that 'they do not plan to marry for the rest of their lives' (NIPSSR 2007b). Further, the support for singlehood cited earlier has receded, and the 2005 survey shows that more than half of the married women respondents (52 per cent) did not support singlehood (NIPSSR 2007b). The institution of marriage is clearly still strong.

Even though marital norms remain strong, a heterosexual dating culture is not well-established in Japan (Yamada 1999; Atoh 2000). Forty-five per cent of never-married women between 18 and 34 years old have neither a steady boyfriend nor casual male friends. Most of these single (never-married) women tend to live with their parent(s), rather than on their own. In 2005, about 80 per cent of never-married women aged between 25 and 34 were living with their parents (NIPSSR 2007b).

What the foregoing sketch implies is that weakening marital norms and the near non-existence of a heterosexual dating culture may have made it easier for lesbians to 'pass' as unmarried women who do not have any intention of getting married. At the same time, while some lesbians also felt tremendous pressure to marry, the agony they felt set them apart from heterosexual women experiencing similar pressure. Further, whether one intends to 'pass' or not, the apparent similarities between lesbians and (heterosexual) single women do render lesbians invisible. The weakening of marital norms also should not be exaggerated, particularly in view of the lack of legitimated alternatives to marriage such as cohabitation or long-term dating relationships. A combination of these factors is probably behind the total lack of public discussion of same-sex relationships. Same-sex partnership has not entered into the statistics, and there is no law that recognizes such relationships either as marriage or as any form of legal unit, although it is also not against the law to form such a relationship.[3]

The 1990s saw a so-called 'gay boom' in Japan during which lesbians and gay men, previously invisible and silenced, suddenly received a lot of media attention. The boom waned, but we might be seeing some quiet changes. For example, the first openly lesbian politician, Otsuji Kanako, a council member of Osaka prefecture, ran for national office, albeit unsuccessfully, in the July 2007 election. Generally, more attention has been paid to gay men than to lesbians. Indeed, while there are openly gay men and male-to-female transgender personalities on TV, there are no openly lesbian celebrities.

Beyond individuals, there are several centres/organizations for lesbians/sexual minority women, including Regumi-studio, a lesbian-feminist group; and LOUD in Tokyo and QWRC in Osaka, both multipurpose sites for sexual minority women. In addition, there are a number of small women's bars as well as 'mixed' bars open to women, a few club events, and so on (Welker 2004; Maree 2007; see also Kamano 2005c for individual accounts of 'entering' such communities).

These spaces, while important, are concentrated in city centres, unlike Internet sites that have developed notably in the past ten years and now connect lesbians in cities and rural areas. Many lesbians meet through the Internet, access lesbian communities through it, and obtain information from it. At the same time, access is likely to be affected by socio-economic status and living arrangements. For example, a young woman mentioned in our study that since the computer at home was shared by everyone in the family and those available outside are in the public space, she could not check information on where to meet lesbians.

During the so-called 'gay boom' several books with the word 'lesbian' in their titles were published, starting with Kakefuda's *'Rezubian' de aru to iu koto* ('On Being a "Lesbian"') in 1992 (Suganuma 2006), followed by a few others. The initial flow of books on lesbians soon seemed to be over, even though there were many books on transgender/

transsexuals/gender-identity disorder. Then, in 2005, Otsuji Kanako published *Coming Out*, and in the following year, Horie Yuri published *Living as a 'Lesbian'*, reflecting on her experiences fighting against homophobic discourse in a Japanese Church and addressing various realms of her life (Horie 2006b; see also Horie 2006a).

Overall, therefore, there was a brief moment of lesbian visibility in the 1990s and now again, with a known lesbian public figure in politics. Spaces, channels for communication, and publications for lesbians do exist but cannot be considered vibrant. The current state of lesbian existence in Japan discussed above, plus the changes and stability in heterosexual norms presented earlier, constitute the broader context of the lives of the lesbians who participated in our study. We will present snapshots of their lives, including where they met their partners, the obstacles they face, and the support they receive in starting and maintaining their relationships.

How did they meet and how did the relationship begin?

The lesbians in our study started their relationships between the early 1990s and early 2000s and met their current partners in a variety of settings open to lesbians, as well as in their everyday lives. The way the relationship developed after the first meeting did not follow any one path. Some resembled chance meetings with neither party looking for a relationship; friendship developed and the relationship took its course. Some lesbians seemed deliberate in looking for a potential partner, while others were in unhappy relationships when they met their current partners. Still others developed a clearer lesbian identity in the process of forming a relationship with another woman. The variety in a small sample suggests an absence of 'pattern' in how lesbians connect with each other and eventually develop a relationship.

A few interviewees shared their experiences of meeting their partners through various activities in the lesbian community, including talks, special gatherings for particular groups of women, reading groups, and organizing meetings in community centres. For example, in the late 1990s, Yasuko[4] and Mayumi met at a talk sponsored by a publisher specializing in sex education, distributed flyers together, became good friends and developed a relationship.

Yasuko: Mayumi told me that she is in theatre performance so I asked her to send me information. Later on, I was going around various events, including club events, to distribute flyers for the [lesbian and gay] parade, and Mayumi was also asking various places to put up flyers of their performances, so we began going around together.

Mayumi: We were fine as friends.

Yasuko: Yes, I thought we could be long-term friends. I wanted to continue our friendship for a long time.

Mayumi: We were quite relaxed with each other. Almost said it would be nice if we could have tea together when we are old. But the timing was right (to start a relationship).

Mayumi: My girlfriend who I was living with found someone else, and I had to leave the place I was living with her. And I did not have a place to go to. So I relied on Yasuko. And then, things just started to take on a life of their own. It just happened.

Similarly, Hiroko and Chise met at a reading group in the mid-1990s at one of the lesbian centres, and got along well. However Hiroko was already living with her partner at the time. Chise was encouraged to disclose her feelings for Hiroko by a friend who knew that Hiroko was not happy in her relationship. It did not seem to be an easy decision or process, as other friends were involved and Hiroko was trying to get out of her relationship. Even though it appeared that Chise has 'stolen' Hiroko from her partner, their relationship seems to have worked out.

While not as 'dramatic', as Chise put it, Yoshiko and Yuko also did not start off smoothly. They met at an organizing meeting at one of the major centres for sexual minority women in 2000. Yuko found Yoshiko nice and interesting: she was different from other women that she had met before. On the other hand, Yoshiko did not have a good impression of Yuko at the beginning. After Yuko persistently sent e-mails to ask Yoshiko out, they eventually dated. Yuko then asked Yoshiko formally to go out with her. As they met more, Yoshiko began seeing the good sides of Yuko. According to Yoshiko, since Yuko was so persistent, she had no choice but to go along with her.

Rather than face-to-face meetings at community events or activities, others met their partners through 'mediated channels' such as magazine ads, up until the mid-1990s, and the Internet thereafter. Some were looking for friends but found a partner, like Eri, Machiko and Takako, while others had more specific purposes, such as Kumiko who placed an ad offering to take any interested parties to Ni-chome, where gay and lesbian bars and shops concentrate. Setsuko replied to Kumiko, thinking that it would be nice to have a friend. Also, she really wanted to go to Ni-chome – she had visited once on her own but stopped short of opening the door of a bar. Setsuko was still married at that time; even though she knew that she preferred women, she was not looking for a lover yet. Setsuko met Kumiko and they had a really good time at Ni-chome. It was love at first sight for Kumiko, although she was seeing somebody else and wondering if that person could become her lover. The beginning of the relationship was therefore quite complicated, what with the person Kumiko was seeing and Setsuko's trying to get a divorce, to which her ex-husband eventually and reluctantly agreed. Setsuko and Kumiko then started a relationship and lived together right away.

Despite their different expectations and circumstances when entering into a relationship, since these women met their partners in the lesbian community, there was a level of 'certainty' that they would find somebody, whether a friend or a partner, who identified as a lesbian. The same cannot be said for those who met their partners outside the lesbian community.

Madoka and Rio met outside of a 'lesbian context'. They attended the same junior high school in a rural area, but they did not go out together until they went to different high schools. Actually, Rio had had a bad impression of Madoka at the beginning. During the few years when they saw one another every now and then with a group of friends, Madoka developed special feelings for Rio and, eventually, they got together.

Madoka: I was trying to send messages that I was interested in her. But she did not notice a thing.

Rio: I did not know at all. . . . Then all of sudden, I was told that she liked me. I just didn't think about it so deeply and said okay (to go out with her). I followed my instinct. So there is no rationale behind starting this relationship. I said okay, since she seemed so desperate. . . .

Madoka: I was about to break down.

Rio: Yes, it was almost like if I turned her down, she was going to die. So I thought, since she likes me so much, why don't I try to put my life into this relationship. If I put all my energy into the relationship and if it still does not work out, then, so be it. No regrets. Also, I felt that it would be unfair to her if I just kept a lukewarm type of relationship. That's how we started and are still together to this date.

The mutuality in feelings, or, rather, being aware that one is a lesbian, or that one could be in a relationship with another woman, was not present when Kazuko and Fumiko, and Sanae and Kayo, first became friends. Kazuko and Fumiko went to the same high school, and met through a mutual friend. Both were trying out for a music school, which was quite rare among their peers, and so they decided to prepare for the exam together, and eventually passed the exam and attended the same school. Kazuko had always been interested in girls while Fumiko had gone out with men a few times. They got into a relationship but after a week or so, Fumiko suddenly broke off the relationship: 'I suddenly realized that Kazuko is a woman . . . and just got overwhelmed with feelings of being gross.' Fumiko left Kazuko for a man, and Kazuko found another girlfriend in the same class 'out of pain and frustration after being jilted'. However, after a while, Fumiko realized she liked Kazuko, worked through her feelings, and got back together with her.

Similarly, Sanae was aware that she was interested in women and developed romantic feelings for Kayo, when they met each other overseas. They wrote to each other when they were staying in different towns and even took a trip to Europe together with another friend. Even though Kayo did not have a lesbian identity or awareness that she could be interested in women, she liked Sanae as a person, did not feel much resistance against her, and decided to go out with her.

Just as there are women who got into a relationship with a woman without a prior lesbian identity or orientation, there were also women who made it sound as if it were not difficult to 'drop' the lesbian way of living if they were not seeing women at a particular time. For example, Machiko, in her mid-thirties, had broken up with her third girlfriend, and for a while, she was 'single'. During that time, her mother was getting weaker, and she seriously thought about going back to her home town. She went through a series of *omiai* (arranged match-making meetings). For her, it was okay to marry since she felt that even her mother was married to her father without much romantic feeling, and that it was just a way of life. A few months later, when she was about to leave Tokyo, she met her current girlfriend through the Internet. It was she who placed an ad looking for a friend, and her current girlfriend responded. Since then, she has remained in Tokyo, trying to see how her life will unfold.

Living the life: resistance, decisions, obstacles and support

In sampling couples only, we could not explore the trials and tribulations that single lesbians might experience in finding their potential partners. Our interview participants gave light-hearted, at times amusing, accounts of how they met their partners and started a relationship. However, putting their accounts in the context of Japan today, where there is a high level of gender inequality and where heterosexual norms are still strongly enforced, one may surmise that maintaining a relationship could be quite a task.

Before looking into how couples decided to settle down and live a life together, it is instructive to first look at the expectations about marriage and how they cope with the pressure. The women who have not experienced any pressure towards marriage are those whose parents have accepted their decision not to marry, independently of their sexual orientation. Mayumi recounts:

> My mother has been living as she wishes herself. So for me, too, regardless of whether I am a lesbian or not, she says that it might be better for me if I do not marry. One of my aunts said it is better to have children but she says that to all the girls. Other than that, they do not pressure me at all.

Kazuko even has the support of her brother. She has told her parents that she is not too interested in marriage. They said if that is the case, it is fine. Also, her brother told her not to worry and just keep on doing whatever she wants and he can take up the role of having children and make their parents feel more settled and relieved. Others are less fortunate and feel varying degrees of pressure to marry heterosexually. Most women deal with such pressure by just ignoring it, but others apparently feel pressured enough to seek heterosexual marriage and/or change their plans to move in with their woman partner.

Sanae and Kayo have been living together for almost ten years, and yet Sanae's mother still constantly mentions marriage. She is not against them living together, working together and so on, and does get along well with Kayo, treating her as one of the family. However, she seems to consider marriage as something separate from their relationship. While it seems that she is acknowledging and indeed endorsing their relationship, she also undercuts it by the constant mention of marriage. Sanae's brother and father reminded her mother that 'if Sanae gets married, Kayo cannot come by and see them as frequently as she does now'. Upon hearing this, she stopped talking about marriage, only to resume before long. As Sanae easily gets upset by her mother these days, her mother has been avoiding her, but basically the issue of marriage – expectations and resistance – has not been resolved.

Yuko is a little different from Sanae as she has told her parents that she likes women and that there was somebody she was interested in at that time. The parents listened, but seemed to have forgotten it a few months later as they brought up marriage. Yuko and Yoshiko have been in a relationship for three years, and yet Yuko has introduced Yoshiko as a friend but not as a partner, which Yoshiko was not happy about. As Yuko has reached 30, her mother is rather relentless about marriage, and the pressure extends even to Yuko's partner, Yoshiko.

> Yuko: These days, every time I see them, they ask me when I am getting married.
>
> Yoshiko: Yes, they seem to look at our relationship as a faked friendship of sorts, and are waiting for us to be done with it. . . . It seems that they think this [liking women] and that [marriage] are separate things. It is fine to be interested in girls but you will get married, right? That type of attitude they have.
>
> Yuko: It was quite shocking the other day.
>
> Yoshiko: Yes, when we visited them, suddenly, we were told that we should think about marriage seriously. Even I was told that. Even my parents do not say that to me, so I was really angry.

While Yuko's parents seem to consider 'marriage' in itself as important, others are concerned about the daughter's financial situation or children, as in Setsuko and Kumiko's case. Kumiko has been pressured to marry for a while, which consisted in going through *omiai* as well. Even her partner Setsuko, who is divorced, is being asked to remarry since she will be financially better off with a man.

In these few examples, the women tried to ignore the pressure. Others might find the pressure strong enough to consider marrying a man, as in Machiko's case:

> I have been told quite strongly that I should get married. I have been asked to come back home. And it seems that they think I am going with a man. And it was after I started to see my current girlfriend that I thought about faked marriage and I am seeing three gay men with an intention to find a partner for faked marriage, so I picked one of them and talk about him as if he were my real boyfriend.

Settling down

Whether women are dealing with the pressure to marry or not, many do settle down with their partner. For some, the decision was almost a non-decision – settling down together took a natural course – and for others, the circumstances were such that living together was desirable. In recounting the development of their relationship, Sachi said:

> We started to see each other, but we lived far apart. It took so long to go see each other, and it was getting troublesome. We said to each other, it is getting really hard. We felt so natural to be together. In a way, it was strange that we were not staying together. Maybe we should stay together, we thought. . . .

And they did, in an apartment Sachi's mother owns. For Mutsuko, Sachi's partner, it was the right time with the right person:

> I did not think about living with anyone though I wanted to come out and have a lover. I did not want interference with my life and I am kind of selfish so I thought I could not live with anyone. My previous girlfriend did ask me to live with her but I turned it down. But with Sachi, the timing was right – it was when I was really feeling lonely and also, with her, I felt at ease.

Setsuko and Kumiko decided to live together soon after they started a relationship, at the time when Setsuko divorced. Realizing that she wanted to live as a lesbian, she chose to live with a woman as her partner. Since Setsuko had nowhere to go upon the divorce, she moved into Kumiko's place. For Yoshiko, it was Yuko's psychological condition which made her feel that she should be near her in order to give her support. At that time, Yuko was having difficulties at work. Since both of them were living on their own already, it was just a matter of finding a place convenient for both of them. They decided on the area and found a place in a day or so. In Hisako and Junko's case, both were thinking about leaving home. Hisako's father was going out with a woman, and Hisako asked him to live with his girlfriend at their home while she planned to move out of it. Junko had never left home, and always wanted to, particularly now that she was in her thirties. The timing was right for both, but it turned out to be quite difficult for Junko to leave home because of her mother's objection – in Junko's mother's world, the only time a woman leaves her parents' home is when she gets married.

Deciding to live together means having to deal with the practical issue of finding a place to settle down. There could be financial problems, given the exceedingly high real estate prices in Tokyo and other cities in Japan. At times, women struggle with not having a full-time job, as in Madoka and Rio's case. A bigger problem, however, except for those who have moved out of their parents' home already, was having to 'justify' the move to their family of origin. At the same time, moving out and living together could also make the (lesbian) relationship more 'visible', and provoke various reactions from their parents and other people.

The process of finding a place to settle down was as easy as Sachi's decision to share a life with her partner, Mutsuko. Her mother owned an apartment and Sachi just rented it from her, and after a while, even the rent became flexible. Sachi's parents do not seem to be conscious of Sachi and Mutsuko being a lesbian couple; they simply do not talk about it. Sachi had explicitly mentioned to her mother about her being 'one of those' and her mother told her father that Sachi is a *rezu* (a derogatory term for 'lesbian'), but they did not really discuss it. At the same time, Sachi and Mutsuko are close to Sachi's parents and they even travel together every now and then. Also, whenever Sachi's mother goes overseas, she gets things for both of them: 'I don't know exactly how they actually think or feel, but at least, they seem to think of us as a "set".' Here we see another example of tacit understanding and acceptance by parents of the couple's relationship, without an explicit discussion of the daughter's sexuality.

Mayumi and Yasuko likewise did not have much trouble finding a place to settle down. Both of them had been living away from their parents already, and so it was first a matter of Mayumi moving into

Yasuko's place, and then finding a place together. Since Yasuko had a stable full-time job, they did not encounter any problem looking for an apartment. They did mention that some real estate offices were not so good, but they had enough options to disregard those with a 'poor attitude'. Others were treated 'positively' by the real estate agent. For example, when they moved out, Sanae and Kayo's agent even said that it was great that they were both women – they kept the place clean. Their story is not unusual – most couples who managed to move out and were able to afford living on their own had no problem finding a place to rent. Some agents might comment on the possibility of one party getting married and, hence, moving out soon – common remarks made not only by real estate agents – but this was not a serious impediment. Further, there is no shortage of agents. As long as each person can provide a credible guarantor, two women can find a place to rent. However, even if one has left home years before settling down with a partner, this does not guarantee that parents will not react negatively or object to the move.

For some the fear of being 'found out' or not accepted was strong enough to prevent them from living together with their girlfriend. Machiko was ready to live together, but her girlfriend was reluctant. It seems that not being able to gain understanding from her mother dominates Machiko's girlfriend's behaviour and plans:

> For her, her mother has the absolute say. She does not want her mother to find out [about her being a lesbian or being with another woman], though she actually knows. . . . And she is also pursing the possibility of 'faked marriage'. But she begins to be concerned about the hassle of living together with a man [should she really get married that way].

Others who went ahead and lived together with their partner also had to deal with parental reactions. When Hiroko moved in with Chise, Chise's mother was suspicious of Hiroko – she was afraid that Hiroko was trying to cheat Chise and would take things from her place, and so on. Other parents see some value in the mutual support two women can provide each other. Kazuko and Fumiko's parents, for example, endorsed their living together in Tokyo. However, they have not told any of the family members that they are actually partners, even though they have been together for almost ten years. Yet others have convenient 'camouflage' that they use. For example, when Kumiko and Setsuko started living together, Setsuko had just had a divorce. Thus it appeared to others that Kumiko was helping Setsuko, an acceptable justification for both Kumiko's and Setsuko's families. Kumiko added that while she had experienced 'strange gazes' when she lived with other women, it did not happen with Setsuko since she had been married once, and, also, she does not look like 'that type of person'. Rather, Setsuko 'looks the type that would have no problem finding a man'.

Still other parents were simply perplexed as to why their daughters needed to leave home before marriage, against the culturally institutionalized practice. Kumiko's mother is one example. Kumiko therefore used her workplace as the major reason for the move – her new place would ease her commuting journey, even if she were relocated to a different store. But even with that, her mother said marriage could solve such problems too. Kumiko ended up leaving home as if she were running away, just taking with her what she could at that moment. Similarly, Eri's parents never accepted her moving out and living with 'a friend':

> I don't think they have accepted it, especially my father, but then, I had some severe stress-related psychological symptoms. Because of that, they tended to tiptoe around me and felt that they had to let me do whatever I want to. I knew my mother was feeling somewhat uncomfortable but she had to agree with me. My father objected to the end, though. . . . But now, when I go back there, they treat me like a guest, asking me what I want to eat, whether I want to take a bath first or to have dinner first. In a way, it makes me feel a bit sad [that I am now treated like a guest and not their daughter].

Others experienced a gradual acceptance by parents, at times aided by other relatives who put in a good word or two. In Junko's case, it was her aunt. As Junko's mother got progressively more ill, her partner, Hisako, also helped in taking care of her. Before she died, she did thank Hisako indirectly and asked Junko to send Hisako her regards. From her aunt, Junko later learned that her mother said something to the effect that she did not know what her daughter was trying to do, what type of life she was trying to live, and so on, but she wanted her daughter to do whatever she wanted to do. Upon hearing this, Junko felt relieved – she had felt that her mother did not accept her sexuality, and this did bother her. However, after all, her mother apparently did understand, at least to some extent, so it was comforting to her. After

Junko's mother died and Hisako went to help with various things, the same aunt went over to Hisako and said, 'Junko seems to really trust you. Please take care of her.'

Kumiko's mother seems to enjoy Setsuko, her partner, as a 'daughter'. As Kumiko puts it:

> Setsuko would put make-up on for my mother, and since I myself am not so feminine, she is happy to have a 'daughter' like this. Picking clothes together, and so on, they can relate to one another as a mother and a daughter.

At times, Kumiko's mother even asks Setsuko to marry Kumiko's brother! Hiroko also feels that she is like an additional daughter to Chise's mother and Chise feels that her mother affirms their relationship:

> Yes, so I told her when I got our place. Right now, it is under my name so that things will be approved more quickly, but in reality, we think we each own half. So I think my mother thinks that I consider Hiroko as my lifetime partner (although I do not plan to 'come out').

Hiroko adds:

> In a way, among all the siblings, we are the closest to Chise's parents. We take them out for meals, we travel together, we go to karaoke, and so on. I think they feel easy being with us.

Here we see another example of tacit understanding and acceptance by parents of the couple's relationship without an explicit discussion of the daughter's sexuality. Hiroko's own siblings, however, have various reactions:

> I told my sisters when I was going to live with her. The oldest one just could not take it. But the second sister sent me a message that she hoped that we would be happy and she would pray for us and that any time we want to, we can go back there, and so on. The other two did not say anything. But they at times send us stuff, and upon my mother's death, they also gave us her mementoes, and so on. So I feel that they are being supportive in their way.

In deciding to live together, lesbian couples both benefit and suffer from being women in a heterosexist society. Setsuko's divorcee status, for example, surprisingly gives her and her partner a status in a heterosexist society denied to never-married women – who might be looked upon as being 'undesirable', and hence not being 'able' to get married. That she has had a man once and is visibly so feminine helps camouflage her lesbian relationship. However, even when two women living together gain the acceptance of the people around them, as in Sanae and Kayo's case, a recognition of the relationship as permanent and 'real', replacing heterosexual marriage, may be harder to come by. Leaving home itself can pose a problem, as Eri and Junko's experiences show, even with a stable full-time job. This is a problem shared by single women in general. However, being lesbians and partnered, some experience anxiety and others have to provide extra justification to their parents. Also, if they have no intention of disclosing the 'lesbian' part of the relationship, there is always a fear of being 'found out'. Parents could ignore the women's disclosure of their sexual orientation, whether communicated directly or indirectly. They could also accept the partner of their daughter as another daughter, hence endorsing the relationship, without accepting the 'lesbian' part of the relationship or changing the expectation that the daughter will marry a man one day.

Conclusion

We looked at the processes whereby lesbians start and maintain a relationship in the context of a heterosexist society that is undergoing a number of changes that weaken heterosexist norms, such as delayed marriage and decline in the rate of marriage. This broader context makes it possible for lesbians to 'pass' and find a niche in society as 'single women', and probably helps lesbians identify with single (heterosexual) women; at the same time, such a niche also keeps lesbians invisible in society, and makes it difficult for individual lesbians to publicly share the fulfilment of living a life with a woman.

Their narratives illustrate the pleasure and the frustration of living a 'lesbian life' in Japan, in particular the joy and the anxiety of starting a relationship and bringing a partner into one's family of origin. While there are trials and tribulations in establishing a relationship, especially outside the lesbian community, our interview participants seem to experience more difficulty and anxiety in maintaining a relationship because one's relationship suddenly becomes 'visible', regardless of whether one has deliberately made it open or not. In a homosocial environment, two women's living together does not pose a pressing problem on a daily basis. The family's indirect acknowledgement or tacit acceptance of a couple's relationship seems valued and yet could also be a source of anxiety. A mother's obvious affection for one's partner could coexist with her constant pressure on both her daughter and her daughter's partner to get married. At the same time, when accepted, the partner is made into a daughter instead of a daughter-in-law, who remains an 'outsider' (*tanin*) in the Japanese context.

What all this suggests is that lesbians do 'extra work' to live the life they want, which could put a strain on the relationship. However, our interview participants also conveyed to us that successfully handling the stress can also become a source of strength. Overall, despite the quantitative and geographical limits of our sample, we can also see a lot of diversity in how they met, how they developed their relationships, how their families responded. Certainly a lot more can still be learned about these women, and what we have seen so far, and shared in this chapter, has been encouraging and inspiring.

Notes

1   This chapter is developed from a larger project exploring lesbian lives in Japan, including examinations of housework division, communities, and how they authenticate and negotiate their lesbianism (see Kamano 2004b, 2005a, 2005b; Kamano and Khor 2006). The interviewees were recruited through personal connections, community events, and the Internet, and among acquaintances of the people thus recruited.

2   Here the term lesbian is used specifically to refer to women who love women and who are not married to a man.

3   There are two methods by means of which same-sex partnerships might obtain some kind of legal bond: adoption and a contract signed by a notary public. Neither is without problems. See Maree 2004.

4   All the names are pseudonyms.

References

Atoh Makoto [阿藤誠] (2000) 現代人口学 (*Population Studies Today*). Tokyo: Nihonhyoronsha.

Horie, Yuri (2006a) 'Possibilities and limitations of "lesbian continuum": the case of the Protestant Church in Japan' in Diana Khor and Saori Kamano (eds), *'Lesbians' in East Asia: Diversity, Identities and Resistance*, New York: Haworth Press, pp. 145–59.

—— (2006b) 「レズビアン」という生き方-キリスト教の異性愛主義を問う

[*The Way of Living Called 'Lesbian': Questioning Heterosexism in Christianity*].
Tokyo: Shinkyo Shuppansha.

Kamano Saori [釜野さおり] (2004a) 独身男女の描く結婚像 ['Images of
marriage held by single men and women'] in Meguro Yoriko [目黒依子]
and Nishioka Hachiro [西岡八郎] (eds), 少子化のジェンダー分析 [*Gender
Analysis of the Declining Birthrate*]. Tokyo: Keisoshobou, pp. 78–106.

—— (2004b) 'レズビアンカップルとゲイカップル—社会環境による日常
生活の相違 ['Lesbian couples and gay couples: effect of social environment
on daily lives'] in Kyoko Yoshizumi [善積京子] (ed.), スウェーデンの家
族とパートナー関係 [*Families and Partner Relationships in Sweden and Japan*].
Tokyo: Aoki Shoten, pp. 117–43.

—— (2005a) 'Housework in lesbian couples in Japan: its division, interpretation
and negotiation', paper presented at 'Women's Worlds 2005: 9th International
Interdisciplinary Congress on Women', Seoul, Korea (22 June).

—— (2005b) 'Doing "couples" in lesbian communities and doing "lesbian
couples" in Japanese society', paper presented at 'Sexualities, Genders and
Rights in Asia: First International Conference of Asian Queer Studies',
Bangkok, Thailand (8 July).

—— (2005c) 'Entering the lesbian world in Japan: debut stories', *Journal of Lesbian
Studies*, 9 (1/2): 11–30.

Kamano Saori and Diana Khor (2006) '"Coming out" for lesbians in Japan:
meanings and implications', contribution to the panel on 'Multifaceted Lesbian
Lives in Japan Today', International Conference on LGBT Rights, First World
Outgames, 26–29 July, Montreal, Canada.

Maree, Claire (2004) 'Same-sex partnerships in Japan: bypasses and other
alternatives', *Women's Studies*, 33: 541–9.

—— (2007) 'The un/state of lesbian studies: an introduction to lesbian
communities and contemporary legislation in Japan', *Journal of Lesbian Studies*,
11 (3/4): 307–17.

National Institute of Population and Social Security Research (NIPSSR) (2007a)
Latest Demographic Statistics. Tokyo: NIPSSR.

—— (2007b) *Report on the Thirteenth Japanese National Fertility Survey, 2005,*
Volume II. Tokyo: NIPSSR.

Suganuma, Katsuhiko (2006) 'Enduring voices: Fushimi Noriaki and Kakefuda
Hiroko's continuing relevance to Japanese lesbian and gay studies and activism',
Intersections: Gender, History and Culture in the Asian Context, 14 (November
2006) <http://wwwsshe.murdoch,edu.au/intersections/issue14/suganuma.
htm>.

Welker, James (2004) 'Telling her story: narrating a Japanese lesbian community',
Japanstudien: Jahrbuch des Deutschen Instituts für Japanstudien 16: 119–44.

Yamada Masahiro [山田昌弘] (1999) パラサイトシングルの時代 [*Era of
Parasite Singles*]. Tokyo: Chikumashobo.

9 Chinese Women's Stories of Love, Marriage and Sexuality[1]

LI YINHE[2]

My study is based upon semi-structured in-depth qualitative interviews with 47 women in urban China, aged from 29 to 55 years. They were technical staff, teachers, company clerks, editors, journalists, doctors, accountants, artists, administrative cadres, military cadres, factory workers, service workers and freelancers. Most of them were educated women, with the majority having university educations. The wider study explores the various aspects of their love and sex lives, covering a range of topics including puberty, sex education, first love, heterosexuality, first kiss, pre-marital sex and sexual pleasure and desire. In this chapter, I focus on three aspects discussed in the interviews: love and sex, love and marriage, and sex and marriage.

Love and sex

The women interviewed held varied points of view on the relationship between love and sex, which generally speaking fell into three categories: love and sex are equally important and inseparable; love and sex are separable but love is more important than sex; love and sex are separable but equally valued.[3]

Only sex associated with love is acceptable
Quotes from interviewees included:

> I think sex and love go together. I completely object to one-night stands and sexual relationships without love; they are just like prostitution. I think such behaviour is bad for the body, morals and social values. They are based upon animal instincts, similar to taking drugs. I can't

178

understand those couples who don't get on with each other but have a good sex life.

Only when you love him, will you have sexual desire for him. I absolutely refuse to do that [having sex] if I don't feel for him. Some people sell sex for money. Human beings should not be like this, even when you are cornered in your life.

I can't accept sex without love. I totally object to sex relationships without love. I feel this is the basic difference between humans and animals. A human being must have love first and then release your sexual desire.

Sex must be based upon love. If you want to have sex with someone that you don't love, at least you have to like this person. It is impossible to have intercourse between a man and a woman without any force or feelings.

A doctor commented:

I have a lot of emotional demands. If I don't feel for someone, I absolutely don't have sexual desire for him. I have a few good male friends. When I hang out with them, I never have any sexual desire. At one time, one of them fell ill. I went to look after him at his home, washing his face and massaging him. But I have absolutely no sexual feeling, but he might have that feeling.

A woman who had divorced and had short-term sexual relationships with many men commented:

Sex and love are difficult to separate. I wish it could be separated so we could take life easy. For a woman, if she doesn't love someone, she can't accept a sexual relationship with him.

An interviewee who had known how to masturbate from very little said: 'Maybe because I knew this [masturbation] very early, I feel love is more important. I feel absolutely I can't do this [sexual intercourse] without feelings for him.' A woman who had no feelings for her husband talked about how she felt towards him when she had another man:

Since that [having sex with her lover], I found it hard to live with my husband. I didn't want to have sex with him. When he was doing that [having sex with me] I closed my eyes and it felt like being raped every night. Even up till now, I can't bear recalling the image of his head hanging on top of me; it is horrible! I can't understand those people who can have several sexual partners at the same time. At that time, I refused to let him touch me. When sleeping, I refused to take off my clothes. He was very angry and smashed the furniture, and was shouting. I couldn't live with him any longer. . . . In the end, I divorced him.

Another interviewee commented:

My idea about sex is to follow your emotions. If I'm not with someone, I don't often think about it [sex]. I believe in fate. When you are emotionally connected with the person, it is a pleasure; if not, it is not good. Doing this with a person you don't love feels like being raped.

One woman talked about the conflicts between her own viewpoints and her boyfriend's on love and sex:

He said to me, because of the social pressure, he couldn't enjoy the pleasure and excitement as he wanted. In foreign countries, prostitutes are allowed and in old society [pre-1949], concubines were allowed. He felt this reflected male biological demands. He felt sex and love were two different types of things. He said to me, 'You need to believe in me, I always love only you. If I go out and play with others [have sex], that's only for a change.' But I feel that sex and love are inseparable so we always fought over this point. He said 'Every [male] hero inside and outside China would feel the same way.'

Many women expressed the view that if they feel for someone, they will like sex; if not, sex life is dull and somewhat humiliating. One interviewee enjoyed having sex originally but when she did not have any feelings for her husband, she hated the sexual relationship with him. Another compared her sexual relationships with her ex-husband and with her lover:

I only first experienced pleasure from my lover. I felt the difference between those two sexual relationships is purely emotional. At that time I haven't watched those videotapes [pornography]. But whenever I was doing it with my lover, I always pulled my legs up. While doing it with my husband hundreds of times, I never did this. I never felt pleasure with my husband. When I was doing it with my lover, I could have that pleasure five or six times a night without any feelings of shame.

Another woman commented similarly: 'When I was doing it with my husband, I felt like a puppet; when I was doing it with my lover, I felt what it was to be a woman.' One interviewee had sex with a person she did not feel for in order to get over with her unrequited love for someone, but she recalled:

> During that period I tried to forget about him, I started to see other people. There was one who was more attractive than him. One day I stayed in his home and had sex with him. I felt terrible; I think it is because I didn't feel for him and maybe because I was still in love with the first man. Anyway, I felt it terribly bad. In the end, I couldn't become this man's lover nor could we become friends with each other.

The relationship between love and sex is reflected upon more vividly by some sensitive women interviewees. For example, one divorcee compared the relationship with her new boyfriend to that with her ex-husband whom she did not feel for:

> When I was doing it with my boyfriend, I didn't feel shy. Because he was completely into it, you felt it was great. This was the best ever since I have known the thing [sex] between men and women. I almost had orgasm every time I did it with him but in the past, I only had orgasm two or three times every ten times doing with my husband.

Some women felt that even if they were only having sex with one person, the state of the emotional relationship with that person would affect their feelings towards sex:

> Love is the priority. Sex and love are inseparable. Without love, you can't have sexual relationship. Even with the person I love, I can feel that. When we are in a good relationship, we can make love well. But when we have arguments, the intercourse feels comfortable but not that emotionally involved.

One woman who had decided to split up with her boyfriend said:

> I felt sex is closely connected with your emotions. At one time, I had a very good sexual relationship with my boyfriend. But later I found that he was not a very nice guy in terms of his personality. . . . Although he was good at sex and giving me pleasure, I didn't regret splitting up with him.

Many women felt that sex and love are inseparable and also should not be separated. One interviewee commented, 'Only when both love and understand each other deeply, can they reach a high level of harmony in their sex life'; another said: 'I feel that sex and emotional love are closely connected. Since I have given my heart to him, he can do anything with me.'

Some women became cold towards sex because of lack of feeling for their partners. However, once they changed the partner, they were passionate for sex again. One editor commented:

> I feel like I am fulfilling a duty. My husband asks to do it frequently so I just fulfil my duty. Sometimes I was deliberately doing editing in the evening to avoid that kind of thing [having sex]. In fact I am not cold towards sex. I have a lover. I want to do whatever he wants to do and enjoy doing it. I can't imagine that I could bear that marriage for so many years.

Another woman who was thought to be cold towards sex said: 'I am willing to do it with the man who can excite my emotions.' One woman who had to make a hard decision between two men said: 'I had been living with him. He was good at sex but there were more techniques than feelings. So emotionally I felt more attached to another man.' However, some women considered that emotional feelings and sex are equally important. As one put it, 'I felt in my relationship with him, the importance of love and sex is 50 per cent each.' A few interviewees felt that once they had a sexual relationship with someone, the emotional attachment would naturally follow:

> I had intercourse with him several times. I felt I needed to love him since I had already slept with him. But later he changed. I asked him whether he loved me or not. Once I said 'love' to him and asked his feelings. He was really rude, saying that I was nagging him. I felt extremely ashamed at that time. In the end, I wrote him a letter, saying that love is not a crime. He was so selfish and didn't know what love was.

One woman recalled her experience with her lover to illustrate that to have a sexual relationship first would lead to an emotional change: 'When I had sex with him, I at first took him as my husband. Gradually I felt emotionally attached to him.'

Some women felt that love was important but life without sex was not good either. One said, 'Pure emotional love is not possible. The two [love and sex] are inseparable, although having sex is not the only way to express love.'

Love is more important than sex

Nowadays people say, sex follows behind love. But in my opinion, love without sex is acceptable while sex without love is unacceptable. Sex with love is beautiful; sex without love is ugly and evil.

Another woman commented: 'I like the feeling of being loved. It doesn't matter whether we make love or not. The emotional satisfaction is most important.' A doctor who had a marital crisis said: 'If my husband and I had problems in our sex life, we could go to see the doctor; but if our love was in crisis, there was hardly a cure for it.'

A divorcee said of her ex-husband: 'Our sex life was no problem . . . but he was from a peasant family and couldn't understand I had emotional needs.' Another interviewee saw it like this:

Comparing sex with love, the need for love will be much greater than that for sex. But humans are sometimes shameless; when you become horny, you just want it. I've had sexual relationships with men once or twice by accident. But afterwards I felt this had destroyed our friendship. I think we should promote the substitution of sex toys so that people won't do silly things just because of desire.

One sensitive and highly educated woman had different ideas from others:

If I love someone in particular, I won't have sex with him because I am afraid of demeaning our relationship after that. I always feel that things get messy if sex comes in. Later as I grew older and read so many books about this, I thought I should try it [having sex]. My principle is that if I love someone, I won't have sex with him; but if I don't love him, I will have sex with him. So I have had sex with one or two men. One of them really liked me and wanted to get married to me . . . but he didn't succeed.

Another woman had a similar perspective but from another angle: 'With men I liked, once I had sex with them, I would be emotionally involved and lose control. So I prefer to keep a physical distance and avoid having sex with the man I really like.'

Some women get used to a relationship where there is no or little sex involved. After marriage, love and sex need not necessarily be in agreement with each other. In other words, love and sex are neither necessary nor sufficient conditions for each other. For example, one couple lived apart for a long time and had virtually no sex life, but the wife said 'Living apart doesn't affect our feelings for each other.' Another woman took her parents' experience as an example to show that a sexless relationship does not affect emotional feelings:

> My parents lived apart for over twenty years and did not get together until they retired but they were always in love with each other. They were high-school mates and paid great attention to the education of children. The reason why they lived apart is because there wasn't a good school where my father worked. For our future, my mother and us kids stayed and didn't follow him.

It is a common belief that sex is extremely important to a relationship and indispensable. Generally speaking, this might be correct, but from the study of individual cases, we can see some examples that contradict this view. For example, from the way a woman who had a very good relationship with her husband talked about her sex life we can see that sex is not absolutely important; in other words, people can maintain a good and stable marital relationship in the absence of sexual desire and activity. This woman (aged over 50) commented:

> Sometimes he suggested doing it, but I couldn't do it (health reasons). He became angry and then lost his desire. I felt that I never had this kind of desire. But sometimes I had dreams where I felt a kind of pleasure such as my heart beating and feeling wet lower down. The man in my dreams looks like my husband but sometimes someone else or a man in an abstract form. But I feel in my real life that I don't have any desire for him. Whenever I am totally aware of our doing it, I feel passive and don't like it. Although I didn't have many bad feelings, the proportion of good feelings is small and I always felt worried about being pregnant. So we always used a condom and as a result of that, he didn't like doing it either. In the end he gave up trying as well. It is a pity that I did this too little in my life. In another life, I probably will ask for more.

A sexual relationship without love is acceptable
An educated woman thought there was an increasing trend towards sexual relationships without love, though she was opposed to this. She said that 'If not connected emotionally, pure biological pleasure doesn't have any deep meaning. But this kind of thing is not uncommon among artists and scholars.'

A woman who had had many sexual partners held that sex and love are completely separable:

> I met a man and did it several times; now I almost couldn't leave him physically. He took this easy. I felt that he was inspirational to my sexuality. I had orgasm with him every time. Ever since the encounters with him, I have had good feelings towards having sex. So I feel that sex and emotional love are separable. I feel grateful to him because he helped me build up a healthy attitude towards sexuality.

In the relationship between love and sex, however, women are more likely to put the emphasis on emotional love than men. This is a common belief in China and was also confirmed by my research. I suggest that it is a result of a double standard of morality. It seems that only men can be allowed to have sex with strangers. By contrast, a woman who gets involved in similar things is considered dirty and disgraceful. Internalizing this view to the extreme made some women accept a relationship with love but no sex so that they would still be 'good women'. However, at the other extreme, some women accept sexual relationship without emotions but become 'bad women'. Thus women hold three positions: that sex and emotional love should coexist; that love can survive without sex; that sexual relationship are possible without love.

Emotional feelings and marriage

Women's comments on the relationship between emotional feelings and marriage fall mainly into the following categories: seeking marriage with emotional love; pursuing love in marriage rather than being unmarried; or accepting a loveless marriage.

Aspiring to a marital life with love
A woman whose parents are highly educated intellectuals married a young man who was born in rural China.

When I chose my partner, I didn't comply with the traditional norms. Of course I'd hoped to be matched in terms of family background, but this is not necessary. On several occasions, I had the chance to go abroad [as an accompanying wife], I gave it all up. I won't consider marriage without emotional love.

A woman who was on bad terms with her husband said:

It would be great joy to be with a person you like in your life, but this situation is rare. Most people are just living together. The one you like doesn't necessarily like you. If you can't find such a soul mate, you will feel very lonely. So I feel only a minority live happily but the majority don't. It is very hard to find one you like who also likes you as a soul mate. I'd prefer to be single than married to a person who I don't love. Were it not for giving birth to a child, I'd have chosen to be single.

Another woman commented: 'If a woman just wants to find a man for marriage, that's easy. A three-legged toad is hard to find but a two-legged man is easy to find. But that's boring; people should have feelings in marriage.'

By contrast, some people set marriage against love, as the common understanding holds that 'marriage is the grave of love'. A woman who had had several flings commented: 'The institution of marriage destroys love.' Another woman recalled that her lover also held a similar attitude but she was quite critical of it:

He was a widower. We had gone out for several years. He felt that I was the most talented among the women he knew. However, he never linked love to marriage. Instead, he perceived marriage as a means: in the end he got married to a Western woman [so as to go abroad].

Being single because of failure to find love
Some women remain single because they have failed to find love. For those whose personality is sensitive, their process of pursuing love is difficult and the hope of success is very slight. One woman who joined a singles' club said:

In the singles' club, there are those who have never married and those who are divorced. Some members who have a very specific goal, to get married, are boring. But as for those who have no goals at all, there is no point in going out with them, either. Society always thinks that we are single because we are too picky. At the age of 24, when

I graduated from the university, I had many chances but didn't meet anyone suitable. I feel that 80 to 90 per cent of families make do with each other. I don't want to comply with everybody else. Perhaps I will be single for the rest of my life: either I will find a companion when I am old or get married to a man (anyone will do) after 40 when I give up hope of love.

A divorcee who remained single for many years said:

I don't like matchmaking. I feel that two people can only get married when they are deeply in love with each other. I feel that one must fall in love and then get married. Once I expressed my ideas to my cousin; he looked at me dumbfounded, saying: 'How old are you? Still as naïve as a teenage girl!'

A woman who had been deeply in love but had failed to get married in the end recalled:

Among my sisters and brothers, all found their partners on their own, perhaps under the influence of my parents who got to know each other by themselves. So I didn't like the matchmaking method. I am not lacking in friends; even when I went to the cinema, there would be friends available to go with me. But I wonder if I still can find my soul mate. I am concerned I will never experience that passion again.

Another single woman said that matchmaking 'felt mechanical' and that she didn't meet anyone she liked. She said. 'I don't feel like having a partner at the moment but I feel the pressure to have one, so have to do it as a task.'[4]

A different view was expressed by a woman who was currently looking for re-marriage:

I tried to find love but nowadays you couldn't be that pure, only thinking of love. You have to take into account economic conditions, for example, whether he had a house, had any children. I know this is boring but I didn't want to get hurt again and nor did I want to be single for the rest of my life. But what can you do about it?

Marriage without love

Among the interviewees, there was a woman who was married but found no love. Everyone's life is a story: the tone of some stories is happy, some are bitter, some are relaxed, some are heavy, some are passionate, some are quite ordinary. Although this woman's story is ordinary, I found that her experience was the most tragic. Its tragedy was further intensified by its peaceful surface. This story is about an excellent man and an excellent woman. Although they got married and had lived together for most of their lives they could not fall in love with each other. Certainly there are thousands and thousands of marriages without love; however, the tragedy of this story lies in the fact that both of them are very sensitive and hold a very clear distinction between the feeling of love and the feeling of being without love. If they had acted less sensitively, just like other couples who were not in love with each other, the degree of their tragedy would have been much less. Below is her narrative:

> I get on with him much better now. He used to love me but I couldn't feel for him. At that time I didn't have any experience; it was my best girl friend that made the decision to go out with him for me. I like men who I can worship in terms of career achievement but he worships me. If at the start he hadn't shown his devotion so obviously and instead been tough to me, I might have felt better towards him. At that time, he kept asking me: do you love me? I said yes. How could I say no? But in fact, I didn't feel for him at all. It doesn't mean that I never felt for someone in my life but I never had feelings for him. Often small things I said would hurt him very much. I tried to cultivate feelings towards him but I failed. When he was deeply in love with me, he was so jealous and possessive. Whenever I went to meet some male friend, he would feel badly hurt. . . . At that time he was madly in love with me but I just couldn't feel for him. Gradually his passion cooled down. At first I couldn't believe and accept the fact. In the end, I did realize that he was no longer in love with me. Once he said to me: nothing in his life left any happy memory. He burnt all the letters I wrote to him and that he used to cherish. He said to me that he couldn't blame me for not loving him because love was uncontrollable. From then on, he never blamed me and never questioned me. He is a very good man. I feel nowadays that I almost can't be without him. I am grateful for the decision made by someone else for me because I feel that one needs career development in addition to sexual needs. Nowadays I am looking after him in daily life and he feels like a life companion to me. His need for me is only based upon the fact that I am a woman rather than myself now.

A divorcee who found no love in her long-term marriage but enjoyed love in her extra-marital affair held a unique attitude towards the relationship between marriage and love: on the one hand, she pursued romantic love and considered it as a necessary condition for marriage, yet felt it was impractical; on the other hand, she aspired to be a happy couple and attached great importance to marriage. She said: 'I know that my dream is not realistic but I still hold romantic dreams. Although I am very old now, I haven't enjoyed any time as a happy couple.'

A woman who was about to get divorced said:

> I feel that marriage shouldn't be like this. We two almost said nothing to each other in the evening, not more than five or six sentences. Sometimes I didn't feel anything towards him and I felt unhappy whenever I saw him. At those moments, I even didn't want to touch that half of the bed he had slept on and anything he wore. I never washed his clothes for him.

One divorcee recalled the moment when she got married:

> We never felt for each other, no love at all. We got married because of the environment, especially the pressure from the family. They always looked at me anxiously, saying that the higher my qualifications were, the more difficult it would be to find a partner. My previous dating experience always affected me so in the end I agreed to be married to him.

Other women tended to relate their own experiences to others and thus became very pessimistic. For example, one woman whose marital life was not happy said:

> I feel that all other couples are also like this. I don't believe there are any happy ones. Perhaps the happy ones are only 10 per cent, maybe even 1 per cent. So I am just among the others, nothing to complain about.

One divorcee recalled her experience: when she got married, her status was a cadre and her family were intellectuals, whilst her husband was only a worker and her father-in-law was once an imprisoned capitalist. She said:

> Now I understand the traditional principle of being suited to each other in marriage. When I got married, I didn't think of it too much and never looked down upon him. In retrospect, I feel that we differed in many things from the start. For example, he was picky with food but I always felt that nutrition was enough. My major is in fine arts but

whenever I painted, he found it annoying. So we didn't get on with each other at all. I really hate him because I feel that I've given him a lot of time but in the end still got divorced.

Another woman who is now divorced after a re-marriage admitted that she had not married because of love:

We got together through a matchmaker. I had a child and he had two children. We got married for two reasons: first, he was divorced so I felt we had common experiences for communication; second, I was a bit selfish – he was an English teacher so I felt getting married to him would benefit my child's education. And also I felt that we got on with each other so I agreed to be married to him.

One woman formed an unhappy marriage because of her soft-heartedness:

Before marriage I had implicitly expressed that I wanted to break up. Every time he was so upset. During the second time when I tried to break up, he wrote a letter in his blood and drew a heart. I was really frightened. At that time my circumstances were not great; I was from the countryside and my family background was not very good. But he was so insistent and refused all the other introductions. From that letter in blood, I decided to be committed to him. Later I went to the university and he also waited for me for several years. So I had no reason for not marrying him. I got married to him as soon as I graduated. I had a simple wedding and felt cold about it. Although his work unit and family background were excellent, I felt little emotionally.

One divorcee had also agreed to get married out of sympathy, which led to unhappiness in the end:

At that time we got on with each other very well. But I only felt we were getting on well, nothing about love. At the time when he went to serve in the army, he expressed his desire to go out with me. My first response was no, because I felt that I was too young and also that such a thing was dirty. Several days later when I saw him, he seemed upset and even ignored me. I was sympathetic towards him so agreed to be with him. Even when we wrote to each other while he was in the army, we didn't know what love was. We only wrote about each other's experiences and felt calm when we read each other's letters. I hardly felt any happiness or passion. I just felt I was entering a role and that I should enter this role.

Another woman regretted not choosing more carefully:

I was dating when I was 22 and felt it was boring. He was six years older than me, introduced by an acquaintance. He was tall and good-looking. He was very keen on me. At that time, I didn't know very much and thought, since he initiated it, I should just go out with him. If I had been in the current era, I would have known that common interests mattered more. He didn't like talking, so when we were together it was really boring.

A survey in the former Soviet Union showed that marriage formed on the basis of love was more likely to be unhappy. This survey seems to confirm the statement that marriage is the grave of love. My explanation is that the romantic colour of love comes into conflict with the greyness of marital life. Accordingly, my question is whether people should pursue a marriage with love or be satisfied with a marriage without love. My study showed that some people did find love. I also did a survey with citizens in Beijing on their marital life. Almost half of the participants claimed that they loved their partner very much and their partner loved them very much, and that they were thus satisfied with their marital life. I feel that no matter how pessimistic people felt about the relationship between love and marriage (the majority have had an unhappy marital life) and no matter how difficult their pursuit of a marriage with love was, a marital life with love is always something they desire, and the reality is not as hard to find as people have imagined.

Sex and marriage

The common understanding is that sex life is the most important element that affects the quality of marital life. Does the reality reflect this? My study shows that some women hold different views on this point. Although many people consider sex an important reason for a marital life, sex is not necessarily the most important thing in marriage. Some women even consider that a sex life separable from marriage is more enjoyable.

Sex is an important foundation for marital life
One woman said: 'The basis of love is biological need, an expression of basic instinct. I agree with a Western lecturer when I was

in the university. I asked her what marriage meant to her. She replied, sex.'

> We were back together several times. During a period, he couldn't get it up during making love. I helped him to get it up. He was dependent upon me and felt that I was better than him at sex. Later he decided to marry me. I felt his decision was related to sex in a way.

A woman who was working in a hotel also felt that sex life was related to desire for marriage. But she interpreted it through a different logic. Judging from her girlfriends, she concluded that girls who had had sexual experiences all wanted to get married. She said that she had several boyfriends and one of her relationships had lasted for almost four years. She felt that 'people should enjoy it when they are young. After experiencing all things, people should settle down.' She admitted that she particularly wanted to get married after playing around.

Sex is not necessarily the most important element in marriage
Some hold that a good sex life is the most important component of marriage, but my findings contradict this. In many marital relationships, the couple do not have a good sex life, but they still have a happy life together because of their emotional feelings towards each other. For example, one woman recalled that her husband could not give her orgasm after many years of marriage and she had to rely on herself. However, at the same time she said that she was satisfied emotionally because she knew that her husband was kind to her and she was willing to live with him until death. This shows that in terms of marital stability, sex life is not a decisive factor. A woman who had a long-distance relationship with her husband said:

> We hardly spent any time together. At one time, my husband found it hard to bear, which was a torture to his body. But he was very serious in sex matters and could not bear having sex with another woman. In the end, he had to solve it by himself. We talked about divorce several times just because of this. But after talks we hardly put it into action. So after a while, we were back together.

She added: 'In a marital relationship, time plays an important role. The things that accumulate in a marriage as time goes by are difficult to give up.'

A sex life separable from marriage is enjoyable

A divorcee compared sex life within marriage and extra-marital affairs:

> We sometimes had sex as lovers after we got divorced. Within marriage, once in ten times I had one orgasm. By contrast, outside marriage, I had nine orgasms every ten times. I felt this was because sex within marriage was like a duty. But now sex was a need, a mutual need. He is now seeing someone but he comes to see me behind her back. He comes to see me almost every month.

A single woman claimed that 'Whether I get married or not is not important; the important thing is to have a sexual partner.'

In marriage, sex is an important factor, but it is not as necessary as people would imagine, at least among some people. Among some 'conservative' people, sex is considered as something that a marital life can include or not. Among some 'fashionable' women, sex outside marriage seems more attractive. Judging from both groups, it seems that they both separate sex from marriage. I would suggest that as Chinese society opens up, the social norms that consider sex within marriage as the only legal channel are becoming less and less restrictive; the social constraints on pursuing happiness via one's body are weakening, and thus social opinions on sexual morality are becoming increasingly tolerant.

Conclusion: love, marriage, sex and morality

Morality changes according to time and space, although time-bound human beings find this hard to accept and imagine. For example, in ancient China, men and women who met before marriage went against the morality of the time. In contemporary China, dating before marriage has become a common practice without infringing morality. Furthermore, cohabitation before marriage has become a choice of the majority in Western European countries. However, in Chinese society, cohabitation before marriage is still seen as immoral. In sum, there is no universal norm on the relationships between love, marriage and sex; there is no universal moral norm. We can only try to find the most reasonable arrangement to minimize harm rather than try to punish anybody.

Notes

1 This chapter is based on my book, *Chinese Women's Viewpoints on Feelings and Sex* [中国女性的情感与性] (1998).
2 Translated by Liu Jieyu and edited by Woo Juhyun and Stevi Jackson.
3 There are, though, considerable variations within these three categories.
4 Editors' note: for a discussion of the matchmaking culture in China and the pressures to marry see Liu (2004).

References

Li Yinhe ［李银河］ （1998) *Chinese Women's Viewpoints on Feelings and Sex* [*zhongguo nvxing de qinggan yu xin*, 中国女性的情感与性]. Beijing: Today's China Publishing House [今日中国出版社].

Liu Jieyu (2004) 'Hold up the sky? Reflections on marriage in contemporary China', *Feminism and Psychology*, 14 (1): 195–202.

10 Talking about 'Good Sex': Hong Kong Women's Sexuality in the Twenty-first Century

ANNE HAU-NUNG CHAN

Hong Kong is a significant site for the study of social and cultural processes for two main reasons. First, Hong Kong culture is often cited as a unique blend of 'East meets West', where elements of traditional Chinese culture coexist with Western values and ways of life (Evans and Tam 1997), thereby providing an excellent background for the examination of cultural change and adaptation. Second, rapid economic growth in the decades after World War Two. has led to highly compressed social and economic development, making Hong Kong an interesting place to study processes and mechanisms of social change (McDonogh and Wong 2005). It is therefore no surprise that studies on family and gender in Hong Kong are solidly situated within these contexts. During the early colonial years women were treated as the inferior sex, bounded by the Chinese patriarchal family and economic dependence (Jaschok and Miers 1992), and so studies on this period typically focus on women's subjugated status in the family and society. In this vein, Hong Kong women were very much studied *as* Chinese women, in the Chinese family, in a Chinese society. But as the status of women changed rapidly in the latter half of the twentieth century, differences between Hong Kong's Chinese women and their mainland counterparts grew apparent (Shih 2001); with this, their status as 'Chinese women' has evolved somewhat. Industrialization and the implementation of nine-year universal education in 1978 have had far-reaching consequences for women's economic independence and social and familial status (Salaff 1981). The modern Hong Kong nuclear family values equality and individual rights, and women today are often portrayed as having a higher social status than ever (Cheung

195

1997). The enactment of ordinances opposing discrimination on the basis of sex or family status in 1995, the establishment of the Equal Opportunities Commission (1996) and the Women's Commission (2001) further the impression that women's rights are well-protected. Although studies have shown that the magnitude of such progress is somewhat exaggerated (see Chan and Wong 2004; Chan 2006; Chu 1997; Lau, Ma and Chan 2006; Lee 1995), there is little doubt that Hong Kong has seen great improvements in women's life chances. With increased opportunities in education and paid work, it is easier for women to become economically independent. And with the nuclear family being today's norm, women's place in the family household has also changed. With a consistently low total fertility rate (0.9 in 2006), the hegemony of procreative heterosexuality is facing unprecedented challenges. Older women's plight was obviously a world apart from that of today's young women (Association for the Advancement of Feminism 1998, 2002).

How do these compressed and far-reaching socio-cultural changes affect the private lives of women? In traditional Chinese societies, women's sexuality has always been more about danger than pleasure (Dikotter 1995; Evans 1997). Patriarchy demands women's sexuality to service the social reproduction of (male) inheritors of property and power. Non-reproductive sex (and women) were cast outside the boundaries of acceptability. Despite the many changes that have occurred in Hong Kong and mainland China in the past fifty years or so, women who demand sex for pleasure are far less socially acceptable than those who demand equal opportunities in education and the workplace. The normalizing of the marginalization of women's sexualities has resulted in limited space for alternative female sexualities (non-heterosexual, non-dyadic, non-coitus-centred) to develop. The only exception is perhaps exemplified by the emergence of lesbian groups, which have managed to bring issues of female sexuality to greater public visibility. But compared to gay men's groups their voices are still relatively muted.

Although Hong Kong is a sexually conservative society, the mass media are going through a process of 'pornografication'.[1] Images of sexualized women posing alluringly or innocently fill the pages of weekly glossies and tabloids, advertisements and billboards. In these depictions, the sexual desirability (not desire) of women rests on the shapes and sizes of their body parts and their varying degrees of exposure. Ironically, women have become desexualized by the media's treatment, as their visibility as sexual *subjects* is masked (Attwood 2002; Chan 2007). In these representations women's job is to service desires and pleasures, not to possess them (Vance 1992). How do these representations compare with the 'real' picture of Hong Kong women's sexuality? While studies have been done, most were designed from a health or family planning perspective. The Family Planning Association (FPA) has conducted several surveys on women's sexuality, but they are either targeted at young people or focused on knowledge and practices related to sexual health (Hong Kong Family Planning Association 1986, 1991, 1997, 2001, 2002). The general picture gathered from these surveys was that more young people were having sex earlier,[2] but their knowledge about sex was deteriorating.[3] Other non-government organizations have also conducted surveys on sex but they mostly focus on behavioural and attitudinal aspects of sex (Breakthrough 1994; Christian Family Service Centre 1999; Chung and Mak 1995; Yeung and Kwong 1997).

Surveying sex in Hong Kong

Our survey was conducted by the Association for the Advancement of Feminism (AAF) with the aim of exploring how women's sexualities have adjusted and responded to rapid, compressed social change.[4] The self-administered questionnaire consists of 96 questions (a mix of multiple choice and open-ended questions), divided into nine parts.[5] In March 2003, 2,500 questionnaires were distributed to potential respondents[6] and 250 completed questionnaires were returned via mail. The low response rate is not entirely surprising in view of the sensitive nature and extraordinary length of the questionnaire. It is likely that our respondents are a self-selected group of women who are more willing and more equipped to articulate their own sexuality than others.

Table 10.1 presents a summary of the basic socio-demographic characteristics of the sample, which is skewed towards the younger, better-educated and higher-income women in Hong Kong. Even though some of our questionnaire distribution channels specifically targeted teenagers, lower-income, and less-educated women, the fact that we still failed to capture many of these respondents suggests they might feel less comfortable with talking about aspects of their sexuality, albeit anonymously.

Table 10.1 Socio-demographic profile

	Sample	2003 female population
Marital status (N=246)		
Single, separated, divorced, widowed	58.1	42.2
Co-habiting, married*	39.4	57.7
Others	2.5	NA
Personal income (N=241)		
No income	22.8	**
Under $10,000	27.8	60.0
$10,000–$20,000	26.6	23.4
$20,001 and above	18.8	16.6
*Household Income*** (N=235)*		
Under $10,000	9.8	24.1
$10,001–$20,000	27.2	28.3
$20,001–$40,000	25.3	29.4
$40,001 and above	27.7	18.3
Economic activity status and occupation (N=230)		
Housewife, retired or unemployed	14.3	47.0
Student	28.1	7.7
Lower service class	33.9	21.2
Upper service class	17.2	12.7
Other occupations	6.5	14.5
Educational attainment (N=247)		
Primary and below	6.8	31.1
Secondary and tertiary	41.6	57.3
University and above	50.4	11.7
Age (N=248)		
12–15 (10–14)****	1.2	(6)
16–20 (15–19)	6.0	(6.4)
21–30 (20–29)	45.2	(13.7)
31–40 (30–39)	26.4	(19.9)
41–50 (40–49)	16.0	(19.2)
>50 (50 and over)	4.4	(34.8)

* Co-habitants are excluded from the official figure as they are regarded as single
** Figure includes only employed women with earnings
*** Population figures refer to 2001
**** Population age categories differ slightly; as presented in brackets
Source (for official figures): Census and Statistics Department (2001, 2004)

In terms of sexual experiences, 22.2 per cent (N=247) of our respondents had never had sex with another person at the time of the interview. Amongst them half were under 20 years of age; one-third were aged between 21 and 30. Most respondents (63 per cent) had their first sexual experience between age 18 and 20;[7] 25 per cent said they had such experiences before age 17; and the remaining 12 per cent between ages 26 and 35. Of valid responses (N=154), 80 per cent said they had a regular sex partner at the time of the survey.

How sexually active were our respondents? About one-fifth (21.6 per cent) of valid responses indicated that they did not have sex with another person in the three months prior to the survey, and only 2.6 per cent had had sex at least twice a week within the previous three months. Of those who were married or cohabiting, 13.8 per cent did not have sex with another person in the past three months; only one respondent who was married or cohabiting had sex more than seven times per month. This is in line with surveys which have found that Hong Kong men and women do not have sex frequently.[8]

Good sex and intimacy

In what follows, I will present and discuss findings from the survey based on the premise that sexuality is a means or medium whereby women express the sexual side of their selfhood. Sexuality therefore includes sexual arousal and physical pleasure, the relationship between physical pleasure and intimacy, and other experiences which are related to sex. I will begin by discussing findings which will help provide an overview of Hong Kong women's sexuality, such as their ideal intimate relationship, their sexual fidelity, views on sex and intimacy, their sexual practices, and views on orgasm and masturbation.

Most respondents said that a partner who 'understands me' and 'respects me' are the most important considerations in an intimate relationship – 95.9 per cent of our respondents named these two as one of their top three criteria of partner choice in an intimate relationship (this was an open-ended question). 'Personality' was also considered to be very important, and 'a good heart' (31.6 per cent), 'cheerful' (27.7 per cent) and 'responsible' (25.8 per cent) are some other traits that ranked highly. Fewer women considered financial status (3.2 per cent) and career prospects (20.6 per cent) to be important. As women's ability and opportunities to be financially independent increase, the qualities they desire in a relationship shift towards the non-material and the emotional.

In another open-ended question we asked women to describe what they think is a 'good sex life'. Most respondents thought that a good sex life should include love and understanding (26.6 per cent), mutual satisfaction (34.4 per cent) and compatibility (12.9 per cent). Only 3.7 per cent gave more weight to the physical side of things and said that a good sex life is one where sexual activity and orgasms are featured. Over 92 per cent thought that a good sex life is either important or very important in an intimate relationship. Good sex is seen to enhance and improve the relationship, deepen mutual understanding between partners as well as reduce conflict. So far the findings from our survey resonate with those of similar surveys conducted on women's sexuality in the West (for example, Hite 1976), where many women tend to perceive a strong association between the physical acts of sex and intimate relationships, as illustrated by the quotes below (case numbers in brackets):

> Very important, because making love feels good, and to maintain a relationship, sex is a very important factor. Sometimes after sex, it feels like problems are solved. (61)

> Important. Although sex is not everything, it really can make you and your partner know more about each other's bodies, it can be very enjoyable. Can improve the relationship. (62)

> Very important. Sex can increase love, sex is a sign of the closeness and intimacy of two people. Psychologically humans long to be held, to be close. (178)

> Not the most important, but can be one way to show how you feel about each other. (202)

Feminists believe that sex should be a means of self-fulfilment and actualization, rather than a site that validates and reinforces existing power structures of dominance and subordination between men and women (Lemoncheck 1997; Wilkinson and Kitzinger 1993). To what extent do Hong Kong women agree with this view? To what extent can they achieve self-fulfilment and actualization through sex?

We asked respondents if they have a good sex life in their current relationships, and 44.3 per cent answered 'yes', 4.6 per cent replied 'sometimes', while the 26.2 per cent who said 'no' seemed much less knowledgeable about sex than those who said they have a good sex life. For instance, 27.4 per cent of women who were not happy with their sex lives were unsure what an orgasm was, compared to only 7.6 per cent amongst all who claimed to have a good sex life. Similarly, 23 per cent of the women who were dissatisfied with their sex lives had never seen their own genitals, compared to only 9.8 per cent of women who were satisfied. A slightly higher percentage of the former either did not know or were unsure about where their clitoris is (27.5 per cent), compared to the latter (18.1 per cent).

In traditional Chinese culture virginity is extremely important for women. Although the social reproduction of male inheritors is no longer significant in today's Hong Kong, only 42.1 per cent of our respondents said that virginity is unimportant. For the 48 per cent who thought it to be important, some think that virginity is a matter of moral responsibility while others admitted that they were still affected by traditional thinking even though rationally they could not see why it should be so important. Nevertheless, fewer than 15 per cent held the traditional attitude that virginity is something which a woman needs to treasure. Around 10 per cent think that the high value placed on virginity is absurd because sex is a natural need, while some likened virginity to women's shackles rather than something to be treasured. Degree holders in our sample were more likely to think of virginity as unimportant (53.3 per cent) than those without degrees (31 per cent). As our sample is skewed towards younger and better-educated women, it is likely that the percentage of Hong Kong women who place a high value on virginity might be greater than that found here.

Views on fidelity are much more homogeneous than views on virginity, with a majority of our respondents affirming the value of fidelity (83.7 per cent). They believed that fidelity represents trust and respect, and is an important basis for an intimate and long-term relationship:

> Important. Because if you are not faithful, the partner will feel very hurt. (203)

Important. If the other party is not faithful, I will feel ill at ease in my heart; feel that I am not important. My fidelity is important also. (175)

Important. At least honesty is important. But if both people accept an 'open relationship' then it is no problem. Although personally I don't believe open relationships will work in the long run. (212)

Only around 10 per cent of our respondents value honesty with one's partner more than fidelity. Those who did not think fidelity to be very important also tended to be more liberal in their other values towards sex (for example, they were more likely to accept one-night stands and accept having more than one sex partner at any one time).

So far we can see that our respondents are generally positive about sex and perceived a positive relationship between sex and intimacy. Sex is acknowledged as important, its value in an intimate relationship is ascertained, and sexual fidelity is seen to represent trust and respect for one's partner. The importance of virginity, however, long held by some feminists to be a means of oppressing women's sexual freedoms and self-worth, is still held close to many women's hearts. Although the young and well-educated are less likely to place great importance on virginity, a sizeable proportion of them still do.

Knowledge and experiences of various sexual activities

I will now turn to respondents' sexual knowledge and experiences. Four out of five women (82.8 per cent) said they knew what an orgasm is; only 2.8 per cent said they did not know, and another 14.6 per cent said they were 'not sure'. Nearly all (96.8 per cent) said they knew what masturbation is, but only 75.3 per cent knew where their clitoris is. Forty-five women said they have not seen their own private parts, a quarter of whom said there was 'no need' to look. I found that it is not necessarily women with little or no sexual experiences or without a partner who are lacking in sexual knowledge. For instance, amongst respondents who were married or cohabiting, 8.2 per cent either did not know or were unsure what an orgasm is, and another 13.4 per cent did not know or were unsure where their clitoris is. This shows that although the women we surveyed seemed to be generally knowledgeable about sex, there is still a significant percentage who were quite ignorant. Our sample was unable to capture a wide range of age groups, but it is not necessarily the oldest or youngest women who lack basic knowledge about their sexual anatomy.

In an open-ended question we asked respondents to describe the general 'run down' of their typical lovemaking:

> Kissing, fondling, usually in bed, sometimes on the living room couch, on the floor, or standing, then insert finger, sometimes oral sex. (48 lesbian)

> Kissing, touching, foreplay, penetration. (236)

> First kissing, then touching (undress, leaving just underpants), touching of genitals, fondling some more (first me above him below, then him above me below, or him entering from behind) (213)

> He kisses me first, and then uses fingers to stimulate my clitoris, or puts his fingers into my vagina. Then he puts his penis into my vagina, penetrates and withdraws, until a certain moment he puts on a condom, continue, until he ejaculates. (63)

It is clear that the general process of lovemaking is still procreation-oriented − starting with kissing, touching, 'foreplay', ending in male ejaculation (very few respondents mentioned their own orgasms in their descriptions). Coitus is predominantly regarded as the sexual norm, and respondents' experiences with other forms of sexual activities are limited.

When we asked respondents to describe the types of sexual activities in lovemaking they most enjoyed, more women preferred 'foreplay' − such as kissing, embracing and touching − than liked vaginal intercourse. From Table 10.2 we can see that only 25.7 per cent like performing oral sex on their partners, 38.7 per cent enjoy receiving oral sex, and only 2.6 per cent said they like anal sex. Only a very small percentage had experience with sex toys such as vibrators and dildos, or with role play and S/M practices. In short, respondents may have very positive attitudes about sex, but a sizeable proportion were not very knowledgeable when it comes to their own pleasures (and pleasure centres). The large percentage who disliked oral sex and the use of sex toys suggests that norms that disapprove of non-procreative sexual contact (e.g. oral and anal sex) are still in place, thereby limiting women's range of sexual experiences.

Table 10.2 How do you like the following activities? (%)

	Like	So-so	Dislike	N
Kissing	83.0	15.5	1.5	194
Embracing	98.5	1.0	0.5	194
'Dirty talk'	73.6	23.6	2.7	182
Touching	92.2	7.8	0.0	193
Vaginal intercourse	79.1	15.0	5.9	187
Performing oral sex	25.7	40.1	34.2	187
Anal sex	2.6	9.0	88.4	155
Receiving oral sex	38.7	35.5	25.8	186
Sex toys (e.g. vibrators, dildos)	10.5	24.2	65.4	153
Role play	10.7	25.3	64.0	150
Sadomasochism	3.3	8.7	88.0	150

Deviating from the norm

Are women open to the possibility of new experiences that deviate from the prescriptions of traditional Chinese norms regarding female sexuality? We now look at respondents' views on two traditional sexual taboos – homosexuality and masturbation. Only 3.6 per cent said they will *not* consider having sex with men (these I assume to be lesbians), but a surprising 31.8 per cent, most of whom are women with higher educational attainment, said they *will* consider having sex with women; I assume this figure to include lesbians, bisexuals and 'bi-curious' women. Although the question is hypothetical ('Will you consider...?'), it is nevertheless significant that nearly one-third were not completely unquestioning of the normalcy of heterosexual hegemony.

We also asked whether respondents *like* having sex with men or women. This question rules out the hypothetical element as it is hard to say whether one likes something unless one has actually experienced it. Only 6.7 per cent said they did not like sex with men – this probably

Table 10.3 Will you consider/do you like having sex with someone of the opposite sex, the same sex, with yourself (masturbation)? (%)

	Will consider	Like	Will not consider	Dislike
Opposite sex	96.4	93.3	3.6	6.7
Same sex	31.9	11.3	68.1	88.7
Yourself	74.6	26.2	25.4	73.8

includes lesbians as well as women who did not enjoy sex with men, yet are not necessarily lesbians. Those who said they liked sex with women (11.3 per cent) probably include both lesbians and bisexuals (Table 10.3).

A high proportion (74.6 per cent) said they will consider masturbation but only 26.2 per cent said they liked it. This shows that masturbation is not a taboo for most women, but is still considered an inferior way of gaining sexual satisfaction. In an open-ended question we asked respondents to describe their views on women who masturbate. Here, 59.9 per cent are positive (regarding it as normal, healthy and natural), but some think masturbation is justified only when one has no sex partner or when sex is not satisfactory, and others think of it as a slightly better choice than a one-night stand. Some even felt that it is disgusting or embarrassing (Table 10.4).

Again, a high proportion (78.2 per cent) said they have tried various methods to satisfy their partners, such as the use of pornographic materials (48.8 per cent) and sexy underwear (32.6 per cent). But when we asked for respondents' views on pornography, only around 30 per cent were positive or open-minded about it. The majority variously considered pornography to be disgusting, distorting the realities of sex, demeaning and objectifying women, or having a bad influence on young people.

Table 10.4 What are your views on women masturbating? (%)
N=222

Normal, healthy, natural, basic need, personal habit, both sexes have the right to masturbate, not that different from men masturbating	59.9
Explore and understand own body, satisfy self, get sexual satisfaction and orgasm, independence	14.0
Feel uneasy, disgusting, embarrassed, guilty, stupid	6.8
When there is no sex partner or satisfactory sex, then need to masturbate	5.4
A better choice than one-night stand, promiscuity	1.8
A social taboo, mystery	0.5
Other responses	11.7

Orgasms and sex

Of the 190 respondents who have experienced sex with another person, 94.7 per cent have had orgasms. However, fewer than 40 per cent of these women often have orgasms during sex with a partner, with 45.4 per cent who 'sometimes do', and 15.3 per cent who 'rarely do'. Two-thirds of women (66.7 per cent) said their first orgasm happened 'naturally', whereas 32.2 per cent said it happened only after many attempts. More than half (54.6 per cent) agreed that orgasm is important in sex, followed by 33 per cent who said it is 'sometimes' important, and 12.4 per cent who think it is unimportant. Most women think that orgasms are important because they enable one to feel satisfied and happy, but only 17.1 per cent think orgasms can increase feelings of intimacy with their partners. This shows that a significant proportion of women do not place great importance on orgasms during sex, and for those who do, there are more who think orgasms are important for their own pleasures than those who think it enhances intimacy with their partners.

We tapped how often and how easily respondents reach orgasm through three questions. First is a multiple-choice question on how they can eas Normal, healthy, natural, basic need, personal habit, both sexes have the right to masturbate, not that different from men masturbating ily reach orgasm. Here, the most popular answer was through intercourse (65.2 per cent), followed by manual stimulation of the clitoris by one's partner (58.2 per cent), masturbation (46.7 per cent) and oral sex (30.4 per cent). This seems to contradict other surveys on women's sexuality (such as *The Hite Report*), which have consistently shown that masturbation is the singularly easiest and quickest way for women to reach orgasm. In the second, open-ended, question we asked 'usually under what circumstances can you reach orgasm?', and answers here reveal a clearer picture. Here, respondents mentioned the importance of their psychological and physical readiness in order to achieve orgasm. A third (also open-ended) question asks respondents under what circumstances can they achieve orgasm through penetrative intercourse. Here again, responses show the complexities involved in achieving orgasm during intercourse, and respondents said that clitoral stimulation and adequate foreplay are slightly more important than the frequency, impact and rhythm of penetration (tables 10.5a, 10.b and 10.5c). In terms of sex positions or actions which respondents find most pleasurable, the missionary position (29.9 per cent) is preferred to the woman on top position (17.4 per cent) and side by side position (17.4 per cent).

Orgasms can be had, and they can be faked. Half of all valid responses said they had faked orgasms in the past. Reasons include: it arouses their partners (25 per cent), they did not want to upset their partners (20.2 per cent) or just wanted to get 'it' over and done with (15.5 per cent).

The overall picture shows that there is considerable divergence in women's experiences of orgasms during lovemaking with a partner. The large percentage who admitted to having faked orgasms shows that there is still considerable unease when it comes to communicating with partners about sex. For these women, their partner's pride overrides their own sexual enjoyment, and many described sex as a chore when the frustration of being unable to achieve orgasm sets in. When we

Table 10.5a Which of the following methods allow you to easily reach orgasm? (%) N=184

	Easy	Not easy
Masturbation	46.7	53.3
Manual stimulation of the clitoris by partner	58.2	41.8
Oral sex	30.4	69.6
Intercourse (vaginal penetration)	65.2	34.8
Vibrator	8.2	91.8
Others	11.4	88.6

Table 10.5b Usually under what circumstances can you reach orgasm? (%) N=158

Vaginal intercourse	10.1
Adequate 'foreplay'	5.7
Clitoral stimulation/oral sex	23.4
Masturbation	12.0
Sexual fantasies	0.6
Good psychological and physical readiness/arousal	25.9
Good cooperation from partner	4.4
Not sure/don't know	17.7

Table 10.5c Under what circumstances can you reach orgasm through vaginal intercourse? (%) N=158

Appropriate frequency, strength, and rhythm of penetration	15.5
Specific positions	8.1
Clitoral stimulation, adequate foreplay	18.9
Partner's response and cooperation	6.1
Sexual fantasies	1.4
Masturbating at the same time	1.4
Good psychological state (relaxed, aroused, good atmosphere)	19.6
Specific physical state	2.7
No specific circumstances	14.9
Rarely orgasm through vaginal intercourse/no experience with vaginal intercourse	11.5

consider this together with the findings on how important women think orgasms are, and how easy it is for them to reach orgasms, a somewhat complicated picture emerges. Even though most of our respondents seem reasonably articulate about the circumstances under which they can reach orgasm, some of them put a high value on orgasm and can often get it during lovemaking, whilst others are less successful.

Talking about sex

Being able to talk about sex with other people increases channels of acquiring sexual knowledge, while adequate communication with one's partner is undoubtedly an important contributor to good sex and intimacy. Two-thirds of our respondents (66.8 per cent) said they have shared their sexual experiences with others, and it appears that more educated women are more open about their sexuality: 78.4 per cent of those with degrees have done so, compared to 57 per cent of those with secondary and non-degree education, and only 50 per cent of those with primary (or less) education. However, more than half said they have never told their partners they could not reach orgasm during sex. Amongst them, over half said they felt unease about raising the subject; 24.4 per cent said it is okay not to reach orgasm during sex, or that orgasms are not that important. Of the 80 women who said they have told their partners they couldn't orgasm during sex, nearly 30 per cent said their partners were disappointed, felt guilty, or found it hard to accept (tables 10.6a, 10.6b). Are those who have never told partners they couldn't reach orgasm also the ones who think orgasm is not important? I found that 88.9 per cent of those who have never told their partners how they like to be touched have never told their partners that they could not achieve orgasm during sex either. Of all the women who said that orgasms are important, 55.9 per cent said they have never told their partners they could not orgasm during sex. When asked why they did not tell their partners, more than half said it was because they felt embarrassed and did not want to upset their partners. Four out of five (80.7 per cent) said they have told their partners how they would like to be touched. For those who have never done so, embarrassment (40 per cent) and there being no need (30 per cent) were the most common answers. This shows that many Hong Kong

Table 10.6a You have told your partner you could not reach orgasm during sex. What was his/her response? (%) N=80

Tried to improve	36.3
Disappointed, guilty, depressed, unhappy	23.8
No particular response	13.8
Tried to understand why	11.3
Accept	8.8
Can't accept, can't understand	6.3

Table 10.6b You have never told your partner you could not reach orgasm during sex. Why? (%) N=82

Did not want him/her to be unhappy, feel bad, feel pressure, didn't know how to say it	51.2
It is okay to not have orgasm once in a while, no need to tell partner, I don't mind, orgasms are not important	24.4
Rarely fail to orgasm	13.4
Partner knows without me having to tell him/her	7.3
I don't know what orgasm is	2.4

women either still have difficulties expressing what they want with their partners, or did not think it important to communicate this verbally to their partners; and that many tend to put the needs of their partners before their own.

Perhaps action speaks louder than words? How do our respondents fare when it comes to initiating sex? While 80 per cent said they had the *experience* of initiating sex in a relationship, only 3.1 per cent said they are *usually* the one who initiates sex with their partners. Women who said they would consider or like having sex with other women are more likely to say that there is no fixed pattern in who usually initiates sex.

Although many of our respondents are affirmative about sexual pleasures, few are comfortable with talking to others, including their partners, about sex. Much of this is revealed in an open-ended question towards the end of the survey, where we asked respondents to write down what they think about the questionnaire:

I feel that I don't want others to know, I had to hide in my room to complete this. But in life there are very few chances to talk about such personal things, so as I wrote, I got very interested in keeping writing. (63)

Some questions involve personal privacy. Although it is anonymous, I still feel uncomfortable answering them. (202)

When I was writing this, I didn't want my mother to see it (she was sitting nearby), especially the section on sexual violence. I still feel upset thinking about the experience. (105)

Please remember to keep the questionnaire 100 per cent confidential. A bit embarrassed. (106)

On the other hand, there are also many women who felt positive about the experience of completing the survey; many also said that the questionnaire made them rethink aspects of their own sexuality:

Very interesting, very bold. Is this another step forward for the discussion of feminist issues? But after this, what? (122)

I feel that I need to be more proactive in making sexual requests. Need to learn how to reach orgasm during sex. Rarely can I talk to others about sex. (51)

The questionnaire is very long, and it is tiring to answer it. But it is quite fun: totally expose my own sexual history, I have never done this before. (94)

Felt great! Not often get a chance to talk and talk. Some questions helped me to sort out my own thinking. Thanks! (82)

As expressed by many respondents, completing the questionnaire provided them with a rare opportunity to re-think their own sex-related attitudes, experiences and behaviours. This process forced them to confront their own sexuality, and while many find it liberating and helpful, there are also many who found it embarrassing and uneasy.

Women and sex in twenty-first-century Hong Kong – some concluding remarks

It is evident that despite the many social and economic changes that have taken place in Hong Kong, and the tremendous impact these have had on women's social and familial status, traditional norms regarding women's sexuality still operate in Hong Kong. The plasticity of sexuality as described by Giddens (1991) is neither practised nor approved by most of our respondents. Instead, sex is perceived to be in close relationship with confluent love, in which sex is a means to attain, as well as to express, intimacy with another person.

The skewed nature of our sample prevents us from providing a truly representative picture of Hong Kong women. Nevertheless, we can still see that despite having a large proportion of highly educated and younger women in our sample, the findings show that many Hong Kong women are still quite conservative and traditional when it comes to sex. Although they realize and acknowledge the importance of good sex, most were unable to talk about it with their partners. Even though they know that virginity should not be that important anymore, they still could not shake off the feeling that somehow it still is. Even though procreation no longer bears a close relation to sex, most respondents were still ill at ease with sexual activities and practices that are not related to reproduction. Even though many of them know what an orgasm is, and recognize its importance and desirability, most do not reach orgasm regularly during sex. Even though it is not through vaginal penetration that women most easily reach orgasm (as revealed in the open-ended question), they still chose that answer. Even though most respondents have experiences of masturbation and acknowledged that they can achieve orgasm through it easily, many still regarded it as an inferior form of sexual pleasure.

These findings portray Hong Kong women as variously liberal, independent, positive about their sexuality, yet at the same time bounded by traditional norms, inhibited from freely speaking their minds and asserting what they want from their sex partners in an intimate relationship. Improvement in women's socio-economic status, educational opportunities and rights in the public sphere took place at a much greater speed than cultural and normative aspects regarding sexuality. All this, coupled with a capitalist economy which relies heavily on the sexualization of women and their bodies to sell products and services, has created and maintained a highly sexualized culture which ironically neglects women as sexual subjects, who are capable of and demand sexual pleasure. It is against this context of rapid and compressed social change, and the vehement culture of capitalist commodification, that the many contradictions of Hong Kong women's sexuality can be situated and understood.

Notes

1 By pornografication I refer to the process whereby images of women are portrayed using the same styles and techniques of representation found in mainstream pornography. Women's bodies and sexual pleasures are portrayed in such a way as to serve men's sexual desires and arousal.

2 The percentage of young women who have had premarital sex increased from 18.9 in 1986 to 22 in 1991 (Hong Kong Family Planning Association, 1986, 1991).

3 The FPA's 1991 survey found that over half of all teenage girls studied thought that pregnancy is impossible if there is no orgasm (Hong Kong Family Planning Association 1991).

4 This study was supported by a seed grant from Hong Kong University.

5 Namely: intimate relationship, sex knowledge, sex life, orgasm, safe sex/contraception/abortion, masturbation, sexual fantasy, sexual harassment and sex violence, and pornography.

6 These were distributed to women's organizations and NGOs, community centres, arts associations, schools, tertiary institutions, the AAF's website and through AAF members' personal networks.

7 A separate question asks the age of first experience with masturbation, so here 'first sexual experience' refers to sex with another person. Although it is not clearly stated as 'sexual intercourse', it is generally understood to mean that. However, it is possible that respondents refer to sexual experiences other than intercourse.

8 According to the Durex Global Sex Survey 2004, Hong Kong people on average have sex 79 times a year (second from the bottom; Japan ranks last at 48 times per year), compared to the global average of 103 times per year, and the French who have sex 139 times a year. http://www.durex.com/cm/gss2004Content.asp?intQid=398&intMenuOpen=11

References

Association for the Advancement of Feminism [新婦女協進會編寫] (1998)又喊又笑: 阿婆口述歷史 [*Laughing and Crying: Old Women's Oral History*]. 香

港：新婦女協進會 [*Hong Kong: Association for the Advancement of Feminism*].

—— (2002) *16+ 一少女口述歷史* [*Young Women's Oral History: 16+*]. 香港：進一步出版社 [Hong Kong: Stepforward Publishing].

Attwood, Feona (2002) 'A very British carnival: women, sex and transgression in *Fiesta* magazine', *European Journal of Cultural Studies*, 5: 91–105.

Breakthrough (1994) *Research Report on Hong Kong Youth's Sex Role, Attitudes And Behaviours*. Hong Kong: Breakthrough.

Census and Statistics Department (2001) *2001 Population Census: Main Report Volume One*. Hong Kong: Census and Statistics Department.

—— (2004) *Women and Men in Hong Kong: Key Statistics* (2003 edition). Hong Kong: Census and Statistics Department.

Chan, Anita Kit-wa and Wong Wai-ling (eds) (2004) *Gendering Hong Kong*. Hong Kong: Oxford University Press.

Chan, Hau-nung Annie (2006) 'The effects of full-time domestic workers on married women's economic activity status', *International Sociology*, 21 (1): 133–59.

—— (2007) 'Sex in the city: female bodies and female sexuality in Hong Kong', paper presented at the workshop on 'Bodies and Urban Spaces', Kwan Fong Cultural Research and Development (KFCRD) Programme, Lingnan University, Hong Kong, 10 March.

Cheung, Fanny M. (ed.) (1997) *Engendering Hong Kong Society: a Gender Perspective of Women's Status*. Hong Kong: Chinese University Press.

Christian Family Service Centre (1999) *Study on Elderly People's Sexual Attitudes, Behaviours and Ways of Coping with Sexual Distress in Hong Kong*. Hong Kong: Christian Family Service Centre.

Chu, W. C. (1997) 'Who is doing what? The implication behind housework sharing', in S. K. Lau, M. K. Lee, P. S. Wan and S. L. Wong (eds), *Indicators of Social Development: Hong Kong 1995*. Hong Kong: Hong Kong Institute of Asia-Pacific Studies, the Chinese University of Hong Kong, pp. 203–32.

Chung Ting-yiu and Mak Kit-ling Kitty (1995) 'Young people's attitude towards sex and related matters: summary report', Social Sciences Research Centre, University of Hong Kong.

Dikotter, Frank (1995) *Sex, Culture and Modernity in China*. Hong Kong: Hong Kong University Press.

Evans, Grant and Maria Tam (1997) *Hong Kong: The Anthropology of a Chinese Metropolis*. Surrey: Curzon Press.

Evans, Harriet (1997) *Women and Sexuality in China : Dominant Discourses of Female Sexuality and Gender since 1949*. Cambridge: Cambridge University Press.

Giddens, Anthony (1991) *Modernity and Self-Identity: Self and Society in the Late Modern Age*. Cambridge: Polity Press.

Hite, Shere (1976) *The Hite Report: a Nationwide Report on Female Sexuality*. New York: Macmillan.

Hong Kong Family Planning Association (1986) *Working Report on the Survey of Adolescent Sexuality Study 1986*. Hong Kong: Task Force on the Study of Adolescent Sexuality of the Family Planning Association of Hong Kong.

—— (1991). *Youth Sexuality Study 1991*. Hong Kong: Hong Kong Family Planning Association.

—— (1997) *Knowledge, Attitude and Practice (KAP) Survey Report*. Hong Kong: Hong Kong Family Planning Association.

—— (2001) *Youth Sexuality Study 2001*. Hong Kong: Hong Kong Family Planning Association.

—— (2002) *Knowledge, Attitude and Practice (KAP) Survey Report*. Hong Kong: Hong Kong Family Planning Association.

Jamieson, Lynn (2000) 'Intimacy transformed? A critical look at the "pure relationship"', *Sociology* (August 1999): 477–94.

Jaschok, M. and S. Miers (eds) (1992) *Women and Chinese Patriarchy*. Hong Kong: Hong Kong University Press; New Jersey: Zed Books.

Lau, Yuk-king, Joyce L. C. Ma and Chan Ying-Keung (2006) 'Labour force participation of married women in Hong Kong: a feminist perspective', *Journal of Comparative Family Studies*, 37 (1): 93–112.

Lee, Ming-kwan (1995) 'The family way' in Lau S. K. et al. (eds), *Indicators of Social Development: Hong Kong 1993*. Hong Kong: Hong Kong Institute of Asia Pacific Affairs, the Chinese University of Hong Kong, pp. 1–20.

Lemoncheck, Linda J. (1997) *Loose Women, Lecherous Men: a Feminist Philosophy of Sex*. Oxford: Oxford University Press.

McDonogh, Gary and Cindy Wong (2005) *Global Hong Kong*. New York, NY: Routledge.

Salaff, Janet (1981) *Working Daughters of Hong Kong: Filial Piety or Power in the Family?* Cambridge: Cambridge University Press.

Shih, Shu-mei (2001) 'Gender and a new geopolitics of desire: the seduction of mainland women in Taiwan and Hong Kong media', *Signs: Journal of Women in Culture and Society*, 23 (2): 287–318.

Vance, Carole S. (1992) *Pleasure and Danger: Exploring Female Sexuality*. London: Pandora.

Wilkinson, Sue and Celia Kitzinger (eds) (1993) *Heterosexuality: a Feminism and Psychology Reader*. London: Sage.

Yeung Chan So-tuen Caroline and Kwong Wai Man (1997) *A Survey Study of the Attitudes of Pre-Marital Couples toward Marriage in Hong Kong: Implications for Service Planning*. Hong Kong: City University of Hong Kong in association with the Hong Kong Catholic Marriage Advisory Council.

11 Becoming 'the First Wives': Gender, Intimacy and the Regional Economy across the Taiwan Strait

SHEN HSIU-HUA

Male infidelity has long existed in Taiwanese society. However, its pervasiveness and its implications for those involved and for society more generally have escalated exponentially over the last two decades. To a very large extent, these changes have resulted from the emergence of the Chinese economy and the migration of thousands of Taiwanese business people, mainly men, to China to take advantage of the opportunities offered by this growth and its availability to Taiwanese investors and entrepreneurs.

Extramarital affairs between Chinese women and Taiwanese businessmen in China are very common (Shen 2003). Many of them are initiated in karaoke hostess bars and other similar settings where Taiwanese businessmen entertain their male business associates on a regular basis to develop their business networks, and where hostesses, locally called *xiaojie*, or 'Miss', are available to serve their customers by participating in drinking, singing and dancing, and by providing sexual favours, including sexual transactions. Some affairs, however, are instigated within small-sized firms between their owners or senior managers and their Chinese female subordinates.[1]

Two major types of relationship result from these activities: One is the casual sexual transaction which is purchased and usually takes place in rooms provided in bars or hotels, or in the dormitories or homes of these men. The other type is some sort of stable relationship which lasts for several weeks or months and can even result in marriage. This type usually results from the preference of some Taiwanese businessmen for the continuing company of the same hostesses or from the need for a stable sexual and/or emotional partner while they are away from home (Shen 2008). In addition, these frequently become romantic relationships where the women quit their jobs and become 'live-in lovers', either as temporary wives

216

or long-term mistresses, in return for living expenses and a regular specified amount of money. Both of these types of extramarital affairs are generally described as *bao ernai,* the phenomenon of keeping a mistress. Both types reflect a masculine, flexible and consumer-oriented logic of intimacy.

As a result of this phenomenon, the wives of these men, whether they stay in Taiwan or migrate with them to China, are automatically 'upgraded' and represented as 'the first wives', a title and status which conflicts with the institution of heterosexual monogamous marriage.[2] This particular type of institutional arrangement not only establishes a legal boundary for the marriage norm but also creates meanings and symbolic boundaries for the actors involved, providing guidance on how to act in a marriage relationship and on how to deal with disruptions within it. The extramarital affairs of Taiwanese businessmen and the collective status of Taiwanese wives as 'the first wives' provide an interesting case study for exploring the changing social settings, including intimate familial relationships, resulting from the development of a regional economy in contemporary East Asia and transnational migration.

Based on ethnographic fieldwork and secondary documents, including newspapers and Internet discussion forums,[3] conducted and gathered in Taiwan and in coastal China[4] between 1999 and 2007, this chapter describes the way in which Taiwanese wives of Taiwanese businessmen in China have become 'the first wives', the so called *da lao po* in Mandarin Chinese, as a result of their husbands' affairs with Chinese women in China. While the development of a regional economy across the Taiwan Strait has attracted great attention from economists and political scientists, this study will examine its impact on intimate and family relations, and most particularly on its meaning for the Taiwanese wives of Taiwanese businessmen in China.

The Asian regional economy and 'the first wives'

The emergence of the Asian regional economy is one of the most influential trends in the world political economy over the last two decades. It has resulted from economic globalization, and particularly from investments by the Newly Industrialized Economies (NIEs) – including Hong Kong, Singapore, Korea and Taiwan – in regional production and from the development of these NIEs as large importing markets for the region (Dicken and Yeung 1999: 113). Intensive economic cooperation between Taiwan and China, including Hong Kong, has produced a powerful regional grouping called the Greater China Economy. According to official data from the Chinese Ministry of Foreign Trade and Economic Cooperation up to August 2007, the cumulative number of Taiwanese investments in China totals 74,036, and the cumulative capital invested amounts to more than US$44.8 billion.[5]

Since the emerging Asian regional economy has usually been discussed as an economic or political matter, it seems odd at first to claim a close association between it and the emerging collective status of 'the first wives' in the region. However, with the migration of large numbers of Asian businessmen throughout the region for extensive periods of time, stories about them taking mistresses in host societies have been spreading across borders for some time.[6] According to reports, many Hong Kong and Singaporean businessmen in China, and Taiwanese businessmen in both China and Vietnam, for instance, have developed affairs in host societies.[7] Even in China itself, local Chinese businessmen have adopted this practice.[8] For these foreign or local businessmen, local women facilitate business connections, provide emotional comfort, satisfy sexual desires, express masculine privileged status and identity, and craft male bonds.[9] However, as a result of this *bao ernai* phenomenon, the wives of these businessmen become collectively 'the first wives'.[10]

Scholars have long recognized the profound impact of the development and transformation of capitalism on intimate relationships. Friedrich Engels argued that the modern patriarchal monogamous family emerged in response to the development of class-divided society and private property, as bourgeois patriarchs sought ways to keep their wealth and privileges in their families (Engels 1972). Contemporary scholarship finds that intimate and family relations become flexible, situational, and 'commercial' in response to the rather uncertain and insecure state of working and family lives in an environment of market capitalism with its emphasis on flexible accumulation and mass consumption (see Dizard and Gadlin 1990; Hochschild 1997, 2003; Stacey 1990; Swidler 2001).

As a result of the development of a regional economy in Asia, intensive exchanges of capital, people and images create many 'contact zones' (Pratt 1992: 7) where societies and people interact closely with each other. How has the formation of a Greater China Economy between Taiwan and China shaped the patterns of intimate and family relations and the role of Taiwanese women in these relations? How has the status of Taiwanese wives as 'the first wives' been constructed through the perception of Chinese women as the other women in these transnational contact zones? What emotions do these Taiwanese wives experience and what strategies do they employ to deal with their husbands' affairs? How have the meanings and feelings of intimate, family relations been shaped for these women by becoming 'the first wives'? How has the influence of capitalist transformation on intimate and family relations across the Taiwan Strait simultaneously reinforced and/or undermined gender inequality and politics for the women and men involved?

The popular representation of 'the first wives' in Taiwan usually refers to the Taiwanese wives of Taiwanese investors, managers, and personnel in China. However, it is so pervasive that it is now even applied to those Taiwanese wives whose husbands have just decided to go and work in China. Three major themes emerge from my research into the experiences of 'the first wives': the domestication of Taiwanese women as stay-behind single mothers or trailing spouses; the immorality of Chinese women as the other women; and flexible intimacy in relation to Taiwanese women's gendered self-realization.

Domestication of Taiwanese women

When Taiwanese men go to China to work, their wives are primarily considered as housekeepers, responsible for protecting the family and the marriage. Even when they work full-time, those who stay in Taiwan during the long absences of their husbands become stay-behind 'single' mothers to their children and distant spouses to their husbands, who visit them for a week or so once every two to three months but are otherwise free from daily family duty. Those wives who move to China are identified as 'trailing spouses'. They usually give up their jobs in Taiwan and rarely return to the workforce in China because of the limited job opportunities or the relatively low-paid jobs available in local Chinese firms. Only the wives of the owners of small firms avoid the status of housewives because they usually become the leading figures in running these firms.

Taiwanese business people entered China in large numbers in the late 1980s to set up and manage Taiwanese firms there. During the first decade, the majority of wives stayed in Taiwan with their children because of the then rather uncertain working, living and educational conditions in China, and because of the disruption to families associated with the move from Taiwan to China. Those who did relocate during this time were usually the wives of business owners involved in their husbands' businesses or those with young children not yet in school. However, during the second decade, when China became a more mature foreign investment destination, and when wives of Taiwanese businessmen became more aware of the *bao ernai* phenomenon, more of them relocated to China with their husbands, particularly to major Chinese metropolises such as Shanghai, Beijing or Shenzhen, where living, working and educational conditions are considered to be better.[11]

Taiwanese wives consider the decision to relocate to China a back-and-forth, difficult process: the various factors involved include children's education, working and living conditions, jobs in Taiwan, care for elderly parents, and family life. For example, a Taiwanese wife of a Taiwanese manager at a computer-related firm had travelled between Taiwan (to visit her family) and China (to stay with her husband) since 1993. She told me her story in Dongguan in 1999:

> When my husband first came to China, I was pregnant. So I didn't come with him. That situation lasted until my first child was one and a half years old. Then my husband was here and I was in Taiwan feeling dormant. I had to take care of my child by myself and was very unhappy. I was worried that my husband might have affairs. Women here [in China] usually throw themselves into the arms of Taiwanese men.

Another Taiwanese woman I met in Dongguan in October 2007 was visiting her husband for two months. He had worked in China for two years and she was still struggling with the question of moving to China. Her children were halfway through their school education and unwilling to move to China. She also had a good job in a computer firm in Taiwan. However, she was worried about her marriage. After chatting with me about her problem, she said to me, 'There are my children and here is my husband; which one should I care for first?'

Given the number of Taiwanese businessmen in China who have affairs, the move to China with their husbands is framed as a means to express Taiwanese wives' 'sovereignty' over their husbands and is often seen as the right decision to protect their marriages. It is constantly reinforced by the earnest advice offered by families and friends, and provided at various Internet discussion forums. In responding to the concerns of a stay-behind Taiwanese woman over a Chinese woman's special attention to her husband in China, a participant who logged on as 'Doesn't get it' wrote that 'Once the husband has gone to mainland China, the wife should immediately follow him. No man in China can get away without having affairs. The wife shouldn't feel she could be lucky [to avoid the *bao ernai* phenomenon].'[12]

However, even those who have relocated to China with their husbands are not always able to get away from being 'the first wives'. Many of the Taiwanese businessmen and wives whom I studied made it very clear to me that, even with their wives in China, the husbands can still use work opportunities and business trips to carry on affairs. For example, a group of five Taiwanese women I met one evening during my trip to Dongguan in October 2007 had all gone through or were still going through their husbands' various affairs with Chinese women.

The immoral other Chinese women

As a result of the collective infidelity of Taiwanese businessmen in China, 'the first wives' and Taiwanese society more generally view Chinese women as disreputable others, the temptresses responsible for the marital and family problems with which they are dealing. As a consequence, they attribute negative economic and social characteristics to these foreign interlopers into their marriages, calling them 'gold diggers' and 'trashy' husband stealers.

While China went through dramatic socialist revolution between the 1950s and 1970s, Taiwan (with US foreign aid) went through processes of industrialization and modernization. Compared to China, Taiwan's more advanced economic and social development has equipped Taiwanese businessmen with the economic and cultural capital to present themselves as 'more modern and cultivated' people to the Chinese as they enter China. Thus, with their economic capacity and their internationally mobile status, Taiwanese businessmen become rather attractive and competitive candidates on the dating scene in China, in comparison to the majority of Chinese men who do not have such economic and cultural capital. A Taiwanese woman, identifying herself as 'a boring person', wrote:

> Once Taiwanese men go across the other side of the Strait, they are like precious treasures in the eyes of Chinese women. These Taiwanese businessmen also feel that they themselves are like generous, rich boys with numerous charms and that hundreds and thousands of Chinese women are waiting for their rescue.[13]

A Taiwanese wife I met in 2001 also stated that, 'in the eyes of mainland sisters, Taiwanese men represent new hopes'. As China transforms itself from a socialist to a market economy, some Chinese women take a flexible stand toward intimacy and see a relationship with a rather well-off man as a way to climb up the social ladder. However, in their narratives, many Taiwanese wives tend to categorize all Chinese women as gold diggers, skilfully looking for material gains rather than love in their relationships, and willing to leave these relationships once they get enough money from their Taiwanese lovers. In my interviews with Taiwanese wives, they often describe what they have heard about or experienced with Chinese women who use various tricks, such as family emergencies or personal needs, to exact more money and even property, including houses or apartments, from Taiwanese men.

According to Chinese law, children born outside wedlock have the same rights to their parents' money and property as the 'inside' children. Consequently, Chinese women present a threat to Taiwanese wives because these 'gold diggers' constantly seek a substantial share of their marital property and money, and, if children result from these extramarital relationships, such children have the same legal right to the inheritance as their own children.

In the eyes of many Taiwanese wives, Chinese women are not just gold diggers; they are also aggressive, skilful, low-class husband stealers. Chinese women are described as 'shamelessly' using various sexual and other services to please these men in order to reach their economic goals. For instance, a Taiwanese woman left an online message about a discussion which she had seen on a popular Taiwanese TV talk show:

> The young, pretty women across the other side of the Strait are very skilful. They know how to play innocence by pretending that Taiwanese men are their first sex partners. This makes these men feel

sorry and loving toward them. They massage these men for three hours every night, including licking these men from head to toe.[14]

This woman ended the online message with a quote from the TV talk show host, 'I see! We, the first wives, only can feel sorry that we are unable to compete with this kind of treatment. We have no such skills.'

In contrast to their views of the Chinese women, many of 'the first wives' see themselves as moral, respectable, good women, motivated by love for their husbands and families which is sanctified by the legal institution of marriage. As a result, they find themselves in a somewhat unbearable situation when they learn that their husbands not only have casual sexual transactions but also develop emotional and serious relationships with Chinese women from the sex-related industry. A Taiwanese woman who discovered that her husband had become involved in a ten-month relationship with a Chinese karaoke hostess, who had previously been a lover to five other married men, wrote:

> I am not sure how to think about it [my husband's affair]. I feel sad if it happened only because of his sexual urgency. I will feel both sad and embarrassed, if he really has a feeling for her. This woman is sixteen years his junior. Their lives and thinking styles are so different. How can my husband love someone like that?[15]

Many Chinese women who work in the sex-related industry are young, have primary or middle-school educations, and originate from the poorer parts of China. The woman quoted and 'the first wives' more generally cannot believe that their husbands would put them in a situation where they are compelled to compare themselves to and compete with Chinese women with such a 'low', 'disreputable' social background. They are embarrassed by it because it undermines their own self-esteem and social status. Their husbands and themselves are often better-educated and hold 'normal', 'respectable' jobs. They wonder how much they really know about their husbands and what kind of relationships their husbands could have with these new Chinese lovers. In addition, based on my conversations with many Taiwanese wives, they have great concerns about sexual diseases, including AIDS, which Chinese women originally working as bargirls and sex workers might pass on to their husbands and later to them.

The construction of Taiwanese women as 'the first wives' is based in part on their particular views of and relations with Chinese women. It is often reinforced by massive flows across the Taiwan Strait of images and people representing Chinese women as economically, socially and politically dangerous others to Taiwanese society because they can lure Taiwanese men's hearts and money to China, a country which has aggressively opposed Taiwan's claim to independence in the international community (see Shen 2003). Such macro representations of Chinese women as the other women in Taiwan help legitimize the negative generalization of Chinese women by Taiwanese women and their feeling of being superior 'first wives'.

Flexible intimacy and gendered self-realization

In 2002 a popular marriage consultant in Taiwan, Wang Ren-chih, published *Love Me Tender, Love Me True* (Wang 2002), a book revealing her story of being betrayed by and divorced from her husband who had worked in China. Ironically, three years earlier, she had published another book, *My Husband Is a Taiwanese Businessmen [in China]* (Wang 1999), in which she proudly described the various strategies she had adopted to remain close to her husband. Shortly thereafter, she 'surprisingly' found out that he had had a long-term affair with a Chinese woman who had originally worked as a bargirl. In her story, Wang provides a dramatic, yet common, account of the marital infidelity of Taiwanese businessmen in China.

Before she discovered her husband's affair, Wang occasionally joked with him about the need to 'pack some condoms for him to take to China' or told him that 'as long as you told me the truth I wouldn't scold you for your affairs'.[16] What she said or did was not unusual among many Taiwanese wives. Because of the distance, wives in Taiwan cannot know the real state of their husbands' lives in China. While they utilize these means to ease their worries or share their suspicions with their husbands, they are not completely consumed by them. As the main care-givers to their children and family, and often as women with full-time jobs, they are very preoccupied by their daily tasks. A Taiwanese wife described her emotional state:

> Just don't think about it [*bao ernai*]. I am here and cannot see him [her husband]. What is the use of thinking about it? If I am going to constantly worry about him, there are only two ways to solve the

situation: one is to follow him to China and the other is to ask him to come back to Taiwan. Since neither way is possible, I only can hope that he does not cheat on me. When he comes home, I often chat with him about the stories I heard about other Taiwanese men's affairs in China. He always responds that he did nothing.[17] I only can believe him. I am worried, but it is useless to think about it.[18]

With the long separations and believing that men are by nature sexually more aggressive than women, many Taiwanese wives actually take an 'opening one eye and closing the other eye' attitude towards their husbands' affairs as long as they only engage in safe, casual sexual affairs that do not bring diseases and children home, continue to make their home visits, and provide financial support. Nevertheless, Taiwanese wives do feel a strong sense of betrayal when they learn of their husbands' serious affairs in China and of anger if they learn that their husbands are financially more generous towards their Chinese lovers, who are seen to be only interested in material gains, than towards their wives and families in Taiwan.

For instance, a Taiwanese woman who divorced her husband because of his affair sent the following message to an Internet discussion forum:

> When my husband went to China, we were just newly wed. Because he wanted to pay the mortgage and the credit card debt from our wedding, my husband wanted me to stay at my job in Taiwan and not go to China with him. He wouldn't even let me phone him or go to see him because he wanted me to save money. But he ended up co-habiting with a [Chinese] woman and got married to her after she became pregnant. . . . This woman quit her job once she moved in with him and he even hired a housekeeper to serve her. Taiwanese men want their wives to work hard for the family, but are happy to give a large sum of money to mainland sisters to spend.[19]

In many cases, Taiwanese businessmen provide clues to their infidelity by changing their financial arrangements. Because of the financial needs associated with affairs, many reduce the amount of money which they send home once they become engaged in extramarital relationships. Some stop sending money home altogether after they establish another family in China. In other cases, they provide clues by avoiding intimacy with their wives once Chinese women become the primary objects of their sexual desires.[20] Wang Ren-chih remembered that her husband had started to show less sexual interest in her after he had gone to China for a year, even though they only got to see each other every two months or so (Wang 2002: 38–9).

When their affairs become known to their wives, and if their intentions preclude divorce,[21] the usual reaction from Taiwanese businessmen is to minimize the significance of these affairs and to expect their wives to forgive their transgressions. Their flexible attitude towards monogamous marriage is supported by a local cultural practice which tolerates men's extramarital affairs and often frames them as 'casual play'. To forgive or not forgive their husbands' infidelity in this context is a gendered matter because, according to my research, the majority of their husbands would not have forgiven their wives if it were female infidelity. A woman, identified as Xiao-chien, learned that her husband had had an affair in China in 2004. Because she wanted to keep her family together for her children and because she still loved her husband, she intended to forgive him. However, she found out that he maintained his contacts with his girlfriend in China even after he returned to Taiwan to save his marriage. Xiao-chien was emotionally torn by this process and told her story to an Internet discussion forum:

> After several days' reflection, I have a deep recognition. For men the role of a wife is to take good care of the family, to overlook their husband's indiscretions if they go out to drink or engage in prostitution or gamble. Although women are hurt by their husbands' affairs, they are expected to forgive their husbands. It is women's own business to heal themselves. I wonder how many men would forgive their wives if they were having the affairs. Maybe some men do, but I have never heard about it.[22]

My research in Shanghai found that some Taiwanese wives had to seek comfort and strength in religious gatherings and bible readings which encourage women's tolerance and forgiveness towards their husbands.[23] The five women whom I met in Dongguan in 2007 had had direct experiences in confronting their husbands' affairs.[24] One once caught her husband with a Chinese woman in a hotel room and fought with him for many days. The other, in her late fifties, had tolerated her husband's sneaky affair with her housekeeper at home for months before she asked this housekeeper to leave.

Children, financial and emotional conditions, and cultural tolerance of men's infidelity play key roles in keeping many Taiwanese wives in marriages, even though their husbands' affairs are uncovered and/or their marriages are no longer working. Thus, Wang Ren-chih's immediate decision to divorce her husband right after she confronted him about his affair is not particularly common. Wang's rather stable economic condition, her connections with several women's groups, and her sense of identity through her work helped her make such a decision.

Family life and marriage become rather uncertain and insecure for Taiwanese wives of Taiwanese businessmen (and for these men too). Children and their well-being grow in importance as these mothers try to find certainty in a world of uncertainty. Over time, the role and meaning of husband and father gradually become less significant. Many of these wives voluntarily or involuntarily choose to 'give up' emotionally or to play down the importance of their husbands in their lives. One woman suggested to other women in an Internet discussion forum that they try 'to remove him [the husband] from life. To treat him like it doesn't matter whether they have him or not so that your emotions won't be turned upside down by him.'[25] They redirect the meaning of family and its members to signify the mother and children, as in a single-mother household.

Many Taiwanese women who have experienced their husbands' infidelity over the years have developed common 'realizations' to set their husbands aside and to take care of themselves. For instance, one such wife sent this message to an online discussion forum for other women with similar experiences: 'I really recommend that all the sisters no matter what should start a new life by loving oneself. . . . Because we have already lost our husbands' love, we cannot give up on ourselves.'[26] Whether they choose to stay in the marriage or seek a divorce, they all seem to adopt this survival strategy. In implementing it, they usually focus on efforts to obtain a good share of the marital property and money, to find a stable job and income, and/or to make themselves feel physically beautiful and mentally strong.

Because 'the first wives' have devoted themselves so much to their families and to their husbands, and because they believe that they have been treated unjustly when their husbands share their property and money with their Chinese lovers, most focus first on obtaining a significant share of the marital financial resources. After learning of her husband's affair, a professional Taiwanese woman in her early fifties wrote:

Don't expect he [her husband] will change. Without telling him, [I] just changed our property to my name to protect my rights and my two children's rights. . . . At this point, I have changed the title of three houses to my name. The rest of the property, I will gradually change too.[27]

The background of her ex-husband's Chinese girlfriend encouraged Wang Ren-chih to get a medical test to determine her risk of contracting AIDS right after she found out about her husband's affair. In her agreement with her husband, she received a commitment to approximately US$290,000 in compensation if she became infected with any sexual disease within a year of the date of their divorce.

In their efforts, 'the first wives' have received the support of Taiwanese society generally and, particularly, of women's groups. On 14 January 2003 the government passed the so-called 'anti *bao-ernai* article', an amendment to the Code of Civil Procedure which attempts to ensure that wives have easy access to their share of their husbands' property and the marital property if they ask for a divorce as a result of their husbands' affairs. Ironically, this legal reform also works to reinforce the collective status of Taiwanese wives of Taiwanese businessmen in China as 'the first wives'.

Many of the Taiwanese wives who stayed in Taiwan emphasize the importance of their jobs in terms of gaining financial security, occupying themselves during their husbands' absence, and feeling a sense of accomplishment. A Taiwanese wife in China left an Internet discussion forum message saying that it is useless for Taiwanese wives to try to control their husbands' infidelities by moving to China. She 'chose to return to Taiwan and find a job to restart my life there. . . . Rather than stubbornly making myself stay in the family, [I] should make myself strong.'[28]

Finally, many Taiwanese wives use commercial services to make themselves look and feel good. Because their husbands are spending their money on Chinese women, some of them feel a strong sense of entitlement, and perhaps a measure of vengefulness, against their husbands, and a sense of competition with Chinese women to treat themselves with marital money. A woman identifying herself as 'Spicy Mother' wrote that 'taking good care of oneself is the most realistic thing to do. If possible, one should take more money from one's man to love oneself.'[29] Another woman, named Chuang

Chuang, described her life after going through her husband's affair:

> Recently I have been taking lessons in belly dancing and pilates. I also swim regularly. I try to make my body healthy and in very good shape. I also plan to take lessons on make-up. I feel very good when I am busy with these things. . . . I want him [her husband] to be surprised with my changes. . . . He will realize that to lose me is the worst loss he will have in his life. . . . I want him to know that without him my world may be better.[30]

Many similar messages appear online to encourage 'the first wives' to manage their finances wisely, to focus on their work, and to pay special attention to their physical and mental health, and their attractiveness.[31] For Taiwanese wives in China, Taiwanese expatriate communities provide opportunities for them to seek each other out and to form groups and organizations where they can share their experiences and find solutions to the problems resulting from *bao ernai*.[32] For some of them, energetic participation in these organizations provides confidence and identity.

According to a newspaper report, a psychiatrist who has treated many Taiwanese wives of Taiwanese businessmen in China has observed a change in the attitudes which 'the first wives' have developed over time. In the early years, these women came to her over the problem of their husbands' infidelity in China and the possibility of separating from them. However, in more recent years, they complain about the disruption in their lives when the husband returns home, because they have established their own life rhythms and social circles during his long absence. Some of them, according to this psychiatrist, even talk about divorcing their husbands once they have saved enough money (Huang 2007).

In response to their husbands' (and Chinese women's) flexible approach towards monogamous marriage, many Taiwanese women adopt a flexible approach towards marital relations by minimizing the importance of intimacy and the role of men in their lives. Given the insecurity and instability associated with their positions in these marital relationships, they tend to transform their roles from emotionally and/or economically dependent wives to rather independent, strong women. Furthermore, they tend to place a premium on the importance of financial resources in providing meaning in their lives.

Conclusion

The development of regional economies in Asia has resulted in a corresponding emergence of 'the first wives' in many societies in the region because of the opportunities presented to their husbands for marital infidelity. This study of the phenomenon in Taiwan shows its influence in three major ways on intimate and family life across the Taiwan Strait. First, it has changed the pattern of family arrangements and reinforced the role of Taiwanese women as family care-givers. Many Taiwanese families become transnational families in which most wives and children of Taiwanese businessmen stay behind in single-mother households while their husbands and fathers are away and free from daily family responsibility for extended periods. At the same time, for those Taiwanese families relocating to China, the wives often migrate as trailing spouses, many of whom have to give up jobs in Taiwan and return to families as housewives.

Second, the development of the regional economy and the opportunity for marital infidelity presented by it has introduced the image of nationally defined (Chinese) other women into the marital bedrooms and gender politics of Taiwan. Taiwanese women portray themselves as the 'moral' first wives, victimized both by their husbands' infidelity and by Chinese women represented as immoral gold diggers and 'trashy' husband stealers.

Finally, it has also changed the meanings and feelings of intimate and family life for many Taiwanese families. In response to their husbands' masculine-oriented notion of flexibility towards intimacy and family, the first wives experience a painful emotional and economic adjustment which has significant implications for the gendered self-identity of some Taiwanese first wives. They assume a flexible stand with respect to intimacy and family by minimizing the significance of men in their lives and by emphasizing the importance of financial security and self-fulfilment. They recognize their disadvantaged gender position and take actions to minimize this disadvantage. They become more assertive in their role as family gatekeepers, more aggressive in their demands upon their husbands, more confident in their ability to support themselves financially, and more willing to look after themselves physically and emotionally. They develop a greater sense of gender independence. Given the role of the other Chinese women in their marital lives, however, they are also divided from women across the Taiwan Strait who might in other circumstances be sharing common gender concerns.

Notes

1 Larger firms tend to prohibit office romances, particularly between married Taiwanese businessmen and Chinese women.

2 Although some wives of Taiwanese businessmen in China are Chinese women who met their husbands after coming to work in China, in this representation it mainly refers to Taiwanese wives of Taiwanese businessmen.

3 The Internet discussion forums I study focus on issues and experiences related to 'the first wives'. Thus, the wives of Taiwanese businessmen who participate in these online discussions tend to be those who have already discovered their husbands' affairs and, in some cases, obtained divorces because of their husbands' infidelity.

4 My Chinese research sites include coastal cities and economic zones: Dongguan, Shenzhen, Xiamen, Shanghai and Kunshan.

5 Sources from the website of Taiwan's Mainland Affairs Council, MAC, wwwhttp://www.mac.gov.tw/english/index1-e.htm (accessed 22 November 2007).

6 However, the men developing affairs are not limited to the ones who migrate without families. Because having affairs has become a dominant culture among the majority of Taiwanese masculine expatriate business communities in China, many married men whose wives have relocated with them are also having affairs.

7 For Hong Kong men's affairs in China, see Lang and Smart 2002; Tam 1996; and So 2003. For Taiwanese businessmen in China, see Shen 2005. For Taiwanese businessmen in Vietnam, see Kung 2004. For Singaporean men in China, see Yeoh and Wills 2004.

8 For a close connection between economic development and Chinese men's practice of sexual consumption of Chinese women, see Jeffreys 2004; Zhang 2001; Zheng 2006.

9 According to Zheng (2006), sexual consumption became a business ritual during China's transformation from a communist to a market economy and provided the emerging class of Chinese businessmen with an opportunity to pre-select potential partners and to establish social trust and alliance between themselves and the Chinese political authorities. For Taiwanese businessmen in Vietnam, with language and cultural barriers, local women are sources of establishing local connections; see Kung 2004. The sexual consumption of Chinese women by Taiwanese businessmen is often articulated as a way of experiencing, displaying and intensifying their upward move in position and identity as privileged, transnational businessmen in China; see Shen 2008.

10 Polygamy was a rather common and public practice among rich men in China before the Communist Chinese Party took over the country in 1949 and introduced strong regulations against it. Influenced by this Chinese culture,

the practice of concubinage has long existed among rich men in Taiwanese society, even after the Nationalist Chinese implemented monogamous marriage as the only legal form of marriage soon after it took over Taiwan in 1949. Consequently, 'the first wife' has also long existed on the island. Historically, the term referred to the wife who went through ceremonial marriage. Concubines were not considered as wives, but as mistresses or maids (see Kiang 1930). Currently, the term refers to the wife who is legally recognized as the only legitimate spouse of a man.

11 According to my research in five major Chinese coastal cities since 1999, the proportion of wives staying in Taiwan with children is still larger than those relocating to China.

12 Posted at 23:50 on 31 August 2003, 'Taiwanese women's online discussion forum', http//forum.frontier.org.tw/women/viewtopic.php?mode=viewtopi c&topic=6946&forum=8&start=0.

13 The message was posted at 16:12 on 10 July 2004, 'Taiwanese women's online discussion forum', http//forum.frontier.org.tw/women/viewtopic.php?topic =11571&forum=8&start=30.

14 This woman identified herself as 'A sister of Taiwanese wives of Taiwanese businessmen'. She posted the message on 22 August 2007 on the EATaiwan website, http://www.eataiwan.org.tw/discuss/Detail.asp?TitleID=20187&dis cuss_id=.

15 This woman identified herself as Chiu-hsin, who had been married for eighteen years. The message was posted at 20:35 on 19 October 2007 on pchome.com, 'The first wife club' discussion forum, http://mypaper.pchome. com.tw/news/chiuhsien/3/1238984177/20040526192544.

16 Wang 2002: 33. Both Wang and her husband were in their forties and, according to her, they had a regular sex life before he went to work in China.

17 According to the Taiwanese businessmen I talked to and the secondary data, the only right response to their wives' enquiry on the question if they have affairs in China or not is 'no'.

18 The wife of a Taiwanese businessmen who had gone to China in 1994, this informant was working in a factory manufacturing musical boxes in a north-western Taiwanese city when I met her in 2001.

19 This woman identified herself as 'An experienced person' and posted her message at 15:02 on 9 September 2003, 'Taiwanese women's online discussion forum', http://forum.frontier.org.tw/women/viewtopic.php?mode=viewtop ic&topic=6946&forum=8&start=0.

20 I have previously argued elsewhere that there is an international division of intimate, familial labour provided by Taiwanese and Chinese women to Taiwanese businessmen in China following Taiwanese investments there. While Chinese women are seen as their primary sexual interest, Taiwanese wives are expected to act as care-givers to their families. See Shen 2005.

21 According to my research, unless Taiwanese businessmen plan to marry their lovers in China, they don't usually seek divorce from their wives.

22 Posted at 12:40 on 7 July 2004, 'Taiwanese women's online discussion forum', http://forum.frontier.org.tw/women/viewtopic.php?topic=11571&forum=8.

23 Christian groups are among the most active groups in Taiwanese expatriate communities in Shanghai. Over the years I have observed that some Taiwanese wives, who were not Christian in Taiwan, have started to attend bible study and/or Sunday services to seek support in coping with the problems of relocating to a new place and dealing with their husbands' affairs.

24 For the wives in China, the process of finding out about their husbands' affairs usually involved more direct confrontations with their husbands than the wives in Taiwan, who were less likely to witness these affairs.

25 Message posted by a woman identified as 'Refreshing' at 15:01 on 28 April 2007 on pchome.com 'The first wife club' discussion forum, http://mypaper.pchome.com.tw/news/chiuhsien/3/1238984177/20040526 192544.

26 Message posted at 23:16 on 19 October 2007 on pchome.com, 'The first wife club' discussion forum, http://mypaper.pchome.com.tw/news/chiuhsien/3/1 250232655/20050815033042.

27 This woman identified herself as 'Family protector', posting her message at 10:12 on 22 November 2007 on pchome.com, 'The first wife club' discussion forum, http://mypaper.pchome.com.tw/news/chiuhsien/3/1251614401/200 50923085731.

28 This woman, identifying herself as 'Passenger', posted her message at 01:55 on 29 July 2004, 'Taiwanese women online discussion forum', http://forum. frontier.org.tw/women/viewtopic.php?topic=6946&forum=8&start=30.

29 Message posed at 17:31 on 4 June 2007 on pchome.com, 'The first wife club' discussion forum, http://mypaper.pchome.com.tw/news/chiuhsien/3/12516 14401/20050923085731.

30 Posted at 13:29 on 4 December 2007 on pchome.com, 'The first wife club' discussion forum, http://mypaper.pchome.com.tw/news/chiuhsien/3/12391 29868/20040605181249.

31 The number of Taiwanese wives who have access to or know how to use the Internet is still very limited, and many of the wives staying behind in Taiwan are still isolated within their individual families as they try to deal with their problems.

32 There are numerous groups formed by Taiwanese wives in China. For instance, within the Taiwanese Entrepreneurial Associations, the major Taiwanese business organizations in many Chinese towns, cities and economic zones, there are Taiwanese Entrepreneurial Women's Associations organized by Taiwanese wives and Taiwanese businesswomen. In Shanghai, a 'Wives' Club' was established by several hundred Taiwanese wives in 2004.

References

Dicken, P. and H. W. C. Yeung (1999) 'Investing in the future: East and Southeast Asian firms in the global economy' in K. Olds, P. Dicken, P. F. Kelly, L. Kong and H. W. C. Yeung (eds), *Globalisation and the Asia-Pacific*. London: Routledge.

Dizard, J. E. and H. Gadlin (1990) *The Minimal Family*. Amherst, MA: University of Massachusetts Press.

Engels, F. (1972) *The Origin of the Family, Private Property and the State*. New York: International Publishers.

Hochschild, A. R. (1997) *The Time Bind: When Work Becomes Home and Home Becomes Work*. New York: Metropolitan Books.

—— (2003) *The Commercialization of Intimate Life: Notes from Home and Work*. Berkeley, CA: University of California Press.

Huang, T. Y. (2007) 'No stop pestering, Taiwanese wives feel crazy' [回來碎碎念 台商老婆抓狂], *China Times* (online edition), 9 December, http://news.chinatimes.com (accessed 9 December 2007).

Jeffreys, E. (2004) *China, Sex and Prostitution*. London and New York, NY: RoutledgeCurzon.

Kiang, K. H. (1930) 'The Chinese family system', *Annals of the American Academy of Political and Social Science*, 152: 39–46.

Kung, I. C. (2004) 'The sexual politics of foreign capital: exchange relation between Taiwanese capital and local women in Vietnam' (the author's original English title) [跨國資本的性別政治：越南台商與在地女性的交換關係], *Taiwan: A Radical Quarterly in Social Science* 55: 101–40.

Lang, G. and J. Smart (2002) 'Migration and the "second wife" in South China: toward cross-border polygyny', *International Migration Review*, 36 (2): 546–69.

pchome.com (since 2004) 'The first wife club' [大老婆俱樂部]. Online discussion forum since 11 May 2004. http://mypaper.pchome.com.tw/news/chiuhsien (accessed since 2006).

Pratt, M. L. (1992) *Imperial Eyes: Travel Writing and Transculturation*. London: Routledge.

Shen, H. H. (2003) 'Crossing the Taiwan Strait: global disjunctures and multiple hegemonies of class, politics, gender, and sexuality'. PhD thesis, University of Kansas.

—— (2005) '"The first Taiwanese wives" and "the Chinese mistresses": the international division of labour in familial and intimate relations across the Taiwan Strait', *Global Networks*, 5: 419–37.

—— (2008) 'The purchase of transnational intimacy: women's bodies, transnational masculine privileges in Chinese economic zones', *Asian Studies Review*, 32: 57–75.

So, A. Y. (2003) 'Cross-border families in Hong Kong: the role of social class and politics', *Critical Asian Studies*, 35 (4): 515–34.

Stacey, J. (1990) *Brave New Families: Stories of Domestic Upheaval in Late Twentieth Century America*. New York: Basic Books.

Swidler, A. (2001) *Talk of Love: How Culture Matters*. Chicago: University of Chicago Press.

'Taiwanese Women Online Discussion Forum' [台灣婦女網路論壇] (1998–2006) Online discussion forum. http://forum.frontier.org.tw/women/viewforum.php?forum=8&201627 (accessed 22 October 2007).

Tam, S. M. (1996) 'Normalization of "second wives": gender contestations in Hong Kong', *Asian Journal of Women's Studies*, 2: 113–32.

Wang, R. C. (1999) *My Husband is a Taiwanese Businessman [in China]* [我的老公是台商]. Taipei: CCTV Publisher.

—— (2002) *Love Me Tender, Love Me True* (publisher's original English title) [終於學會愛自己：一個婚姻專家的離婚手記]. Taipei: Psygardern Publisher.

Yeoh, B. and K. Wills (2004) 'Constructing masculinities in transnational space: Singapore men on the regional beat' in P. Jackson, P. Crang and C. Dwyer (eds), *Transnational Spaces*. London: Routledge.

Zhang, E. (2001) 'Goudui and the state: constructing entrepreneurial masculinity in two cosmopolitan areas of post-socialist China' in D. L. Hodgson (ed.), *Gendered Modernities: Ethnographic Perspectives*. New York: Palgrave, pp. 235–65.

Zheng, T. (2006) 'Cool masculinity: male clients' sex consumption and business alliance in urban China's sex industry', *Journal of Contemporary China*, 15 (46): 161–82.

Index